Last of the Fun Bunch-
A seasonal adventure
of fire and life

By Professor Jim (Boomer) Canyon

and

Buck

Thanks to buds

And all the friendship we've shared down the trails and on those dirt roads.

Dedicated to Len (the Wad) Dems

(1958-2010)

and

Ken Castro

(1961-2007)

"May the good lord be with you
Down every road you roam
And may sunshine and happiness
Surround you when you're far from home
And may you grow to be proud
Dignified and true
And do unto others
As you'd have done to you
Be courageous and be brave
And in my heart you'll always stay
Forever young, ..."

-Rod Stewart

<u>**(Buck) Preface**</u>

Forever young, if only in our hearts and minds. Not to dwell there, because as life goes we too must move on. As an anchor point of a solid beginning and shaping of one's future, there was a time in the isolated land known as the North Rim of Grand Canyon, where some daring folks created lasting bonds, took time to know each other, while friendships and respect developed, and cameraderie ensued. This story is based upon many true events, realistic episodes of adventure-seeking souls on a quest for life, in a time past. The people and events featured are real; many names have been changed to protect the innocent and guilty, and some events combined for brevity as well as liberty. These tales are about friend and foe alike; as any gregarious person knows, some events have been embellished in the retellings, thanks to a few rounds (maybe several) but ever so slightly. And well, there is some ramble (blame that on the professor's good smoke).

Many stories have been written by rangers and firefighters in the past. Many of those are good to excellent retellings of the job and what it entails. This is not that type of story. This includes those types of happenings and people, but exposes a vulnerability in the young, grab-life-by-the-balls person that portrays a certain niche of individual, best exhibited by this quote,

"Whoso would be a man, must be a nonconformist."
-Emerson

In the '80's, Grand Canyon's North Rim, unlike it's brethren to the south, was a quiet hamlet. The development, mass tourists and year round access belonged to the other side, ten miles south as the raven flies, and separated by the Colorado River and the chasm it created. This North Rim was on an isolated mountain lying down as the native inhabitants referred to it. It was on a mesa top, jutting up over 8,000 feet in altitude.

Along with its' isolation, the seasonal workforce habitants here were a strong, self-sufficient, individual type breed. One such being was Jim (Professor) 'Boomer' Canyon. A fitting name associated with such a place. Here's his story, in part, with fellow character protagonist, Buck. Together, they found a home, passion for work, and the awesome majesty this place commands, but also a place to be free, to be authentic, to be real, and to live.

"Go confidently in the direction of your dreams. Live the life you have imagined."
-Henry David Thoreau

The shared bond uniting some of these seasonal creatures was to break free from society's norms and find a higher meaning to life. Relating to Hemingway's *"Lost Generation"* as a people coming of age, or Kerouac's (once a fire lookout) *"Beat Generation"* influence, as well as gonzo journalist, Hunter S. Thompson, these non-conformists refused to fit neatly into society's structure. The most influential of these was Edward Abbey, employed on the North Rim as a fire lookout from '69-'71, and in his words, left a, *"stuffed white job"* with good pay to do a, *"man's job"* rather than being in an overheated office all day in a necktie, strangulated with a horde of middle aged females pushing papers and pressing dictaphones. According to him, Abbey's deepest personal tragedy would not be death or dying, which is tragic, but rather to have existed without fully participating in life. Characterizing the essence further, he stated it as such, *"Keep America beautiful, burn a billboard,"* as well the need to be free from the strangulation of the hordes and masses of followers, *"If you can't pee in your own front yard, you live too close to the city."* If you don't get that, don't read this. This is not a sugar-coated Boy Scout story of angelic saints. It is in the soul of the people that live life fully to experience it wholly (blemishes and all).

In the story, <u>The Razor's Edge,</u> author Somerset Maugham creates a character returning after the First World War seeking meaning in life by experiencing many adventures. Disapproval by peers and mentors about wasting time in these endeavors fearing his failure to conform, leads to their observation, *"...if you wanted to get on in this world, you must accept its conventions, and not to do what everybody else did clearly pointed to instability."*

Those aforementioned have shaped and influenced other generations including this one. Sometimes it occurred while searching for meaningful life that others have also been on similar treks and thus paths crossed.

"In Buddhism, there is something called 'dharma'- the path...They believe that our role in the world, the reason we are all here, is to find our path. We begin our journey of self-discovery on a path of learning and gradually, if we're really listening, we find our way to our true path. Having found it, we are to pursue it with all our heart. It is where we should be, where we need to be, and where we will be happiest, most fulfilled, and at peace. There are as many different paths as there are people...The key is to find the path that is right for us, one that will not only benefit ourselves, but others as well. As long as what we do supports nature and does not detract from it, nature will support us. But how do we know when we are on our path?...how do we get there? When we are on our path, 'coincidences' happen naturally...The key to finding our path is to follow our heart and intuition. As long as we do this, we will live a fulfilled and peaceful life, not just one in which we exist by eating, working, and struggling to pay bills."
-Alan Hobson <u>(From Everest to Enlightenment)</u>

Table of Contents

Part One-
Smoldering

Part Two-
Heating Up

<u>Contents continued</u>

<u>Part Three-</u>
<u>Going up in smoke</u>

<u>Part Four-</u>
<u>Live & Let Burn</u>

Contents continued

Part Five-
The Homestretch

Epilogue

Afterword

Appendix

Specifically this story is about one group of National Park Service seasonal workers, the wildland firefighters. Each major western park has their unique resource needs, and likewise, the North Rim of Grand Canyon had for the longest time an elite and historic fire crew known as the "Longshots," made famous in Pyne's book, <u>Fire On the Rim.</u> Pyne, noted fire historian, and a Longshot for 15 years from the '60's on had trained exemplary proteges in Len (the Wad) Dems who passed the torch on to Ken (Day-O) Castro. An extraordinary, proud crew of rugged, willing, and able-bodied individuals collectively united as a team to face the challenges of wildfires throughout the park as well as the west via helicopter, engines, or on foot. The Longshots were a trusted and relied upon crew in the paramilitary organization of wildland fire. Their reputation preceded them and they willingly lived up to the billing. To be a Longshot was an honor and a highly sought after position. Leadership, self-sufficency, intelligence, as well as hard, sustaining teamwork was expected of each member. They worked hard and they played hard. It comes with laying your life on the line and bonding with your brethren. The other park and concession employees had much respect and admiration for the Longshots and loved them when in station. During the '80's, they received the unofficial title as, the "Fun Bunch," due to their highly positive outlook, their friendliness to all, elite status yet curbed egos and passion for life. They knew how to have a good time and enjoyed themselves wherever they were: on a fire, running a chainsaw, or in the saloon.

During the decade of the '80's, parks were beginning to look into managing wildfires differently. Recognizing the value of fire in a natural ecosystem began to shape decisions. Archaic computers were coming on board to help organize, map, and even predict fire behavior. There was no GPS, just old fashion map and compass skills to orient oneself and to triangulate a fire location. Specific to the extreme isolation, no television nor radio reception existed. The only news flowed from the visitors that left behind their read over copies of USA Today (purchased somewhere down off the rim). Affirmative action was being played out to an exhausting level to right our past wrongs in what appeared to be overnight decisions. And as with any beauracracy: politcs, ineptitude, and wrangling occured. All was fine in the land of the Grand, until large beauracratic ego's started exerting their bellowing power trips that would render havoc with the future of this prime, grade A, real estate piece of land. In the year 1986, it would come to a crisis situation and the famed Longshot fire crew would be a target. Due to their notoriety, the fun bunch would be dismantled after manipulative and controlling measures went moot. They were too efficient and made the inept overhead look bad. With reputations on the line, ego's intact, and narrow minded goals in sight to climb the corporate ladder at all costs, sacrificing the Longshots was seen as the scapegoat for government mismangement to proceed. Thus the last of the Fun Bunch was forced to retire and left in 1986. This is also their story.

<u>**(Professor's) Prologue**</u>

"I fight authority, authority always wins."

-John Mellencamp

The standing joke, between my folks and me, was, "When are you going to get a real job?"
"Hopefully, never!" was my usual, heartfelt reply, with a smile. And of course, that was followed by the old, "Get a haircut, and shave the beard" comments. I suppose there are some constants in my life. Another constant in my life was earning a living with the government of our fair land on a seasonal basis. I was in the wildfire business, mostly in that land of smoke and fire called, California. There were, however, several fire seasons spent in that holy place known as the Grand Canyon. It was there that I found home and found my true love. The canyons of the southwest, the ancient lore and legends, the magical lure of the rivers, the mystical landscape, the high mountain meadow respit, and the spiritual sunsets spoke to my sense of being. The people I encountered there often had this zeal for life, to experience it, engulf it, enjoy it, treasure it, and share the love of it.

Thus, I attempted to explore, study, and get to know this new land to me. In my immersion, I fell in love with this place. I often left after fire season, but would return within months to experience some new area or adventure within this alluring beauty. My pals thus named me Professor Canyon.

"This spot where you sit is your own spot. It is on this very spot and in this very moment that you can become enlightened. You don't have to sit beneath a special tree in a distant land."
-Thich Nhat Hanh

Part of this story is of that circle around the sun known as nineteen eighty-six, the last season of the fabled "Longshots." As I write these words here in the sun on the porch of my cedar cabin, I smile. Sometimes when I wake up, I start to look for my White's, that is, my fire boots. Then I realize that's long past. No more fire seasons, flights in helicopters, landings in a meadow miles from any dirt road to seek out smoke. To render that act of lightning into ashes with a shovel, chainsaw, McCleod, or my favorite, a Pulaski. Razor sharp on both the axe head and that root grubbing, trenching hoe side, so sharp that a piece of paper slices clean when held to the edge. If it doesn't then get back on that (mill) bastard file until it does. Don't forget to re-sand the handle then get out the red spray paint can and the lightning bolt stencil to put the mark of the Longshots on it. Final touch is a light linseed oil afterwards. Ahh, that was nineteen eighty-six. Where's my coffee? I've got a story to tell… In a couple of days, I'll be heading back to the canyons to get another fix. In the meantime, let's get this damn thing started.

For some thirty fire seasons, these Longshots, as they were known, existed upon the North Rim.

This tale is about their last season,

I know the story, for I lived it. I say, let the truth be known,

For it festers inside me like a thorn under my skin.

-Prof Canyon

(Buck) Note about quotes

The use of the many lyrics and quotes throughout goes along with supporting our beliefs that while each individual is unique, we have and can identify with many shared experiences, beliefs, emotions, songs and stories. Other quotes are used to underscore a point made by another author.

(Buck) Note about parentheses

At the beginning of each chapter are parentheses which denote the speaker for that section, either the Prof or Buck, sometimes both. It is hopefully obvious to the reader.

(Prof/Buck) Fire Logistics

Fire fighting in the outdoors is different than your local structural brigades putting out fires in buildings. Wildland fire fighting uses water sometimes, if it is available, many times, dirt. Typically, fire is looked at as a triangle, with a heat source, fuel to burn and oxygen to sustain. As wildlanders, we look to take away the fuel (i.e.- trees, grasses, shrubs, etc.) or cool the heat (by dirt or water). In your national parks, fires are most often started by lightning strikes. Oftentimes, a lightning strike to a tree may just involve that tree (the taller the better). This is a typical initial attack response by two firefighters. They may drive or fly as close as possible, but more often than not, they end up hiking in, carrying everything needed to extinguish the flames. Their packs are 45 pounds on their back, plus the tools carried. In tree country, a chain saw and the accompanying web gear of oil, gas, file, etc. are always carried. Scraping and cutting tools are carried in as well (i.e.- shovel, Pulaski, Macleod, etc.). The breathing is filtered by bandanas, not oxygen tanks as in structural fires. Oftentimes working a wildfire consumes time, weeks on an assignment is possible. Before OSHA (Occupational Safety and Health Administration) requirements became mandatory, firefighters would work days on end without any real sleep time. Cat naps were had on the line. That is, napping in the dirt while others monitored the fire.

We worked most diligently during the evening, nights, and early morning hours, when the relative humidity was up somewhat and fires generally would calm. Meals in the early days were the military C-rations, being upgraded (Ha!) by MRE's-meals-ready-to-eat. There are a host of other meal options today.

Most of the wildfires occur in the forests of the west. The vast majority of the work force was seasonal. That means they work as long as fires are burning. Seasonal work means there are lay-offs afterwards, so no benefits and no health insurance is available only workman's comp. One is never guaranteed a job. Hard work, diligence and endurance usually gets the fire fighter invited back. Many do this for years, most trying to gain a permanent position one day in the future. Again, no guarantees. Adrenaline junkies usually apply for fire jobs. There are other seasonal workers in the NPS system. The law enforcement rangers (the other adrenaline junkies) naturalists (interpretive division) entrance station and campground fee collectors, maintenance workers, trail crew, etc. all make up the bulk of employment during the summer season in our national parks.

Meaningful relationships are hard to come by and sustain in this line of work.

There are different types of fire crews for various responses. The type one crews are the elite smoke jumpers and hotshots of the fire world. Type two crews are typically regular forest service fire crews, engines, and helitack (the Longshots of the North Rim did all of these as a type two crew). There are also emergency hires (EFF's-emergency firefighters) during big or project fires. All are trained and must pass a physical fitness test to obtain a red card, your ticket to be called for a fire. As you climb the ladder of experience and training, your red card fills with your qualifications, enabling you more assignments. There are many variations to this.

Some fires grow so large and run for so long that cyclical weather patterns finally extinguish them (such as the classic Yellowstone fire of 1988, with snows of November finally putting it out). So many a firedog construes a different meaning to the line from James Taylor when he sings, *"I've seen fire and I've seen rain"* (snow, sleet, hail, etc.). Fighting fire long enough and you will understand, especially during monsoon season. It is not uncommon to be working in rain, snow, sleet, hail, frost and have wildfires flourishing around you. More common is the grueling hot summer temperatures working in superheated conditions of smoke and fire. As fires grow, so does the amount of people and supplies. Sometimes fire camps grow as large as towns in size and capacity. One of the reasons for more massive and hotter fires in our modern times has to do with the amount of fuel on the ground. Our national policy called for extinguishing the fires. We have been so good at getting to these fires that have ignited (by lightning) that we keep the acreage down, not allowing nature to take its course and clean up the forest floor by the fire's natural mosaic burn patterns. If left to burn, many fires would do their job to keep competing and un-natural vegetation out. However, with the wildland urban interface, many complexities have arrived in the fire world today. Not just more people moving into the woods, but the declining health of the forests have contributed to a dilemma. Forests are becoming more dense and overgrown, choked with an overwhelming amount of fuel that can ignite into cataclysmic proportions with only a spark and some wind. The Longshots fire crew faced this new dilemma throughout 1986. Should we fully suppress the fire as quick as possible? Or maybe, since it was a natural lightning strike and the fuels were thick and needed cleaning out (for wildlife) plus being in a wilderness area, with no people nearby, should we let it burn in the right conditions? Or maybe monitor it awhile and see how the fire goes and the weather allows before responding…

Just a host of other variables and many more considerations, but for the new reader, this story parallels the time of emerging fire management policies.

Stephen Pyne, fire historian and expert has noted: *"As fire management is redefined by the Park Service, it becomes a compromised and ambiguous job. Emergent philosophies of fire management demand not only a retreat from traditional fire suppression, but a complicated program of fire reintroduction that will, until the system is mastered, involve difficult decisions and a quota of public relations fiascos' (1989)."*

Managing a wild-fire?
I know that we sure try and think we know how. In the end, it's nature's course and call.
"Human beings take shelter from hurricanes, flee tsunamis, keep their distance from tornadoes, move indoors when dust storms roll by. Wildfires, they choose to fight."
-Fernanda Santos, <u>The Fire Line,</u> p.142.

Today, even more conditions prevail that add to the severity; trees weakened and killed by insects' infestation and regional droughts make for very tough situations. Most of our national parks are surrounded by national forests. Two different land management agencies with different philosophies. In the wildlands surrounding these areas are home sites built with privacy in mind. For firefighters this adds an extra risk with little to do for structures (i.e.-houses) in the middle of these inferno's that don't recognize political boundaries.
"Federal agencies don't have unlimited budgets to fight fires, but they do spend a lot of money keeping flames away from houses...Yet there's no evidence that the increased spending is doing much to make towns that abut the forest safer. The flames are natural; the homes aren't...the threat wildfire poses to houses and towns can be mitigated- through forest thinning, prescribed burns, and defensible-space work."
-Kyle Dickman, <u>On the Burning Edge,</u> pgs.160-1.

When conditions are right (tinder dry fuels, high winds, dry lightning) conflagrations occur quickly. One such incident was Sunday, June 9, 2002, the Hayman fire in Colorado. Although arson caused, the area was ripe for tragedy. Fire raced 19 miles in 13 hours, spreading advance fires a mile ahead, with heat waves rising 21,000 feet. The fire emitted five times the amount of carbon monoxide and twice the particle pollution than all of Colorado's industry does in a year's time. Carbon monoxide is a by-product of incomplete fuel combustion and adds another hazardous element to the fire fighters, resulting in typical headaches. Fire fighting is an arduous task. Many risks are inherent. Fatalities occur every year. Some more than others.

There are situations trained to watch for, and standard orders to follow, but summarized they are LCES.
L-lookouts are posted and assess and reassess the fire environment,
C-communicate, with everyone, clearly.
E-escape routes, have them, know them, they can change.
S-safety zones, where the crew can retreat to safety from the fire.

If only we'd follow these diligently always... If only...
Maybe there'd be less tragic stories in wildfire since throughout history the recurring common theme of investigative findings cited violations of these rules.

"There are no easy answers to living with fire, not when forests and wildlands pose a bewildering checkerboard of challenges, when human encroachment into wildlands rolls on governed by widely divergent regulations or no regulation, when fires have grown bigger and hotter, when numerous laws can be used to derail and delay work in the forests, and when state, local, tribal, and federal firefighters come to the fire ground with unresolved differences about missions, levels of competency, and communications."
-John N. Maclean, <u>The Esperanza Fire</u>, p.289.

<u>(Prof) Heaven Scent</u>

The developed area of the North Rim is at an elevation of 8,260 feet. Climbing from the desert floor, one ascends up an escarpment. For the most part, it's a gently rolling landscape of large, park like stands of Ponderosa pine trees as the predominant species. Their vanilla scented bark permeates in the clear blue skies typically overhead, comforting and signifying one is home. Interspersed are mixed conifers that include blue and Engelmann spruce, with Douglas and white fir. The many wide open meadows are a wildflower haven of colors with penstemmen and paintbrush predominating. Where fire had burned its' mosaic piece from the landscape, stands of aspens flourish, hiding the mule deer and wild turkey, as red tail hawks soar above searching for Kaibab squirrels. Ravens laugh loudly when the black bear or mountain lion wanders too close to civilization and Rangers are called. Along the rim where updraft desert winds creep out of the canyon below, groves of pinyon pines and junipers live in harmony with the cliff rose, sage, cactus, along with associated wildlife like: lizards, rattlesnake, ringtail cats, and scorpions.

There are no streams flowing through this forested island rising out of the high great basin desert. All of the winter snowmelt and summer monsoon rains percolate through the top stratum of Kaibab limestone, Coconino sandstone and down the various layers until it hits harder rock, where it pours out in waterfalls throughout the canyon. Just when you think you're experiencing a desert in the inner gorge, waterfalls and ouzel nests with lush vegetation appear, to put you in another place, somewhere tropical comes to mind. Down below, from the rim's edge, chants of the Ancient ones can be heard in desert breezes upon Cottonwood leaves.

"The closer you get to real matter, rock, air, fire, wood, the more spiritual the world is."
-Jack Kerouac (Dharma Bums)

As (Major John Wesley) Powell, (Edward) Abbey, along with countless others, from writers and poets to rangers and tour-ons (NPS unofficial language for tourist-moron) have found out, this is truly a grand place. I wrack my brain for platitudes of grandeur to describe eloquently to you the magic that is called the North Rim, as well as the inner gorge, what is known as Grand Canyon, yet no words do justice.

Awe, the *"feeling of being in the presence of something vast or beyond human scale, that transends our current understanding of things,"* notes psychologist Dacher Keltnor. *"It's a dramatic feeling with the power to insprire, heal, change our thinking and bring people together,"* reports Paula S. Scott (<u>Parade,</u> 10-9-16).

If you have any desire to know such a spectacle, get your ass there. Forget your camera, take your boots, and take some time. In fact, take all the time you can. At least a week is recommended. If you can only stay an hour or a day, go to the South Rim instead and join the canned sardines to say you've been there. If you want to truly get to know this place, get down in it, stand on the edge where there are no safety fences, put your butt down on the limestone and dangle your feet over the precipice. Pretend the swift that just passed by your left ear like a feathered jet, is your next existence. It will change your life.

"Look deep into nature and you will understand everything better."

-Albert Einstein

<u>Part One-
Smoldering</u>

<u>(Prof) Beginnings</u>

"There are no strangers here. Only friends you haven't met yet."

-William Butler Yeats

The reflection that struck me on my first ride to the North Rim was the beauty of the meadows: a green carpet leading to the park entrance gate lined with aspen and blue spruce. This scene belonged in the Rockies. My return arrival in May, 1985, at this magical mysterious cathedral in rock had me in awe again. Immense, captivating, excited, yet hesitant to rush the process, I had to reflect at the majesty surrounding me. At this altitude, snows were piled six feet high in the aspen meadow where my government cabin lay waiting. Blues skies, sun shining bright, a flurry of activity already in progress. Arriving with the first shift of seasonals to claim bunks within the various cabins and trailors housed in haphazard fashion amongst the towering Ponderosa pines and aspen forests, I eased into my park service issued quarters.

Ritualistically, I set up my stereo first to blast some unpacking tunes, *"No woman, no cry..."* sang Marley. Having everything I owned in my small Tacoma pick up with camper shell, I was rather adept at the house setting up procedure. In no time at all I was ready, staking claim to a broom closet sized room, with a twin matress on the floor. Opening the door fully was not possible as it would hit the matress. But for future privacy, I would be able to squeeze my body through if I went in sideways. Set about my sheets, threw out my sleeping bag, pillow, headlamp, paperbacks, and voila! Bedroom complete for the season. Will hopefully be sleeping out under the stars more than couped up in here, although my window offered me another entry/exit way and a nice view of some tall boulders strewn about the high aspen meadow.

Packed away dry goods in bins and some of the perishables in the refrigerator. Mice were a constant problem; the chinking between the logs of these Teddy Roosevelt era cabins were spacious. For entertainment in the evenings, while reading in bed, I would hear these furry critters scamper up from outside to the log gaps, only to watch them squat and stare back at me. I knew they'd be in here as I drifted off to sleep and switched off my headlamp. WTF, it was the same if I camped outside in the meadows or forests too. As long as those suckers didn't get into my hard brought food. Usually ninety miles one way to the nearest store (in Kanab, UT) we treasured fresh food brought up when we could get off station.

In the following days, I circled wider and wider in my wanderings, as the official day of my work start neared. Wandering through the forest, I heard an anthem from my past blaring away, *"I Can't get no...satisafaction..."* Directed to this familiar charge of the Stones, I stumbled to the canyon's edge and onto another cabin, this one more reminiscent of typical "log cabins." A tall, svelte, dark featured, guy was unloading his full size Ford pickup.

"Canyon, Jim Boomer Canyon's my name." as I extended my hand.

"They call me Buck." he replied.

"I'll be the assistant foreman of the fire crew this year; last year I worked on the crew as well." I offered.

"Yeah, well I guess we'll be working together. I was brought in as a crew member, worked here in '83 as a ranger." and he reached down into a cooler bringing up two beers.

"Chink" as we toasted a new season, a new crew, a new partnership, and what would become a lifelong friendship.

While shaping up our fire cache for the season, another entourage entered the compound, the off road area of government housing. Haunting sounds reverberating from a green stepside van,

"There is a road, no simple highway,

Between the dawn and dark of night,

And if you go no one may follow,

That path is for your steps alone..."

as the (Grateful) Dead song, "Ripple" came into clarity. Deadheads.

"Howdy" came the call from the lean, blue-eyed, blonde haired driver at the wheel. A cute, blondie female companion accompanied him in the other front seat. Dogs behind the two of them were peeking heads out as the van came to a stop.

"Fire cache, I must be in the right place, Dave's my name." he introduced himself.

"You must be the one we hired from Texas, did some work with BIA (Bureau of Indian Affairs) in New Mexico."

"That's me, and this is my pretty gal Kathan."

"Hi, are you Gussie, the chief ranger?" she asked me.

Chuckling, I replied, "nah, I'm Jim or Professor Canyon as people have taken up calling me. I'm the assistant fire foreman. This is Buck (nodding)."

"Professor Canyon, oh boy, then, when we have questions regarding the canyon for hikes, and hideaways, and backcountry, you can give us some real good tips, right?"

"Yes, indeeeed, honey! I sure can do that." She was a delight to look at, so fresh, so lovely, so blue eyed, blonde, cute, and full of life. It was just a joy speaking with these good hippie folks, so genuine, so real.

"We'll be needing to check in to get set up somewhere around here. We have this family of pets with us and come self-contained, yet we also were told that we'd get electric and water hookups. We'll see y'all around soon enough, take care now."

(Prof) Fire ready

Outside of meeting Buck and Dave, fellow misfits, the fire season of nineteen eighty-five was a rather dull Pulaski. In other words, no huge fires, little lightning, and not much smoke chasing. When one is in fire, that's what one lives for, to get a request to jump in that engine or climb into that helicopter and answer that intriguing call of nature. Most of the summer of eighty-five, the Pulaski's, shovels and McCleod's stayed clean and sharp in their tool racks. Fall and snow came around and the layoffs for the winter did too. The crew scattered off to various parts of the globe. Some went back to school, others to family, while in my case, it was chasing a crazy woman that I'd become smitten with and headed to that green urban jungle called Seattle. It only took the coming of the spring to send me back to the canyon for the following fire season. And lightning waited to strike as a strange wind began to blow...

(Prof) The curse of fire and smoke: Fire season calls and Buck answers

"Humans are creatures with a longer history of living in the outdoors than of living within the confines of concrete and artificial light. We have an atavistic sense of well-being when immersed in the natural world."
-David Miller (<u>AWOL on the Appalachian Trail</u>)

The phone call in early 1986 from the canyon was echoing in his brain, another season as a Longshot. After several seasons of parks, Buck had a normal job now in the thriving metropolis of Tucson, ringed by mountains and saguaro cacti. He even cleaned up and looked every inch of corporate America: from the "Sting" mustache to a suit and tie. Enough condiments of the real dollar world to gag any self respecting smoke bum green.

As the air conditioner droned and hummed a cool artificial envelope around Buck and his fellow workers, his mind and eyes were on the sun soaked desert hills outside the glass windows of the insurance company walls. On the beginning of that long plateau of human life beyond youth, Buck was supposedly seeking stability, a year round job. The phone rang on Buck's desk and he answered quickly. His mind was not with the client, but rather he was wandering in thoughts, still in movement and voice; he was naked and sitting on a rock overlooking Transept Canyon, watching the colors of the rim as the sun's setting rays cast shadows of another day on the North Rim, feeling the desert heat rise as the cooler down drafting currents from the forest above danced about.

Coincidentally, a Neil Young tune was playing on the radio in the background,
"Everybody seems to wonder what it's like down here.
I gotta get away from this day to day running around,
Everybody knows this is nowhere."

Voices of the office and machinery droned on while Buck's hands naturally removed the tie from his throat, and deposited it in the round file known as a wastebasket. As though from a dream, Buck awoke, a wicked smile crossed his face while his eyes rested on the tie in the garbage. Then, the fingers sought the buttons on his shirt, one by one, they popped. A laughter born of freedom escaped from Buck's soul. Bending down to the freshly shined Thom McAn's, the laces were removed, and his dogs barked at the thought of fresh air. Socks were flung with abandon. The voices in the office became still silence; the phone was dropped with a screaming for an answer, while Buck's belt fell to the floor. A snicker from glossed lips attracted Buck's smile as he plucked his truck keys and wallet from his slacks. The voice of management and supervision cut through the pleas of telephones, "What's going on here?"
"Time to catch some sunshine!" delivered Buck as he strode out the door to his pick up. Now fully naked in the cab with fresh air and rays of sun gleaming through, it was time to hit the road. Inside the office it was a brief standstill until the phones' servants answered their summons. Outside, a pick up motor roared to life and the sounds of Marshall Tucker on the stereo declared,
"Fire on the mountain,
Lightnin' in the air,
Gold in them hills,
And it's waiting for me there."

Another season on the North Rim working as a Longshot. Nothing could come close. All other careers could be on hold.

Sally liked the feel of the badge upon her chest. The fear that had once been there when she put on her leathers and gun to go on patrol was gone. She found as she thought she would, that she liked the thin line. That adrenaline rush that came with every incident call. It sure beat waiting tables and the men were a lot more respectful. Sally had been a Tucson peace officer for about five years. Quite a while now, as she was thinking, when her thoughts were stopped by a pickup which didn't at the stop sign. She wasn't laughing when she turned on her lights and siren and radioed in, "Dispatch, unit 94 in pursuit of a 4-19."
"Dispatch copies. Vehicle make and license please."
"Early eighties, white Ford pickup, Arizona plates, Delta, John, Echo, Three, Zero, Two, Four."

"Dispatch copies, location?"
"Tenth and Javelina Avenue."
"Copy."
Buck was laughing when he missed the stop sign. He stopped laughing when looking in his mirror, he noticed the black and white behind him with lights flashing. Pulling over, he went to grab his wallet from his non-existent pants, "Damn! I wonder what the charge is for indecent driving?"
At this point, he was surprised by a woman's voice.
"License, registration, please." Sally started looking at Buck, red face and torso. Taking a step closer, she was startled at Buck's naked state. Then, she laughed. It was a bit before she could stop.
"It just seemed too hot." Buck offered, as he handed over his license.
"Unit 94, status?"
It was definitely hot, Sally thought, as she went to answer her radio.

W.T.F. Buck? (Buck's reply)

"The elderly usually don't have regrets for what they did, but rather for things they did not do. The only people who fear death are those with regrets."
-Author unknown

Not everyone has the same path, passion, and desires. Damn, I tried several times, the typical career path with a good paying job, settling down and the two-week annual vacation. I kept working harder at things I didn't like doing in order to have a type of existence that I didn't care for. It just wasn't for me. Further, certain songs spoke to my soul and I thought they were meant for me.
"Well I try my best to be just like I am, but everybody wants you to be just like them."
sang Bob Dylan (in Maggie's Farm).

So that I wouldn't have regrets for my future, I had to be true to myself.
Driving to my seasonal park appointments in my pickup, I was freed enjoying two lane highways while blasting my mantra by Gordon Lightfoot,

"Now the thing that I call livin' is just bein' satisfied
With knowin' I got no one left to blame
Carefree highway,"

usually followed by wailing open windowed along with the classic, *"freedom's just another word for nothing left to lose..."* (as performed by Janis Joplin on Kris Kristofferson's song, *"Me and Bobby McGee."*

On I went, my journey with life, and the innocence of the ever changing wonders of life. Decidedly taking the path less troden and not worrying about the road not taken. Most people fear death, I feared missing life. The National Park Service provided the settings and opportunities; I plugged in my passion for the outdoors with hard work and play. Picking up seasonal experiences at different parks for a few years allowed me to gain the experience that the bigger parks wanted.

Eventually, after an epic season rangering, I would be asked to return to join the wildland fire crew there on the North Rim. I had been given opportunities to lead and command on fires there that first season, and that was further the curse of fire and smoke on this soul. Pyro-romantism. A fire love affair ensued.

Have you ever noticed a dog that smells something in the air? It begins to sniff the air, with its' keen olfactory senses and pursues to no end the outcome of that scent. Thus, a similar curse happens to many a wildland firefighter, even years after they leave the ranks, and settle into other jobs or careers. A wood smoke generates the ol' fire dog into action. Sniffing it out, seeking the smoke, the direction, magnitude, and then realizing that it's only from a neighboring campground, yet triggering the Pavlovian dilemma-salivating and remembering the glory of yesteryear. As ice cubes crackle in my drink at hand, the oak burning in my fireplace follows note and releases smoke scented wood as Springsten belts out, *"glory days…"* Indeed they were.

Captivated further by this land of mystic proportions yet so real as to have immersed myself with it, the North Rim of Grand Canyon lured me to attempt to conquer its' foothold on my soul. And thus I was captured to this cathedral. A spiritual awakening.

In Sigurd Olson's book, <u>*Listening Point*</u>, he shares some insight about this lure. *"The Canadian French"* (fur trappers/voyageurs) *"had a name for what he felt and what all men feel at times. 'Pays den haut,' they called it, the land of lakes, rivers, and forests beyond the settlements, the lure that had dominated their lives for almost three hundred years in their explorations of the unmapped continent…Back in the days of early colonization those three words explained the virtual abandonment of farms and villages by the 'coureurs de bois,' who had listened to a siren call more powerful than the ties of civilization or the bonds of family. The lumberjack was no different…It was the same challenge of far horizons he had known and the shared realization that once you have seen the blue and known the wilderness, nothing else is worthwhile…Others might find their 'pays den haut' in tiny hidden corners where through accident or design a breath of the primeval has been saved…"*

"Happiness is not a destination. It is a method of life."

-Burton Hills

It was an exciting life with good companions and lifetime friends that commonly understood what we shared was unique. A bond and a love for the outdoors, for the adventure, for being true to yourself, honest, hardworking, and laying it on the line for your fellow crewmember. We were the Longshots. At least for awhile.

Sometimes lives converge and lifelong friendships are formed. One of those happenings occurred in this magical kingdom called the North Rim. This harmonic convergence at the Grand Canyon was not unique in of itself, but to those impacted, their lives would be changed forever. As one player amongst numerous, I was a keen observer, close companion, colleague, and participant that was allowed into the close sanctity of an esprit de corps, an elite, top notch, veteran fire crew known as the Longshots.

And so, to myself, to my core, I just was me. And being me, I became Buck to my friends and colleagues as I was tested repeatedly in my rookie days. Placing a Coke can forty feet away from a tree to fall in saw class, I was instructed to crush the can, "if I was good enough," by dropping the sixty footer on top of it. "Clunk," sang the metal under the weight of the tree, followed by my, "Yahoo!" and given a full can of Coke to consume for the success. Tagged as the saw manager, I was instructed to organize and keep the saws running, all eight of them. With the extra parts that had not been utilized in years, I re-constructed a Stihl 034 saw from just a handle assembly. As fellow crewmembers gathered around, I pulled the cord and smiles erupted as the saw roared to life. We would use it for projects and road clearing all season. Another test came in the form of troubleshooting an old relic, the Mark III pump. Malfunctioning for years, unreliable, testy and not very worthy, I was able to re-wire and get it working for the season on the few fires we were able to draft water. Hose, tools, engines, and on it went, the tests and the proving grounds for reliability, trustworthiness, and excellence. The Longshot tradition ensued. I was glad to be here.

(Professor Canyon)- Orientation

On my first official day back of contracted work on the North Rim, eleven others and myself were gathered in the administration pre-fab trailer for orientation meetings with district ranger, Gustaaf Laarson. Inside the conference room the lighting was indirectly fluorescent, the papers in front of us photocopied, institutionalized chairs were of metal and hardened plastic, with a black painted table of the same cheap metal and a veneer of artificial wood grain on top. How sad and ironic that climbing the ladder of success even in the outdoor agencies meant far removal from the natural world that was the initial lure into the profession to begin with. Many of our acquaintences, colleagues and friends can attest to the rigors of "paperwork, being deskbound, trapped in the office, or stuck in a meeting" as park managers, district rangers, etc. Overburdened with filing briefs, reports, spreadsheets, etc. that removed them from their original "calling" in the outdoors, as they pursued the stability and pay that such advancements brought at the cost of sacrificing their true inner spirit. This dichotomous dilemma was etched on many such faces with heavy hearts.

Indoctrination consisted of rules and regulations with a slew of crapola. Before meeting Gustaaf Laarson, better known as Gussie, I had pictured a portly, jolly, Santa Claus type of figure as the district ranger of the North Rim. It seemed to fit that such a fellow should rule over this Camelot. Rather, Gussie was neat, dark haired with an immaculate beard and facial features. His quick, darting manners and sturdy yet slightly pot bellied body added to his bureaucratic features. His demeanor was one of acceptance, as he understood us and why we were here. He'd been down the same path before and didn't forget where he came from and how hard he worked to achieve his status as chief (unlike so many that do in the ivory tower). Gussie gave us his best speech, "The North Rim is the side of the canyon for those seeking solitude, those who don't want any more development. That's also the way the park wants to keep it. Any last questions before I turn you loose?" The reality of being cooped up in a room for seven more hours greeted Gussie. "Ok then, have a good, productive summer." Before that sentence was over, most of us were out the door, where a blue sky breathed new life into us. The vanilla scent of the Ponderosa's permeated the paths to our primary areas of employment that season: fire, law, interpretation/education, maintenence, and fee collections.

(Prof) Opening Night

"You can discover more about a person in an hour of play than in a year of conversation."

-Plato

Frequently unseen due to their remote work in the backcountry, the fire crew had a favorite hang out at the end of the road, the North Rim Saloon. Small by city bar standards, it was reminiscent of an old fashioned real western movie style saloon: swinging doors, smokey mirrors and even the local cowboys, known here as wranglers. The wranglers worked the horses and mules for public trail rides down the 14 mile North Kaibab Trail. There were no "donkeys" here and don't anyone go calling them such. One would get a quick, loud, and stern talking to about such a mistake. Big ten gallon hats, sombrero's, chaps, and jingling spurs, they were the real McCoy. Some with convictions, jail time, and outstanding warrants, hiding out in this remote region, on the dusty trails, long hours, measly pay, but the pride in knowing that they were working the old western way of life, on horseback. The fact that they were fed and bunked in addition to pay was helpful. Knowing they could drink on discount at the one and only watering hole, the local saloon, while hustling the senorita's was a bonus.
Mostly the wrangler was a quiet drunk; sometimes excitement was provided when a new, young dude, testing his oats, over imbibed, and became belligerent, loud, and

started a commotion, often with fists, chairs and a visit 3 hours away to the local jail in Flagstaff via a park ranger caged vehicle.

In contrast, the Longshots fire crew visited the saloon when not on fires, and were welcomed as a gregarious, fun loving, crazy, partying bunch. They got the local crowd (mostly off duty TW Service employees and some NPS personnel) as well as the visitors fired up, by playing songs on the juke box, and then singing along and dancing to them, whether anyone else sang or danced with them or not.

It was our grand opening down at the saloon and lodge. It had been an annual "get to know each other" dinner for the TW concession personnel and NPS crew. Before the road would be officially open to the North Rim, usually in mid May, and the public hordes invaded the scene, this event was the kickoff. Everyone was there. We made it back from road clearing just an hour prior. After a fine dinner at the lodge, we moseyed on over to the local saloon, where the juke box launched into the seminal favorite (Buffett) song, *"Why don't we get drunk and screw?"* Buck, Pat and some others were on bar chairs (a.k.a., *"the solid gold dancers"*) singing along while tossing various articles of their clothing to a cheering throng. Over in the corner was Gussie, head honcho, talking to Delbert (a.k.a.-Dim) Witt, the law bro, both glancing at Buck, half-dressed standing on a chair, Corona sloshing everywhere. I ordered another Corona. The song ended and a sweating Buck joined me at the bar.

"I think that Dim Witt's gonna have one of his boys stop you tonight." I told Buck. "Ha! I rode my bike down. Hey, I think maybe Dim needs a bit loosening up." Buck grinned as he walked over to Molly, one of the cocktail waitresses. Fifteen minutes after Buck had spoken to Molly, Dim Witt had his back against the wall as Molly's eyes, voice, and cleavage held him captive. Buck was nowhere to be seen.

Dim Witt was interrupted and answered his radio, making his get away through the saloon's swinging doors. Bennie, a waiter and I hustled out the doors as well while other folks in the saloon were now staring out the huge glass windows and laughing in their beers. The patrol car was hitched to two mules and wrapped in a dozen or so rolls of TW's finest t.p. with a bedsheet that hung on the side of the patrol car reading, "Free escort service." Dim Witt was not amused. He was gesturing like a scarecrow flailing in the wind to Jerry, the manager of the scenic mule rides. Jerry was shaking his head. While all of this was going on, I noticed Buck heading up the road on his bike. Going back to the saloon, I ordered another Corona and tried to engage Molly in witty conversation.
"So, what are you doing later?"
"Buck told me he'd have a candle light dinner ready for me when I get off shift." She smiled like a lighthouse through my Corona fog.
"Fuckn' Buck!" was all I could mumble.
I smiled back aloud, "Maybe another time?"

"Maybe." She stated sweetly and picked up her drink laden tray, parting the waters of the bar crowd heading back down to the thirsty diners in the lodge.
"Earth to Canyon." awakening me from dreamland was Bennie. "Want to burn one?" Bennie didn't drink anything other than water, juice or coffee, however, he liked his sacraments, as we both put it.
"Sure."

Staring out from the veranda, moonlight casting a glow into the giant abyss below, I faded into a dream...sweat gleamed on his forehead in the shaft of light through the kiva's rooftop opening. With the ways of the raven, he flew over the canyon, seeing below yellow bodies dancing with smoke and flame. High above the canyon, a column of buzzards reached to the clouds of mother sky and smiled, "You shall walk along the edge; you shall slay that which lays waste, yet you shall not come back and your friends will be scattered to the winds." The light was gone from the sky, yet the raven sat at the opening edge and gave a cry before it flew off into the night. Once again laughing, he climbed into his pickup and drove back to the mesas.

Awakening from my mind's wanderings, this old hippie walked off under a star studded evening to Bright Angel Point. Good stuff!

"In the old days people knew how to dream. They did not have to go to sleep first."
-Nietzsche

(Prof) Whack yo' Ponderosa with a dull Pulaski

With a periwinkle sky, the Ponderosa and aspens seemed to sing the early arrival of a summer song, happy at another upcoming North Rim solstice, reflecting my same sentiments. From my park service house on "Skid row" it was about three coffee slurps to the fire pit (our office). Ken, our foreman was just across at the Ranger workshop offices getting the weather and fire situation report off the computer. After a brief discussion, he informed me of the next day's projects and the anticipated fire season to come. Grabbing some mud for a refill, I wondered back to the pit, where I bumped into Lisa. She was a goddess, cute, muscled, tough, a marathoner, vegetarian, extreme adrenaline junkie, Antarctica search and rescue team member, had worked fire crews around the great North-wet. Grew up on the Washington peninsula with parents that were alternative and progressive. Lisa not only believed she could do better than boys, she backed it up.
"Hard night at the saloon?" grinning with that mischievous look of hers.
"No harder than any other." was my wicked grin reply. I walked past her tight, little running body to my first ever official desk, where I noticed a legal sized yellow page from a pad tacked on the wall above. Somewhat prominently in two by four inch bold markings was the following note:

"Ha!" I laughed and heard Lisa chuckling outside the pit.

"Come on you useless boy, it's time for p.t.'s, put that coffee down!" she yelled and was gone to the fire cache, to round up the rest of us, "useless boys." "My Pulaski's never dull!" I shouted and put down my coffee cup, following after her (and forgetting to check my instructions for the day). The mules brayed from the trail crew corral as the periwinkle sky looked down.

<u>(Buck) Traditions</u>

One of the Longshot annual traditions involved the sunroom of the Grand Canyon Lodge on the North Rim. The infamous, "Brighty" donkey statue had resurfaced there after many years in storage. A famous 1953 fictionalized book and then movie was made that elevated the burro to celebrity status. However, the fact was that introduced donkeys (burros) were destructive to the indigenous desert bighorn sheep competing for the same vegetation. The park service began removing the burros at the time creating a public relations nightmare. To make matters worse, the film producer had a statue made of Brighty which was originally put in the visitor center on the South Rim briefly. Not until years later when the park service had relocated all the burro's and public fervor died down would Brighty re-emerge from storage at the North Rim Lodge.

Attributed to either the Wad, or the professor, the tradition was for us, the crew, to go down one evening to the lodge, and gathering around the statue (with tourists in full bloom) go over to Brighty, and kiss the ass. Yes, literally, kiss an ass's ass! In full view of the public. It was supposedly to bring us good luck and many fires. Yeah, right! But good naturedly, we did so to the look of astonished visitors. More than a few (visitors) followed suit when informed of the good luck. Amazing witnessing the leming effect at work.

<u>(Prof) Reflections from a coffee break</u>

"Love the life you live, live the life you love."

-Bob Marley

To describe the emotion however I was seduced, it was LOVE! No doubt about it. That's the way it was for me with the GRAND CANYON! Ever since I spent four months as a Fred Head (Buck's translation- *he means a Fred Harvey South Rim concessional employee*) in the bowels of the El Tovar's kitchen back between fire seasons in the winter of '80, I had fallen smitten in love. A day hike to Dripping Springs confirmed it with every step down into that Grand ditch.

"The best job I ever had during my thirty years as a ranger was the five years I spent... on the South Rim of the Grand Canyon. I loved the beauty and changing moods of the canyon and I loved the action...nothing topped the Canyon for diversity of experiences."

-Michael J. Meyer, <u>Ranger Stories,</u> p.45.

My initial fire season (1977) and love first occurred during my training. I was handed the nozzle at the end of a hardline from an engine with two strips of flames set before me there on the shores of Lake Mendocino. (Buck's translation-*I think Freud would look into the nozzle/hardline analysis, hmmm*). As the engine drove between the walls of fire, I applied a fog pattern to the base of those flames, turning smoke into steam. That was all I needed. (Buck's translation- *power trip baby, oh yeah, more psychoanalysis needed*). At the North Rim two of my great loves collided, the canyon and fire.

<u>(Prof) Longshots</u>

"Surround yourself with people who make you hungry for life, touch your heart, and nourish your soul."
-unknown

By the time I got back to the North Rim in eighty-six, the fire cache was unpickled, leaving the opening of the fire roads, my favorite task, yet to complete. Good timing indeed. The crew in eighty-six had Ken coming back for his second season at the helm of the Longshots. A big, burly, well seasoned Longshot, Ken had a hearty laugh, with a low key demeanor. Faller extraordinaire, his performance was legendary. Now married to a beautiful park service employee Linda, and their fun loving dog, "Wit," he was a homebody seeking a permanant career for a secure future. A favorite *proverb* comes to mind in describing Ken, *"If you see a friend without a smile, give him one of yours."* Always smiling, always positive, his presence as our leader was the calming in a sometimes hectic environment of fire and management. I returned with the title of fire monitor, a newly created position. Buck, became Ken's assistant. It was Buck's second full time fire season and second on the crew. Buck and I became fast friends and hiking buddies in our first fire season together. Dave, or Tex (eventually named Bucky) also was back for a second season on the crew. Tex being from Texas, fit that soft spoken western part and was as good a hand as one could get. Rode horses growing up, loved animals and you couldn't find a nicer guy in the world. Now at twenty four years of age and still toting that wonderful sweetie, the part that I always think of as his better half, he arrived once again with his beautiful girlfriend, soon wife to be, Kathan. That fun loving, beautiful blonde, granola, with common sense and know how, was now a teacher on the Rez (Navajo). Anything to be together, they were a beautiful pair. Kindness, gentleness, a respect for life, that's what Tex and Kathan carried with them, like halo's. The smiles on their faces emanated from their heart. It was a joy to see both of them back.

"Day-O" was Ken's typical bellow call to order. Lisa led us in warm ups. "Come awwn, let's take a run." Ken smiled emphatically. As chief of this Longshot tribe, he made sure to keep us together.
Lisa led, as Tex and Buck took off running.
"Body Nazi's!" I murmured, and followed behind with the Fox.
The Fox, what a character.

As I arrived at the fire pit earlier, I was to meet another member of our fun bunch. He was a bulldog of a man with chiseled features that fit his frame. Vietnam vet, Alaskan offshore fisherman, rancher, and served on various fire crews. Red hair and beard, a quick wit and quicker tongue. I'll let his first words that he spoke to me, introduce him. "My names the Fox and I come from god's country, Montana. I'm the son of a preacher and a Black Foot princess. I'm here in the quest to slay the mighty dragon that rages of thunder and lightning inhabiting this forest with fire." the Fox then taking a breath, his blue eyes shining, and continuing, "Yes, my friends, my comrades, let us live as legends, let us delight the wood nymphs under the full moon, let us uncork the bottle of passion and slay the dragon of power and fire on four legs. Are you with me?"
His blue eyes now smoldering, implored each of us with his glance, yet we all broke into laughter.
"What planet did you say you're from?" I chuckled and extended my hand, introducing myself, "Professor Canyon, but everyone calls me Boomer, cuz of the thunderous voice and at times, ass."
"Earth, my friend." smiled the Fox and extended his. A legend in his own mind.

The mule in the corral was braying, but the raven found a choice piece of week old Wonder bread. Meanwhile from the cache, music was blaring Willie Nelson as the Fox and I started working on saws.

(Buck's interjection) It goes without saying that a description of the Prof, Jim, "Boomer," Canyon is needed at this point. Physical appearance, he reminded me of a young Jack Nicholson, as in Easy Rider. He was a good looking guy, scraggly due to not shaving that often, but fit and trim from working hard. He was very intelligent with fire knowledge and outdoor saavy, well respected. His taste of music varied and did his best at turning us on to much in the way of rock, blues, folk, and americana. Avid reader, I know he loved Vonnegut, Abbey, Hillerman and SW history. A hippie at heart, his politics were liberal, in fact he was good at debate, and was hard to refute. His mantra was, "anarchy with a smile." Liking those funny cigarettes, he imbibed quite often, though never on the job, and never impairing his performance while doing task at hand. His voice boomed, and he worked us hard his first year as assistant (back in '85) but this year (1986) he mellowed a bit as the fire monitor. He was into "earth muffins" or honeys as he called them, outdoor, cute, petite, fit, granola-type women. He was a real sucker for the type, a hopeless romantic, and a bleeding heart. Smitten with lust way too many times, he would turn on the charm and show them some great times and have exciting adventures with them. To me, he was a great companion, my hiking bud, travel mate, and fellow Longshot, I trusted my life with him.

__Part Two-__
__Heating Up__

__(Professor) Temporary assignment- L'il Test Burn__

Having certification with prescribed fires, I was sent over to the South Rim as an instructor in fire training for their Ranger skills class. To mainatin healthy forest communities, land mangers used to imitate natural lightning fires by setting fire to a plot of land. It was prescribed with specific parameters and guidelines in place to combat the overloaded and crowded forests. Anyway, I left my cronies on the North Rim temporarily for this assignment while they were busy with getting the engines ready and roads cleared.

"Now, ah-mm ah countin' on you guys to kick ass." the words ringing out from the thick lipped spittle laden rusty red and black mustache. I was the only guy with Billy "Joe" Sagebrush, the Grand Canyon's new fire management officer (FMO). By "guys" I figured he meant the North Rim crew. The twang continued, "So, ah-mm ah countin' on you boys to call the shots."
"Let's hope I don't have to kick your ass." I jokingly muttered.
Billy Joe's roomy, alcoholic, blue eyes turned on me and in a serious twang added,"Ahh- might have to git out here tonight, have a brew 'n' do a l'il test burn to see how y'all respond." He turned from me and started walking back to the government vehicle, a pick up.
"He must be putting me on." was all I could think. "He can't do a little test burn without all the protocol and parameters met, who the fuck does he think he is, arsonist moron". On our drive back from Desert View to the South Rim Village, he said no more about a brew and l'il test burn by himself.

That night, when I mentioned Billie Joe's beer and fire comment at the Bright Angel Saloon to the fire expert, Len, the Wad, he shot back with, "He musta been puttin' you on Boomer, have another brew."
Of course I did. Unfortunately, my luck with wayward tourist gals was to no avail that night.

The next day found the Wad and I at Albright Training Academy for the wildfire portion of the Ranger skills class. Park service personnel from all across the United States were there for training in: public contact, law enforcement, search and rescue, and so on and on. Our portion of this class would last a few days, which included a small prescribed burn if conditions were favorable. Len, the Wad, had been in charge of the Longshots when I arrived in eighty-four. He was Buck's roomate back in '83, when Buck was rangerin'. Len had been foreman for four or five seasons, a Stephen Pyne protege, as was Ken, our current foreman on the North Rim. Two-thirds of the way through another season, Len took a job on the South Rim to obtain what's called in the realm of the government, his "status," yep, permanency, including retirement and benefits. Now riding pine, tucked away from the big ditch grandeurs and sitting in a dark room monitoring computers, he was always ready to get back to some action.

So here in '86, Len was taking a break and heading up the wildfire part of the program. "And so remember, fight fire aggressively but provide for safety first, now we'll have a ten minute break and then continue on." The Wad had his usual grin, blue eyes twinkling, his fine blonde hair thinning. He had arrived to the North Rim just out of college, as in Syracuse, an upstate New York Polish-descent boy become a man here on the edge of the Grand Canyon. He hated to hike, but loved playing softball, organizing games any night he was home and free. Into country music, steak, and sausages, he was a genuine nice guy. His positive outlook on life was contagious. Ever the six foot, hundred seventy-five pound leader, he got up to me and gave his usual "chu-uckle" adding, "There's some cuties out there Boomer."
"Yeah boy howdy." I coyly commented. Yeah boy howdy being a phrase I adopted from one of Lisa's friends that I'd been hot on the heels of to no avail. Boy howdy!
"Well now that I'm out of Seattle, maybe I'll get lucky here by the big ditch of love and sex…"
"And rock 'n' roll fire fighters." as Wad finished the phrase, cutting me off as the crowd was back from break.

"For the next part of our fire program, I'm bringing out a smoke bum in the truest sense of the word, Jim, Boomer, the professor, Canyon." Continuing on the Wad added, "Boomer's worked with the California Department of Forestry for a couple of seasons as a firefighter, and then for four seasons drove wildland fire engines for the U.S. Forest Service and Bureau of Land Management. This will be his third season with the park service as a Longshot on the North Rim Helitac crew. Prof was assistant foreman last year and this year will be Grand Canyon's first fire monitor as part of the parks new fire management plan. For now though, he's here to talk about the tools of the trade, so take it away Boomer."

"Take a breath Len, and thanks." I had to reply with a grin to him and turned to face my audience with my so called booming, rambling style.

"It starts right down below." I lifted one of my legs, not to show off my canyon rugged hiking legs, but to reveal the Vibram heeled fire boots. One cute, blue-eyed rangerette had my attention as she giggled at my double entendre.

Classroom continued outside. Demonstrating and hands-on technique prevailed for awhile until looking at each other, we both voiced it, "We got us a fire, Boomer-Wad!" Oftentimes, whether small or large, it's the smell that gives one the first hint one's nearing the proximity of a blessed blaze, at least to a true smoke bum.

"I guess he did it." I stated.

"Who, what?" the Wad turned to me as he slowed down the three vans of Nomex-clad students of fire training behind us.

"Remember what I told ya about Billie Joe last night?"

"Geez!"

You could see the ground fire from where we parked. I put on my old Bullard metal hardhat, grabbed a fire shovel from the back and began to look it over.

"How about you hand out tools appropriately and check out the gear, while I check out the fire?" asked the Wad, grin and Pulaski at hand.

"No problem, there's someone I really want to check out." I smiled looking at the pretty brunette from earlier in the class.

"So I thought." said Len.

This someone piqued my curiosity earlier with the raising of her slender, tanned arm, asking what Nomex was. To which I'd replied, "A treatment to the fabric so we don't go up in flames, however, given enough direct application of flame and heat…" This had produced a delightful laugh.

However, with the situation at hand, I turned my attention to the anxious faces looking at me aware of the smoke and flames.

"We have a little test burn here for you today." I smiled as if it were all planned. Picking up a Pulaski, I handed it to one of the fire experienced students, "Here Ed, you'll be lead Pulaski, behind Len. Remember your balance points on these tools and how I told you to carry them." I barked loudly. As I handed out tools I checked to make sure that all of the safety requirements of personal protective equipment, from boots to gloves, water, fire shelter, ear plugs, eye wear, hardhats, and Nomex (clothing) were in order. I had to trust that all had remembered cotton underwear.

"Boomer."
Pulling my radio handset from the swivel on my leather belt, depressing the transmit
button, I replied, "Go ahead." and moved out of earshot from the students.
"I think we should have the Desert View Engine here, even though I don't think we'll
need it. Also, I'll inform dispatch that we have a small test burn going, in case they get a
smoke report."
"Sounds good." was my reply.
As I got to the fire, I noticed Len had that heightened awareness look that a fire can give
you.
"It's about an acre Boomer, moving slow, jumped a scratch line that Billie Joe must have
put around the oblong shaped spot."
"Well, let's get it then."

The Wad turned to everyone, "Remember stay ten feet from the person in front of you.
Now let's cut some line. Follow me." The Wad stooped over a bit and swung the
Pulaski's razor sharp hoe end to reveal a bit of brown earth, mineral soil, neat as you
please, right next to an eight inch flame coming off the forest ground litter. After twenty
minutes of scraping, cutting, swinging, lecturing on proper tool use and distance, we had
a fire line two feet wide containing Billie Joe's l'il test burn. And the Desert View
Engine had yet to arrive. But Billie Joe was not done yet.

That very same evening the "Pit" was rocking to the strains of Jimmy Wazoo and the
Peach Pitters, one of Flagstaff's finest in the mid-eighties. The Wad and I grabbed
barstools, and I ordered us Corona's and lime, the beverage of choice for a Longshot in
eighty-six.
"Cheers!" toasting and raising his longneck for the ceremonial clank and gulp. I'd no
sooner put my bottle on the bar, when a voice came from behind.
"Care to dance?"
I slid off my stool with a, "See you Wad." smile.
"Yeah, right, chuck, uck, uckle, gulp, gulp." came from the Wad.

Off we went to the old dance floor. During the daytime, the "Pit" (of the South Rim) was
a huge cafeteria for tour busses. At night, it became a bar with occasional bands on the
weekends. We gave our legs a good Wazoo workout that night. Later, she parted with her
student buddies. I took off to the South Rim fire barracks back behind the youth hostel.
There was prescribed burn work to do with Billie Joe tomorrow. Come to think of it, I
never did finish that Corona.

A new day, a new fire. We couldn't catch it. The fire was moving too fast. Now that the
wind had picked up and the flames were getting higher and higher (as the song goes) I
turned to old tomato face, Billie Joe, "Let me pull an engine in here or you'll have to call

the forest service for a crew.”
“Can't do that.” huffed BJ, then added a moment later, “Get me the engine!”
“Shit!” was all I could think as I was getting the engine. Just another little test burn, huh.
Billie Joe wasn't hung up on the rules, he just didn't know them.
As he commanded me, I drove the engine into the fire across the open Ponderosa forest
floor. Going off road over archeological ruins in a government vehicle into the fire,
violated several regulations in the national park. What a dilema, our new boss Billie Joe
breathing down my face and heatedly barking, “Hurry up!” while committing various
illegal acts of impropriety.

I longed for the days of old Norm, the FMO my first two canyon seasons. Norm didn't
know fire, but at least he allowed his experienced personnel to do their jobs
professionally. I fired up the pump and raced off with the hard line to extinguish the
blaze. The wind died down. “Well, we got her now.” I thought as I joined BJ with my
shovel and bent down to cut line stating the obvious, “Let's hope it stays calm.”
Sweat covered BJ's forehead and there was no reply. After we had the fire controlled, we
tried to cover the engine's tracks (over ancient ruin sites). We had little success as there
was too much visible damage.

Neither of us said a word on the way back to the South Rim until I whiffed an immense
scent of shit in the cab. Turning to BJ, I asked him if he accidentally stepped in
something. Sniffing the air in the truck, he responded with, “Sheeitt, stop!”
So I did, at which he leapt out and yanked his trousers down and began sweeping chunks
out with his hands. Apparently when he had pulled his pants down to defecate earlier
that evening in the forest, he didn't squat far enough over for clearance, instead
depositing his soils in his drawers. I choked back my laughter as this dumb ass deserved
what he did to himself. Serves him right for not knowing woods etiquette. We always
dug a small hole, wiped using the 3 inch by 3 inch tissue squares issued to us (or
leaves/needles) and covered our excrement with soil, leaves, and a rock. You just don't
go around shitting anywhere in the woods like an animal. What kind of creature was he?

“I can't seem to face up to the facts
I'm tense and nervous and I
Can't relax
I can't sleep 'cause my bed's on fire
Don't touch me I'm a real live wire
Psycho Killer”
-The Talking Heads

<u>**(Prof continues) New Boss-Man**</u>

"The NPS workforce has become quite accustomed to seeing misconduct openly sanctioned. Many of the most egregious offenders in the agency have been merely relocated and placed, through directed assignments, into increasingly more powerful positions from which they cannot be removed..."

-Paul D. Berkowitz (<u>The Case of the Indian Trader,</u> p.80)

The spotlight followed the frightened eyes, long ears laid back, frozen by the roadside. The guns report tore apart the night. A rabbit twitched in a pool of crimson, under a sagebrush in the dirt. A laugh echoed through the cab of the pickup. One hand clutched a cold Bud, the other the steering wheel, while one foot pressed down on the gas. The hand with the Bud put it up to his mouth, which let some slide down the chin and onto an old, stained t-shirt. Putting the beer down to free his hand, he adjusted the spotlight, still searching for anything that moved or crawled, to blow away. This was Billie Jo's favorite pastime other than drinkin' beer or drivin' like a son-uf-a-bitch. Billie Jo previously had been doing law enforcement and administration, transferring from somewhere back east. That is, until one "uv dem damn woman libbers" filed a harassment complaint. In typical government fashion, rather than rid the problem, they transferred the scumbag into another area, and gave him a promotion while at it. Go figure!

"Fuck 'um, I've got plans for fire, if I can get rid of those damn hippies, Indians and misfits on the North Rim," mumbling incoherently to himself while belching his displeasure, "buuuaaaahhhh!" Billie Jo now reached for a swig of Old Crow, followed by a chaser of his Bud. He hit a hole that was unseen to him, bottle spilling while the can went flying from his hands clobbering his eye.
"Fuck!" his hand on the wheel jerked to his face and the truck leapt off the road, onto its side. BJ's forehead kissed glass at 35 mph, delivering a non-fatal blow. The contents of his cooler, with ice and beers, pissed all over him in the cab of the truck as the engine motored on. Two vertical lights shot into the pinions of the South Kaibab National Forest off the Grandview Fire Road. One lit up the yellow eyes of a coyote, and off in the distance, the yipping-howls of others could be heard, probably on their way to the dead rabbit down the road. Billie Jo moved his legs and arms.
"Whew! Nothing broken." the voice said to itself. One hand went to his forehead and came away sticky.
"Fuck!" The hand then turned the truck lights off, found an unopened can, and proceeded to imbibe.

<u>**(Prof) Trouble Brewing**</u>

"When more people pursue the power of love vs. the love of power, peace will exist."

-Jimi Hendrix

To the eyes of the public, the National Park system is managed and operated by the government, which is really, you and I (as taxpayers). To the eyes of this employee of the National Park Service, it seems that the parks are actually managed and operated for those private corporations that own the concessions in the parks. There's lots of money to be made inside and outside the boundaries of these sacred islands of wilderness amidst the crush of humanity. I always find it ironic and sad that here in America, where capitalism and competition are the laws of the land, businesses that operate in our national parks are granted monopolies. No competition. Contemplate this: those motels and restaurants, gift shops, and gas stations where you spend your hard earned dollars on vacation are nothing more than gold mines for the powerful, select few. Employees of these mega-corporations (i.e.- Curry Company at Yosemite, Fred Harvey at South Rim, TW Services of the North Rim) are treated much the same as the peasants were under a king in medieval times. I know, because I used to be one.

"What if our national parks and monuments became places of conscience instead of places of consumption? How many more T-shirts can we buy, let alone wear, that advertise where we've been? How many different forms of recreation must we create to assuage our adrenaline addictions from wing suits to pack rafts to roller blades? Is it not enough to return home with a fresh idea gleaned while walking in new territory? As I have been visiting our national parks, I keep asking myself: Who are we becoming?"
-Terry Tempest Williams, <u>The Hour of Land,</u> p. 354.

Pecker Tracks was a consummate politician. One had to be in such a highly visible park. He was a big man, with neat, silver hair, tan complexion, stubbornness and a subtle wit. The same P.T. had ordered the horseback mounted attack on hippies in the meadows back in his days as superintendent while at Yosemite. The battle cry of Yosemite became the rallying call for all law enforcement in the National Park Service (translates to heavy-handed). Pecker Tracks as superintendent of Grand Canyon was making his policy known, and word was out that he was soon headed up to D.C. as director. He had to leave his legacy and development for the North Rim was making news.

"Likewise, a disturbingly high percentage of leaders in the NPS, especially park superintendents, have been selected not for their experience or qualifications per se so much as for their demonstrated loyalty and friendship to even more senior officials in a particular regional or Washington office."

-Paul D. Berkowitz (<u>The Case of the Indian Trader,</u> p.61)

<u>**Professor Canyon to the rescue**</u>

"Laugh with conviction. Love with abandon. Live with passion."

-unknown

Her tongue sensuously flicked my neck, while her tan, slender fingers roamed the plains of my jeans. The cute, tan Ranger gal from class was seriously lighting my own fire. Ponderosa's passed us by as my pickup's lights cast an illumination off the South Kaibab Plateau.
"Can't we stop somewhere?" whispered the voice attached to the honey tongued vixen. I knew that soon we'd be off the plateau and on the Rez. My mind raced for remembrance of a place in the forest to stay for the night.

"Yeah." I could barely muster as the action was boiling below. "Hold on, just a little bit further." commenting to both of us. Upon arrival, I quickly took my eyes off the road and planted my lips on solid ground.

Morning found our bodies entangled in the back of Bertha (my truck) a deluxe camper complete with dark tinted windows and a nice bed set up.
"How does breakfast sound?" as I was actually thinking more of coffee than eggs.
"We didn't even get our socks off." she laughed, just noticing.
"Ha-ha!" as I joined in, because that was all that we didn't take off.
"Here." I offered, reaching down to her feet. "Let me take these off for you."
Breakfast would have to wait. I won't bore you with the delectable details of that delightful weekend. I drove her down to Phoenix to catch her jet back to California. Leaving the congested civilization behind, it was a tear strained drive back. I headed north with only one ray of hope, my next stop, the North Rim, my home and my companions.

<u>**(Buck recalling) Early on**</u>

Early in the season, as we were gearing up for the storms and lightning strikes that would arrive soon enough, we were home bound each evening at our duty station. Home is where we were comfortable with each other, with ourselves, quirkiness and all. As individuals, we were unique, yet as a crew united together, synchronized, and synergized for our mission and common goals. All idiosyncracies left when we were on fires together as trained professionals and passionate about our work. We laughed, jested, sang, hollered, and motioned to communicate our intentions to one another. Trusting one another, our strengths melded forming a cohesive unit.

"An early morning walk is a blessing for the whole day."
-Thoreau

Early mornings we typically woke with the sun, strapping on running shoes and hitting the trails for some cardio conditioning. Five to six miles was the norm, returning for some crew games of sand volleyball or strengthening and agility exercises. Lisa tried leading us in some yoga, but we were not quite there in those days as to crew yoga. Morning coffee, some grub and fire reports as well as assignments split between the crew, and we were off on our daily adventures. Three of us might head out road clearing in one engine while three others headed out in another engine for other roads to be officially openend. Road clearing was an annual operation to have access to our backcountry for when the smokes were reported. Road clearing consisted of sawing and removing large timber fallen over the dirt roads from the heavy winter snows. Once a road was cleared to the end, typically a vista, or point overlooking the canyon, we would mark it on our maps and announce it back to dispatch. It was open for action and to be utilized for accessing a smoke report. If a smoke report was in the vicinity, then we'd gear up, ride out, park the rig, and hike, miles upon miles smelling for the smoke, on the compass bearing given, until we found it and acted upon it. Rarely were we able to drive up and put out a fire using our engines and the few hundred gallons they carried.

"Tex, you drive like my grandmother," boomed Canyon.
Smiling, and holding on to the steering wheel two-fisted, while four wheeling up "ball-bearing" hill, Dave kept us all rocking side to side and sliding into each other. Maneuvering the scree, boulders, and steep grade as we ascended the infamous road was always a test of focus. Our mission was to make the Kanabownits (pronounce, can-ah-boo-nits) lookout tower for our lunch rendezvous with the others by noon. They'd be coming in via forest circus logging highways until it hits the park boundary where dirt ruts two feet deep become the road through dense stands of fir and aspen, making their progress slow and tedious with lots of saw practice and winching operations. The irony is that these pitted fire roads follow through some of the prettiest aspen lined meadows around. The final climb out is along piney ridges as one nears the old Kanabownits lookout.
"How's your grandmother drive prof?" finally responding after cresting the hill and seeing the road versus the sky in the windshield.
"Death gripping the steering wheel, and looking like a deer caught in headlights, while moving like she was in a funeral procession." ol Boomer just waiting to jostle.

I was stuck in the middle between the two, arms braced upon the dash mounted radio unit just waiting for the bait to hook. Once ol' Boomer was on a roll there was no stopping his antics; he would pound ya till there was no more rebuttals, replies, nor rebukes. All in his good natured way, of course, and all for the benefit and education of us "young bucks" as he liked to call us.
"Oh wise one, teach me how to go up ball-bearing hill next time without causing you such anguish," Tex quietly smiling, going along with the play.

"WTBH" roared Boomer.
And in unison, we all bellowed back his common admonishment to us.
"Worthless as tits on a boar hog!"

Moving along with road clearing, we rounded a bend and came across a small, dead, punky log in our path. I volunteered to jump out and physically just haul it to the side so we wouldn't have to fire up the saws for more cumbersome work. As I pulled on the log to swing it away, a Kaibab squirrel landed on top of the engine hood. Thud! DOA (dead on arrival)! Looking up into the Ponderosa's surrounding us, I spotted a Red tail hawk perched on a branch overhanging the rig. I watched this beautiful, majestic bird of prey (genus Buteo) wisely and calmly staring down. The uniformly colored tail and dark belly band were definite identifiers of this broad winged hunter. Normally at this point, I would just write this off as another cool happening, except this bird of prey had been occurring more and more in my life here at the canyon. Soaring effortlessly above in slowly turning circles outside my cabin on several occasions as well as while hiking on different paths at different times, and now here, once again, what was this common coincidence? Knocking the dead squirrel off the hood onto the ground, I hopped back in and we ambled slowly away. Looking back I immediately saw it swoop down and grab the squirrel in its talons, sharp bill ready to rip into this meal. However, it just stayed there on the road, looking at me for the longest time. In that encounter between the two of us I felt a connection that I really couldn't explain. Leave it to a feeling, deep inside, but a feeling nevertheless, that somehow, I was appreciative of that bird, and identified with it in some way. I knew that its' terrain was varied and frequented the woodlands, mountains, even deserts but needed open country for survival. Maybe that was the connection that I was seeking, an identification with something wild and free.

Shortly after that incident, further along the road, a huge Ponderosa across our path had caused us to stop once again. Sliding out, this one would put us in saw mode. I was up while Tex and Boomer (prof) cleared out the smaller stuff around my main cut on the leaner. In no time, we had saws buzzing. The four foot diamenter tree had come down partially hung up on other trees blocking further passage until removed. For the next hour, we sawed, bucked, limbed, and rolled logs until we were covered in sawdust, dripping wet in the ever climbing sun. We didn't make the fire tower lookout for our meet up until 1330. The others had come and gone on, clearing further out to Point Sublime.

"Lunchmeat, yum, that little gal at the general store sure makes it special for me and puts in those extra slices." as I teased and devoured my sandwich.
"Just make sure you watch your lunchmeat, and where you put it, ya know Buck?"
"I'm always ready Prof, always ready!"
"Yeaaah, you're just like lunch-meat, always ready. Lunchmeat." And with that reply,

Canyon continued with his infamous evil laugh.

Making our way out to rendezvous with the others at Point Sublime, a rather ironic name at this point in time in history, it is an awe inspiring view when clear and quiet. The Anasazi Ruins below on a cliff, off the point make it a highly toured site from the air. In the short thirty minute reflection break we took together there as crew, no less than six helicopters and two fixed wings had buzzed our vista for the scenic flights provided out of Vegas and the local (South Rim) airstrip in Tusayan. Considered a noise pollution issue as well as an air traffic hazard with the NPS, studies were going on for future management. On average, about every three to four minutes this Sublime Point was inundated with aircraft hauling the paying masses to view the Grand Canyon. Already several air collisons in the area resulted in many casualties but so far, the bottom line was that top dollar speaks. Screw the integrity of the park, making money is what it's about. At all costs, and any means.

Terry Tempest Williams in her book, <u>The Hour of Land,</u> observed, *"Bison are grazing inside Yellowstone National Park, but once they step outside the park boundary they are shot by state or federal agents for fear of their carrying brucellosis, known as undulant fever, which could affect elk. Elk hunting is big money in Montana. Kill a bison to save an elk. It's that simple and it's that political-never mind there is not one documented case of a bison having given brucellosis to an elk. **<u>Most of the issues confronting our national parks today are political.</u>"** (pg.59).

Meanwhile air quality was also degrading in the class "A" pristine environments, such as here at the canyon. Construction dust, auto pollution and particulates were being windswept from as far as Vegas and even California. Obviously, even in the vast west, encroachment and development was taking its hold and effecting the experience of this national park. Set aside for future generations to experience.

Interesting how times have changed. When I was visiting Yellowstone and attended a presentation, it was historical in nature. To attract the public initially to the remote location, paved roads were built for easier access. It showed how the automobile industry had effected that park with masses wanting a wild experience from their vehicles. People actually smeared honey on their infant's face to attract bears to come up and lick it off as they could snap a picture from the comfort of their car. Greaaat picture, dumb ass! Then cry when the bear bites an accidental chunk out your kids face. Demand retribution, threaten lawsuit, and have the critter put down, 'cause you wanted a Disney experience, all from the ease of sitting in your vehicle. Our previously referenced North Rim fire lookout from the early days and major influence in the environmental movement, Edward Abbey, eloquently shared this prophetic dilemma in his famous book, <u>Desert Soitaire</u> (from his time as a ranger at Arches NP in the '60's). Specifically the chapter titled, "Industrial tourism and the National Parks," details the travesty of big business and the pursuit of money at the cost of sacrificing the parks. "Why is the Park Service generally so anxious to accomodate...the indolent millions born on wheels and sucked on gasoline, who expect and demand paved highways to lead them in comfort, ease and safety into every nook and corner of the national parks?" Abbey goes on the relate how the National Parks have become petting zoo's so that the public can drive around to pet nature, knowing that the vast majority of folks visiting National Parks never get more than a mile or two from a paved road.

Back to reality for us was our own issues with our fuel loaded forests. When the fires came, as they did annually, some years bigger than others (as far as size, intensity and numbers) we were dealing with air quality from the smoke output. Mostly I'd just say, "screw it!" and that we need to burn no matter what. However, a consideration that now faced me was that some of our tourists had saved up long and hard for this once in a lifetime opportunity, many from afar (i.e.- Europe and the Orient). To have their vision obstructed by the heavy smoke inversion clouds would suck. Similarly, the evening downdrafts of smoke choking out the canyon floor with the whitewater camps and backcountry sites below making for difficult breathing and spoiling their experiences would not be appreciated. Like nature, a balance was needed.

"When we try to pick out anything by itself, we find it hitched to everything else in the universe."
-John Muir

There were many other variables to consider in trying to manage a wildfire. There were many hats to wear, many mouths to feed. Few decisions were made without all parties taken into consideraton. However, we, the Longshots had each others' back, consulted, gave our input, and then got in line where we were assigned as resources for a particular fire. We reviewed our plans, updated, and revised as needed being open to issues as they came up. Fire is dynamic, so we believed that the humans should be in responding to them.

<u>(Prof) Are we having fun yet?</u>

<u>1986 Longshot prayer</u>
O, great god of lightning,
deliver us from routine,
for thine is the power
to kindle the flame
that blesses this poor Longshot
with overtime plus hazard pay.

Powell Plateau rises like an island off the west end of the inner gorge. Muav Saddle connects to it like an earthen umbilical cord from the North Rim via Swamp Point. Swamp Point was our typical drive-to destination, followed by a hike through the Muav Saddle to the north end of Powell plateau. Walking to the southern point on Powell takes another several hours. This springtime the fire road out to the U.S. forest circus highway (to Swamp Pt.) was still un-cleared due to snow pack and downfall, so it was to be a fly in show for fires out there.

Meanwhile, our crew was still tied up working the park service roads, clearing them for the season.

Powell is home to numerous age old foundations of song and fire. Ponderosa glades that rival the Redwoods occupies the northern half of the island, while the southern half is pinyon-juniper due to the desert climate surrounding it, with the heat from the furnace of the inner gorge. A 70 degree North Rim day is often a 90 degree canyon day. Powell is home to the most spectacular views of the canyon. It is canyon magic to the eyes, and does its name proud. While I'm pontificating on the platitudes of plateaus, I guess I may as well mention the cabin in Muav Saddle. There is a cabin where TR (Teddy Roosevelt) Uncle Jimmy Owen, Buffalo Jones, and others stayed while slaughtering the mountain lions, wolves, damn varmints and all when it was a game preserve. Past thinking was that eradicating the predators would be inducive to bringing in the public and allowing the ranchers with their beefstock safe range.

Thunder bursts and spring lightning strikes quickly occurred.
Buck and Tex had been out on Powell for two days and nights monitoring the fire. In other words, letting the fire do what they've always done in the forests, letting it burn until the dawning of Smokey the bear. This, of course, was before the great Yellowstone fires of '88. However, this was the first season of letting fires burn in Grand Canyon. Yosemite, Sequoia-Kings Canyon and indeed Yellowstone already had this policy in place.

As such, under the fire management plan of the Grand Canyon, there were three different zones. One, a total suppression zone (the developed area) another, a let burn zone, almost all of the inner gorge, and finally, a conditional zone, which is where most of the North Rim's thousands of acres of virgin pines, firs, and aspen lay. Conditional meant if we felt safe and the fire was in a "prescription stage" (meeting all the conditions) we'd let it burn and take action as needed. Finally, only those of us on the North Rim had to deal with the new FMO (fire management officer) factor, Billie Joe, or as Stephen Pyne (fire expert) has noted, that fourth side of the fire triangle, "management."

Lisa and I had been scheduled the night before to take over monitoring from Buck and Tex on Powell Plateau. That was before we learned of a slop over from the rim with fire now into the steep slopes of brush, just off the edge. This activity of the fire set the Billie Joe ass pucker factor into high gear. The BJ factor here was similar to premature ejaculation. Billie Joe decided (on his own) this meant full suppression, complete with a ten person response crew. Hearing him on the radio was reminiscent of a boy's first sex act: quick, loud, and over reactive.

"Cliff White, the wildfire scientist who helped orchestrate wildfire management strategies in Canada's national parks for more than thirty years, says that the fire triangle is actually a square because of another side that no one likes to talk about publicly. Politics, he says, often plays an oversized role in the development of wildfire strategies and the execution of wildfire management."
-Edward Struzik (Firestorm, How wildfire will shape our future, p.26).

The next morning brought a size up from Buck on the Powell Plateau with the slop over. "Cold, cold, cold." claimed Buck who said he did the cold trailing on his hands and knees. The reality was that this fire was out. Billie Joe had no faith, and couldn't back out of his (ego) stated plans from the night before. He went ahead to dispatch the ten person squad out to Powell along with himself to accompany. Lisa and I were now sent to Point Sublime and decide a course of action for a new smoke that was just spotted. Needless to say, I was bummed on not getting to Powell, the beautiful, isolated island in the sky. Then again, no sense getting caught in the cluster fuck out on Powell with BJ and Buck.

As we got into 210, the park helicopter, Dana, the pilot, told us,
"If I don't get you to Sublime soon, you aren't gonna find it."
"Ripper, huh?" I commented facetiously.
Dana smiled and pulled the ship into a nose dive down Transept Canyon. The first flight of the season is always an "E" ticket and I was glad I missed attending the saloon last night. As it was, the morning coffee was starting to head upstream along with the rest of my body. Dana pulled out of the dive smoothly, and looked over smiling, as we headed out south down the Bright Angel drainage, then west over Utah flats and onto Sublime. We got put down almost right on the smoldering duff. Lisa and I unloaded our gear: one Stihl chainsaw, Dolmar container with two and a half gallons of mix, a quart of oil, two gallon canteens of extra water, one shovel, one Pulaski, one Macleod, two overnight packs with our personal gear bags, our two initial attack packs with our fire gear and maps, fire situation analysis forms, fire line handbook, compass, flares, rations for two days, various snacks, four quarts of water apiece, wedges, and chaps for falling. In other words, a lot of shit. While Lisa got our saw together, I did the size up. It was pretty quick. We hammered it out and got it done.

Meanwhile on Powell Plateau, a Grand Canyon fire convention was taking place. Billie Joe, with the entire South Rim fire crew (except Slim Tim, who stayed back to manage the heliport) plus a few South Rim law dog rangers, along with Buck and Tex already out there all met. Ken and the Fox (in an engine) were also enroute cutting and clearing their way out to Swamp Point for an access to Powell. Upon arrival the entire assembled crew had witnessed first hand a "cold" fire. Laughable and incomprehensible, a total waste of government tax payer money, to satisy an ego and an incompetent's untrusting control freak nature. By the time Ken and Fox got out to Swamp Point, Billie Joe was on the radio frantically calling for a flight to exit out of there.

However, Mother Nature began to have plans of her own with gusts of wind on the South Rim registering 45 to 50 miles per hour. Thunderheads were towering over Great Thumb Mesa and the sound of drums from heaven roared while Zeus launched thunderbolts. Billie Joe, grounded due to the high wind advisory, started the long hike across Muav Saddle to Swamp Point with Ken and the Fox waiting. Gussie and chief ranger Dim Witt, would ferry out park vehicles for transporting all the other folks back.

With the winds kicking up, it also meant that I needed to take direct suppression on the smoldering spot of duff at my cold fire. I called in such a course of action, which a reluctant voice declared affirmative. Mucho gracias senor Billie Joe asshole, I wanted to sign off with.
Then, the following transmission was received.
"506 (BJ), fire dispatch."
"This is 506 (BJ) go ahead."
"We have a report of a smoke growing rapidly on the South Rim."
"Copy. Contact forest service. They've got three engines and a twenty person crew stationed there."
"Dispatch Copies."
"509, this is 506 (BJ)"

Slim Tim, as I knew 509, promptly responded from his heliport manager duties to take over the fire. I laughed thinking of all the South Rim folks being here on the North Rim for a cold, slop over, and now hiking all day across Muav Saddle, while it sounded like Tim and the forest service were riding to glory on the heels of a romping pinyon-juniper fire. I hit the ground laughing triggering Lisa to choke on her sliced peaches as she joined me in laughter too. It was going to be quite a fire cluster fuck season.

'Twas a fourteen mile walk out, hoofing a 15 pound saw and fourty-five pound pack. Lisa was loaded to the gills carrying 60 pounds of gear and keeping me at a brisk clip. The Fox had been reassigned the job of transport, but hadn't gotten too many miles past the basin, when we ran into him; more importantly, he was carrying food, cold drinks, and driving. Lisa and I stashed most of our gear in the back of the chase truck. Seating ourselves amidst our packs, the Fox started up the truck, and we were down the road headed home to the rim. Many were the trees cleared off the road as we went by them. As we came upon a nearby seasonal snow melt stream, a mandatory stop was required. Taking off our boots we soaked our feet awhile. The most important part of a firefighter, the feet. Ahhh!

From the Fox we learned the forest service was mopping up another PJ fire which made its run and burned out in the coolness of the night. Buck and Tex were ordered to stay on Powell, monitoring the scenery. My mind was dreaming of a real dinner at the Lodge. In reality, I was craving ice cold Corona's with lime at the saloon and one of those foreign visitor gals...

Overhead, a red tail hawk cried high in the spring blue sky. A fire down, a whole season to go.

(Buck) Easy come, easy go

"Nothing is worth more than this day."
-Goethe

Arriving from the Northwest parks, a holier than thou Ranger named Bryce was assigned a temporary abode with some others until the housing situation settled and maintenance opened up more living quarters. Having the broom closet room in a trailer with a Native (Indian) and a Mexican were not to his liking. Furthermore, it was the antics of some serious partying with off duty loud music, dancing, and socializing. I know 'cause on several occasions I was there "Wang Chungin'" at night. A very quiet guy, wound a bit tight, too serious, and not very adaptable, he checked daily for openings to another residence. Meanwhile, his sweetheart from up Northwest way came for a surprise visit to the Grand. Lost amongst the ruins, she bumped into the prof, inquiring directions to her beau's place. Graciously, happily, mischieviously, Boomer invited her down to the saloon for a welcome drink. Being the type he loved: cute, petite, shapely, and granola, one drink quickly became several. On duty Bryce appeared in the saloon, surprised as all hell, red faced at seeing his gal Margie all cozy and giggles with Canyon. Seeing her ol' Ranger-man standing there, she threw herself upon him and with one of her two faces, planted a big smooch and whispered to him something sexual in nature. Oh yeah, that's what I'm talking about!
Now the professor is an understanding kind of guy, not into stealing what is not rightfully his, but matters here didn't seem to jive. She was definitely into games and one was being played out here and now. Canyon, astute, and having been around the block a few times, let it go, turned to his drink, and gulped it down, ready to boogie on reggae

woman. Margie, now that Ranger-man Bryce was gone, flung herself upon Canyon. Sensuously moving her parts where other parts responded, whispering sweet somethings, and craving a lustful adventure, it was exit, stage left, swinging doors out the saloon to skid row palace for some rockin' and don't bother knockin'. Wow! Could it be love, again? Between Margie's visits with celibate Bryce and her hot and steamy adventures with Jim, it was playing out as a soap opera on epic proportions. We all were waiting for the showdown (music reverbeates from the flick, *"The good, the bad, the ugly"* in my head at this point). Obviously, the rugged pirate look won out over the clean cut, straight-laced teatotaler. A week long episode and she was gone, but only in her physical presence. Her care packages arrived weekly, addressed to her new flame, or flavor of the month, whatever, to Canyon. He loved the home-made cookies, strong coffee, and little gifts found amongst the assortment. Too much to take, as the mail arrived and the rangers picked it up and distributed to everyone, it was only obvious the gal had made her choice and it didn't include Bryce anymore. Frustrated with his housing, the roomies, the heartache, Bryce was a short timer and left for another park, somewhere far away and removed. Ahh, such is life. Bittersweet.

(Prof) The Buckskin Tavern Incident

Up on the plateau from our rendezvous point, I could barely see Buck's tail lights across the north Kaibab meadow. Turning my lights off, I drove by moon glow. The two lane highway turned into a silver ribbon. We were high-tailin' it eighty nine miles to town, a border town, Fredonia (at the Arizona-Utah line) to the Buckskin Tavern. Tonight it would be drinking and dancing, tomorrow, an off day, we were Buckskin Gulch bound for an overnight backpack trip in BLM wilderness. As soon as the meadow moonlight was gone, my fossil fuel burning beast was in the night forest shadows and lights came back on as my eyes went on "Deer Alert!" The North Kaibab Plateau has one of the largest mule deer populations of any forest I've ever lived in. This, thanks in part to Teddy Roosevelt and Uncle Jim ridding the predator wolves and most of the lions. Driving speed was 45-50 miles an hour tops, day or night. I've learned through being with another friend that hitting a deer then skidding into a 200 year old fir and being in a vehicle don't all mix. The vehicle and the deer lose. My friend lost his memory as well that night and I lost a few doobies.

The band came on to play, a Lynyrd Skynyrd opener,
"...Gimme three steps toward the door?
Gimme three steps, gimme three steps, mister
And you'll never see me no more."
I took a pull off an ice cold long neck. Looking over at Buck, there was a slender white hand with blood red knife blades for fingernails planted palm down on the small of his white t-shirted back. Upon further review, I could see tight blue jeans, a bare thin midriff

and long black tresses. With peripheral vision I scanned a gang of bikers looking intently at us.

"Would you like to dance?" a honey laden voice asked Buck.

Moving up close to be within earshot was a huge, hulking biker, scar-faced, skull ringed, and reeking of alcohol, pressing his body against Buck. I looked over at Buck, who was studying his long neck brew. I nudged him from the other side with my knee. Turning to me with a smile he picked up his beer and said, "Cheers!"

We tipped our bottles and drained them, chug-a-lug.

Buck turned to the raven tress, knife blade nail woman, and politely stated, "No maam. Me and my hippie amigo are boogie-n' on out."

The hulking figure next to her said, "Good timing asshole!"

I didn't see what happened next, it was so fast. Scar face was now a heap on the floor.

"Let's go professor." Buck quickly responded.

As we headed out the door, the gang at the jukebox started coming our way until a wildcat voice from the bar called, "Don't move a muscle fleabags or I'll spread you all over the walls!"

Buck and I looked at the legendary bartender, Sam, who was holding a sawed off shotgun on the gang with very steady hands. I laughed, Buck laughed, then Sam laughed. We were all laughing in the bar, except for the bikers by the jukebox. We knew she was legend in these parts, now they would too. Ahhh! The wild, wild west. *Bad Moon Rising"* appropriately played on my tape as we headed into the clear desert skies with a big, bright moon overhead.

We camped only a few miles away off some dirt road. Our reasoning on staying close to Kanab, Utah, just a few miles from the border was to hit Paula's Gold Dust Café for breakfast before heading out to the trailhead. Paula's homemade muffins were reason enough, but she was nice, always pleasant, smiling and probably always had been for her 60 or 70 spins around the sun. It was fun to see some locals too, like Ol' Nick there, a cantankerous old fart. He always had some of the prettiest young women in town around him. Hmmmm! While Buck and I ate muffins, ham, eggs, potatoes, coffee, and more muffins, Nick told of his latest trout expedition. Right then and there, Buck and I developed serious plans of converting young women to our "Church of the What's Happenin' Now Saints." With such dreams in our head, we paid our bill, bid Paula adios, and Nick good luck, some wishful see ya's to the waitress, and we're out the door, trail bound.

(Prof) The Gulch

"If a person does not see, hear, or smell civilization, he or she is in wilderness."

-Roderick Nash

The Pariah trail head is only an hour or so of two lane from Kanab. Soon, I had my truck Bertha, parked and with my backpack, off we went in Buck's truck. Driving to Wire Pass trail head was five miles of two lane followed by a dirt road through House Rock Valley to Vermillion Cliffs for another 8 miles of rocks and hardpack sand. My truck would be waiting for us at the take out, then we'd drive down to Buck's truck for our completed shuttle. Thus, we could just do one way hiking (for our time limited days off). Got that? Well, we arrived at Wire Pass, had a beer there and got our packs ready.
"Buck, I'm gonna put my keys in your glove box, so I don't lose them."
"Fine." Buck looked up from busily tying his boots (obviously not paying attention). Obviously in our haste and focus upon our task ahead, neither one of us caught the future dilemma, my keys should've stayed with me or left somewhere safely back at my truck. We both put our packs on and headed down the trail.

Wire Pass is a side canyon of the infamous Narrows of Buckskin Gulch. We had to turn sideways to pass the chute with our backpacks off, looking up one hundred foot walls. The Buckskin Gulch is twelve miles of narrow slot canyon. Tree logs from flash floods jammed between canyon walls high above us spoke of thunderstorms. Sunlight was by chance of the canyon bending, where the sun was resting in the sky at that moment. The canyon floor for the first three to four miles was of firm packed sand with damp pockets of mud interspersed. These pockets of mud turned into quicksand and even log jammed stands of muddy water between canyon bends. First these stretches started out ankle deep, then became knee deep, going up to thigh height, huevo depth, and climbing higher. I led the way, and as I would round the corner, my words would ring out, "Oooooh, Buck, it'ssssss cooooold!"

At one bend, a log jam created a very noxious floating pool of cow turds and green scum with debris floating in it. Being about five foot ten inches tall and one hundred sixty pounds, I negotiated log to log with quick footing. Towards the end I had to chimney up to where I could get a hold of rock to pull myself up to the top of the jam.
I'd no sooner pulled myself up, than I hear a crack of the log behind me and Buck yelling, "Fuuu...lllppp"

Buck, being six foot and one hundred eighty pounds or so was treading fast in green slime. He was up to his newly bearded chin in green goo, with a cow patty floating by his mouth, eyes bulging, arm reaching out towards me. As I looked helplessly on, Buck came flying out of the pool, pulling himself to the top.
"I can see the headlines, hiker killed by scum pond." laughed a crust coated Buck.
"I'll take a hit off that bottle we have stored for dinner."

(Buck's reflections) The prof is a scurrier, lightweight, quick, and scampers up rock and ledges faster than a ram following a ewe. As I tried following his same path, I encountered different conditions with my weight breaking the old rotting log where Jim flew right over. With the loud crack, I went immediately down into the pond scum below. Immersed in smelly, stagnant green-black water, dead animal carcass and floating cow turds surrounding my face, I collected my frantic energy in an effort to extract myself. Disgusting. Gross. Slimy. Stinky. I would have to remain camoflaged for the rest of the trip or until we found cleaner water for me to wash up. All in the adventure though. A story to tell (as I am presently relaying).

(Prof continues) Buck and I figured we were a couple of miles from where Buckskin and the Pariah Narrows converged. It was then that I had the revelation.
"Buck, guess what?" I queried.
"What?"
"Guess where my keys are?"
"Where?"
"I fucked up."
"The glove box" we both harmonized in the silence that seemed to only break with our words at the wing beats and chatter of the ravens.
"Looks like you're gonna have another hike" commented Buck.
"Looks like it."
Twelve miles of Buckskin Narrows over with and no stuck cows in quicksand as was written in (Edward) Abbey's tale, Buck and I continued three or four more miles of Pariah Narrows. The Pariah Narrows greeted us with fun moments of some knee but mostly ankle deep sand jelly quicksand. Nearing the end of our day, we burst into open sky. Finding a nice soft sand bank, we dined on cheese and crackers, and a bit of brandy.

Buck cleaned up in the sand, a dry loofah experience instead of the water he was hoping for.

With a blessing to the constellations amidst the dwindling light I lit my pipe as we lay down on our bags, feet feeling the cool soft sand between our toes. Philosophized until our eyes were full of stars and dreams took hold of us. It was a good Buckskin of a day (even though Buck still reeked of pond scum).

(Prof) Strumpets !

Morning brought the sound of howling coyotes. We stayed in our bags until the shadow of the canyon walls which lay with us was replaced by the warmth of that blaring ball in the sky. As the sun shone, the coyotes quit their song. Buck heated water on his camp stove, and we enjoyed a breakfast of instant coffee, oatmeal, and real oranges. It was a quick four mile jaunt to my truck, where to no avail, I looked underneath for the spare key I'd taped there years earlier, and probably a few years earlier had fallen off. Handing me his keys, I hit the highway while Buck reclined in the shade of my truck, yelling out to me my favorite line, "WTBH" (worthless as tits on a boar hog).

It was a hot mid morning already in the nineties. I had two quarts of water with me.

Walking up the two lane asphalt road for about an hour when a sports sedan pulled over with two beautiful women "Lady luck," I smiled. They were Salt Lake City-ites, vacationing at Lake Powell, out for fun. We all laughed when I told them of my keys. Expressing my concern about the trek in the sun, they invited me in.
"Come with us to Park City." one said rather coyly.

I thought of Buck while I looked at the two beautiful babes with long sun tanned legs in the front seats. The road to Wire Pass stared at me ahead from the window. I had a decision to make. Frost's poem came to mind, "I took the road, the one less traveled…it made all the difference." I offered up a doobie. They giggled, accepted, and took out a bottle of wine they had stashed in a cooler.
"Is it true?" one asked rather demurely.
"About what?" I responded.
"About pot, does it make you horney?"
I could only muster my evil, wise professor laugh and twinkle my eyes in Dirt Road Nicholson fashion.

After a desert mirage fantasy, or was it real, we parted ways at the turn off. Four miles went fast with my re-fantasizing of the Salt Lake Mormons gone bad.

Priorities first, I grabbed a warm beer from Bucks cooler, then the keys to his truck from my pocket, got in and started her up. Before we went back in our separate vehicles, I took Buck aside and told him of my hard, hot time in the desert getting to his truck, slowly emphasizing with enunciation some of the details. "Hot, Buck!" and laughed with my best evil laugh. He could only smile and shake his head, mumbling some incoherent gibberish, "F**#!"

"Reality leaves a lot to the imagination."

-John Lennon.

(Prof) Engine cab talk

Buck and I flushed a lot of turkeys driving towards Point Sublime a few days later. Our mission was to check on the previous, hmmmm, fire and declare it officially out. The saws were operating well and it was nice to be here. One of those crisp, clear days when every breath feels good, at least in between choking on sawdust and saw exhaust.
"How about Zion Narrows for our next days off, oh professor of canyonology?" blurted out Buck, while sharpening his chain.
I looked over at the freshly bearded, brown eyed smiling face of Buck, responding in the affirmative to his question and then asking one of my own.
"How'd you level that guy last weekend?"
"Did I ever tell you of my D.C. upbringing and world travels?" came back Buck.
"No." I responded.
"Good." he retorted.

I looked over and Buck wasn't smiling. I then asked about his decision to leave the law enforcement rangering behind and transition into wildfire.

(Buck's reply)-When I first got into the Park Service, it was as a naturalist. A fun job educating the public with very positive interactions. As government budget cuts occurred, the only way to continue with the Park Service was to attend a law enforcement academy and gain experience in the smaller parks before applying to the most sought after ones. At first it was all good but with time it became a very different experience. More and more crime came to the parks and we, as rangers, had to deal with it just as the local police and sheriff deal with their issues. Burglaries, car thefts, sexual assault, batteries, vandalism, and a host of other incidents kept me attending magistrate's court monthly testifying in the government's behalf as key witness working with the assistant district attorneys. With time, more cases evolved where we were dealing with escaped convicts, felons, and wanted criminals with violent pasts. When drug runners and outlaw biker gangs arrived, we were sent out for stand downs and possible, "shoot-outs" at our boundaries. However, the bad guys had been equipped with an arsenal of automatic weapons overpowering our government issued six-shooter (typically a Smith & Wessen .38 Special) and a .12 gauge shotgun.

At the GS-5 level of seasonal hire status (read- no benefits and only temporary work at $7.25/hour) it doesn't take a rocket scientist to figure out that this wasn't a fair pairing. Now it was an adrenaline rush to have these encounters and live to tell about it. No denying that. With the increasing demands and lack of support it became a very negative factor in dealing with the hostile elements in the parks. Wearing your weapon and defensive gear while on patrol around the public elicited many negative comments and harsh critique. Actually, this type of "real" action and desired presence was now attracting several of LAPD's (Los Angeles Police Department's) finest in applying to the permanant vacancies on the South Rim. Many of them expressed their pleasure in leaving the big city behind and working in such a place doing what they loved best, deterring crime, and that usually meant in a heavy handed way versus the laid back approach that I was originally taught back in my academy days. To each his own. And being true to oneself.

(Prof continues)- When we got out to Sublime, we turned off our park radios and went out to the point. The view was incredible this day. Once again, a never ending parade of helicopters took their turns during daylight hours suspending tourists and noise over Sublime, while the sun burned its ever changing rays to cast shadows and a myriad of colors upon the rocks. Buck's favorite activity at Sublime was to moon the flights as they pulled up for views of the ancient dwellings. With night came silence to this sublime place. The way it was intended to be revered.

The next day, we headed back to the rim after lunch, extracting the rest of the gear from the Sublime smolder, which was still dead. Buck had that grin again once I informed

him that Corona's were on me tonight. We headed back to the skid row palace where already gathered were a motley crew. As I walked in the door I heard voices back in my room. But first order of business was the fridge and a case of Corona.
"Bless you, oh friends." I thought aloud while handing Buck a cold one.

"Hear, hear!" cried Buck, plucking a couple of lime wedges already sliced from the cutting board. Walking further into my place, the crew was gathered. Snake, from the naturalist division was philosophizing or politicizing about something. As always. Snake was of Irish origin, raised in Jersey. His goals of being an actor were being played out on the stages of various national parks, as a living historian. Snake was also a rabble rouser. Rollo was there from the STP, or "turd herder" as those in the sewage treatment plant industry referred to themselves. Tex and his sweet gal Kathan were there reunited once again for the season.
"I'll come back every other weekend until you're up in a month and a half to join me." soothed Tex.
"wooof!" Echo, his trusty hound dog, barked.
"With all four dogs and three cats, too." Tex smiled laconically Texan that he was.
Kathan assured her handsome man, "It's okay Dave (refusing to call him by his crew designated nickname) I just worry about the fires."

"Well, I'm gonna make this my last season as a Longshot." Tex prophesied more than he realized. A coyote laughed off in the distance.

The smoke bums were all gathering on the back steps, downing cold ones.
It was then that I saw my roommate for this upcoming season arrive. Already a month later than the rest of us (just out of school). A tall, 6'4", two hundred-thirty pound New Yorker that I had played chess and jammed with back in Flagstaff times. The "Dove" had his guitar in hand as he climbed out of his Subaru, which looked as if it was outfitted for desert survival for the next forty years. It was packed with odds and ends past the windows. The door opened with a smiling Dove, "Grab your harp old man." bellowed my favorite playing partner. The skid row palace would be rockn' tonight. From the bedroom came another bellow, "Where's those Corona's?" I smiled clear down to my toes.

"Music is what feelings sound like."

-author unknown

<u>(Buck) Other duties as designated</u>

Even with fire as our main mission, we also wore many hats and assisted with other park duties, some fun (like our campfire program in the amphitheater) and some not so fun. Whenever we heard the call for distress, and if we were in station or off-duty, we responded as a trained resource for assitance and overtime pay. A common occurance on the North Rim (due to its' elevation) was "S.O.B.'s" or short of breath folks, usually older, commonly referred to as, "tourosauruses" that took the tour busses on a vacation with an overnight here. Called out in the middle of night, one of us ended up administering low pressure oxygen via nasal canula, while another drove the ambulance transporting towards Kanab (Utah) medical facility, an hour and a half away and at lower altitude. We would exchange the patient somewhere in the middle of the drive (somewhere in the Kaibab forest) meeting with the upcoming ambulance from town.

Another common call was, "hiker in distress," coming from other hikers ascending the long and arduous North Kaibab Trail, 14 miles from the river and Phantom Ranch below. Rough, rocky, hot and dry during tourist season, it was not a day hike or one to just mosey on down. Running down the trail with our "jump kit" (emergency medical supplies) we would encounter some really questionable types down in the big ditch. Often out of shape, overweight, restrictive health problems, and no plans for the desert wilderness, they cried for help. Mostly, they needed water, lots of it, and a baby-sitter. It went something like this...

Touron: "Help me, help me!"

Responder: (giving water, and taking vitals) "Drink this water with electrolytes and tell me what happened?"

Touron: "We just thought we'd take a quick peek at the Grand Canyon and see what it looks like from down below. We started down a few hours ago, but I began to feel faint, and quesy, and tired and now sick."

Responder: (on radio to dispatch) "We have a .... year old patient with a history of....vitals are all clear times 3, we have a code W. Will be walking up with patient."

Dispatch: "Dispatch copies, clear."

Touron: "Can you fly me out with a helicopter?"

Responder: "Well, that is restricted for emergency cases, and we'd have to hike down further to a safe helispot. It would cost you $3000, but we are restricted due to high winds."

Touron: "What? That's ridiculous, how 'bout a mule ride up?"

Responder: "Well, we'd have to arrange that with the private concessionaire up above, and to have them come down with a mule will cost you $300. If you are over 200 pounds, then they cannot transport you."

Touron: "Hmmmf! How 'bout you carry me?"

Responder: "Well, I'd be glad to carry your personal items in my pack, and walk with you back to the top, but there's no way for me to personally carry you up."

And so it went, we would talk to them distracting their attention while we walked them up, back to the rim, monitoring vitals, hydrating and baby-sitting. The code "W"signified that we had a "wimp," typically someone not prepared for such an excursion in this wilderness. It was surprising how many people we encountered that went beyond their capabilities, disregarded their health issues, and thought this was a stroll in the local park, jeopardizing not only themselves, but family and sometimes the responders.

A typical summer day at the park with throngs of visitors each one snapping their picture of a lifetime to document the momentous occasion was a common sight. Just as I was finishing up from a shower and headed out for my day's off, a call came out for EMS (emergency medical services) and SAR (search and rescue) staff to respond down to the BA (Bright Angel) Point for an emergency. Arriving at the scene I was immediately put to work as a belayer on rope number two, next to ranger Pat on rope one belaying paramedic Steve, already rappeling down the cliff face. Apparently a couple on honeymoon had been walking the short trail and wanted a better picture. The new bride, a nurse I was told, instructed her "hubby" to go off trail, climb on a rock and pose. Still not pleased with the viewfinder shot, famous last words were, "take a step back" so that she could capture a more dramatic photo. Which led to his fall, a vertical plunge of ninety feet only to land in a pinyon pine, breaking through that and continuing to tumble another fifty feet on a scree slope, resting at a ledge with thousands of vertical feet below. Paramedic Steve arrived to the victim, and radioed up that the patient was still breathing. Following orders from the doctor (on the South Rim for this very reason) he administered the designated drugs and saline via an IV. Meanwhile I was instructed by teammates to be the second belayer for the stokes litter basket that was to extract the patient. As I finished with my seat harness, a new Ranger, one that I barely knew, and one that we questioned based upon his antics previously, had become assigned to anchor me in (to a boulder) as my body would be on the edge of the cliff. Ranger Dudley hastefully clipped three cams (spring loaded camming devices) into a crack in the porous rock and then rushed off for crowd control. In all the commotion, looky-lou's, helicopter noise overhead, and mayhem that ensued it was a clusterfuck for awhile. In the process paramedic/Ranger Steve was headed up the ropes with the patient in front of him in the (Stokes) litter basket. I pulled slack as they continued their progress up the rock. The first "friend" (as these cams are sometimes called) popped out and I slid further (over the edge) by a few inches. I still had two in the crevice holding me. Not much longer and another popped out now sliding me further out forcing me to arch my back and find unbalanced seating on my butt at the rim's edge. One cam held me, the patient in the litter, and Ranger Steve (that was administering to the patient and clipped in to this litter now). It was a precarius position, unsafe, and I called out, several times for assistance. No one heard as they were too far away and all the commotion and eyes were on the action down below. Ranger Pat belaying near me (anchored in via rope around a tree) couldn't move as he was pulling rope for Ranger Steve. At that point I thought how stupid it was to not check the cams myself, no matter how quick and chaotic the situation was. What a painful way to go, all three of us going down scraping skin against rocks, bruising, breaking, and hopefully knocking unconcious our heads in the ensuing fall or killing us instantly. Obviously I am here to relate this incident and thus that one cam held. In review, our team at the safety de-briefing came up with future solutions. In voicing our concerns we addressed and practiced weekly simulations that would improve our future responses with safety for all as paramount for success. In the process of performance review, Ranger Dudley was let go never to be seen in the uniform again. Word on the patient was he survived having spent several months at Flagstaff hospital. How he fared after with his new marriage, we never heard.

"A man's errors are his portals of discovery."

-James Joyce

As park service employees we were all "Rangers" to the visiting public. To the touron, we were at their beck and call. An incident comes to mind when I encountered a station wagon pulled over on the shoulder of the road, a few miles from the lodge. Still maintaining my commission (for law enforcement) I stopped my government vehicle, got out and proceeded over to the man under the open hood.

"What seems to be the problem?" I asked curiously.

"Problem...PROBLEM!!! you think I have a PROBLEM! I don't have any PROBLEMS, I am perfectly FINE!" as the guys voice raised quite a few octaves yelling his statement.

I cautiously backed away, looking inside the vehicle at four kids and one crying baby in the arms of I suppose his wife; a vehicle packed to the gills with stuff and anxious looking people. Leaving them there was not my intention, however, this guy was having a serious melt down. I got the hell out of there, and thanked my lucky stars that it was him and not me. Arriving back to the developed area, I notified the local mechanic of the broken down vehicle. Maybe he'll have better luck. I learned never to ask if there is a problem (no matter how misinterpreted it could be, it wasn't worth it).

"Life is complicated with its: ifs, ands, and buts; it's alright to be crazy, just don't let it drive you nuts."

-Jimmy Buffett (Simply Complicated)

An isolated place like the North Rim and as servants in the public realm, we were exposed to the diverse crowds of visitors when in the front country, as in at the lodge vicinity. Quickly identified by our various uniform apparel, we literally couldn't escape without questions of all sorts posed to us. Mostly, we loved the encounters with the diversity of folks, sharing a bit of their backgrounds and reasons for being there. But there are always a few...you know what I'm talking about...those few, found everywhere in life, in the nooks and cranies of WTF? Well, I believe it was Laurel, yes, sweet, innocent, chief Ranger's fiance, Laurel that came up with the idea of a "tacky touron" party theme. What that amounted to, was dressing in flashy and bright colors of floral print tropical shirts, Bermuda shorts, dark socks, sandals, some kind of straw hat, and big, dark, funky sunglasses. Individual attire differed, but that was the starting point. The park lost and found was helpful in procuring the necessary items. It was a real smorgasbord of Goodwill fashions lost by our wonderful visiting public. Drinking beer, barbecuing dogs and burgers, American flag flying, with our asses planted in our lounge chairs on the sand (of our volleyball court) we played tunes and proceeded to pick out of a box the various questions that most the naturalists, rangers, and other park staff had heard. After reading aloud, we all hoisted and toasted the tacky touron for our wonderful presence. A sampling of the questions were as follows:

Where are the restrooms? (the number one most often asked question in a national park).

When are you going to build a bridge across the canyon to connect the two rims and lessen the long drive?

Why don't you have a hair salon on the North Rim like they do at the South Rim?

Did Evil Kneivel jump over this on his bike?

Where are the geysers?

How often do people fall over the rim? (just once).

Where is the elevator to the bottom?

How many Indians live here?

Were Thelma and Louise here?

Will the sun set tonight?

Is there a golf course here?

Is there anything to see here?

Appropriately at this very gathering, a call came out for an EMS (emergency medical service) response required down at the lodge parking lot. Apparently a woman was reported in labor and ready to give birth in the middle of the asphalt lot blocking hundreds of other vehicles. I was on call, so I headed down, reporting in to dispatch my arrival. Sure enough, there in the middle of the parking lot was a crowd gathered around a woman laying there moaning, while a man comforted her. I immediately began to prepare for a delivery but not without some questions to direct my assistance. The guy that was there by the woman's side informed me that she was experiencing, "rebirth" and just needed to lay there, refusing further aid. I inquired again about whether I heard correctly the term, "rebirth." Yes, he stated, she is, "going back into her childhood and the womb."

"Okayyyy..." as I hesitated and thought this was a new one for me. Reporting to dispatch this information, I was instructed to just monitor and keep her safe there in the lot while she went through her rebirth. Crowd dispersal and traffic control was my next step. About twenty minutes later, with traffic flowing again, I came over to check on the patient, now getting up slowly. As they made their way to a vehicle and left, I notified dispatch as the incident was over. Several radio's throughout the park gave me smart ass comments like, "congratulations on a successful delivery."

Ahh yes, serving the public in need, indeed.

(Prof/Buck) School's out

"Fear an ignorant man more than a lion."

-Turkish proverb

The Longshots ended up providing fire training for other park employees to be red carded (qualified to fight fires arduously) for the hot season ahead. On one such session, while still in the classroom, we were dispatched by an afternoon smoke report just down from the developed area. It had been burning in a mess of firs and aspens, consuming about an acres. Due to its proximity to our structures, we immediately stopped the classroom and brought them to the real fire for a full suppression attack. Hands on experience. They were split into squads and went about the business of scraping lines into mineral soil to contain the fire. Day became night, and we had finally encircled this mess of dog hair thicket stands of trees. Winds began to pick up, and thus we hurried to improve our lines by moving in towards the fire, removing combustible burning material (green to green, black to black). One tree, a nasty old fir, about ten feet inside our line, had been engulfed by flames. Maybe sixty feet in height, but fully encompassed by fire, it was threatening our hard work by blowing embers over our line towards the non-burned forest downwind. This called for typical saw work. We ran Stihl chainsaws. Buck was faller/sawyer on this fire, being swamped (assisted) by the Fox.

BJ, our idiot boss man, happened to be on the North Rim that day for who knows what. Being the pyro he was, he loved being around flames, and stopped by to visit us as evening approached. Upon seeing the roman candle effect of the burning fir, he quickly ran over and dismissed Fox so that he could swamp for Buck. As he moved in to the tree, flames were well over two to three feet height on the ground. Enough burning fuels existed on the ground to make it a real hot situation. Adding to the difficulty was the tree had fire coming out from the inner base, a cat's face. Due to being the source tree of ignition from lightning, the top was also actively burning, although partially blown away. We tried cooling the area down with a few squirts from our "piss pumps" which dropped the flames height momentarily but added too much smoke to see. Buck went over with the chainsaw whirring for his front pie cut, the fuel oil mixture and lube combined with the fire all around creating the effect of a flame thrower. In the night forest, with active flames all around him, Buck was literally standing on fire, dancing around with hot feet, trying to drop this tree into the burn. It was a picture of Dante's Inferno. He was immersed. Flaming ground fuels heated up once again, his Nomex pants burned up past his calves, unaware, he continued sawing away.

I'll let him continue...

(Buck)-

 As I walked over to fall this engulfed tree, I felt the heat, and stinging in my eyes from smoke and sweat, but felt like I could do this rather quickly with Fox swamping me, just as our foreman, Kenny taught us, the Longshot way.

With earplugs in, my whole world was in front of me, intensely cutting the tree to drop it. All my focus was on my cut, heedless to any outside influences. I had my spotter, my trusted, and accomplished Longshot companion, Fox, watching above and around me. Arms length away as my swamper, or eyes, ready to alert me in a moment's notice, even pulling or pushing me to safety if needed and as trained. My eyes were stinging from the smoke and sweat within the goggles. With fire dancing around me I thought I could drop this tree before my treated pants went up in flames as well as myself. My feet heating up intensely elicited a shuffle, one foot to the other. A shroud covering my neck to keep fire brands from traveling down my shirt, was a fountain of sweat as was my body at this point. Intensely at work, but knowing and trusting that my swamper was there nearby with falling axe, wedges, and a safety signal kept me with the task at hand. A push in the back, and I, the sawyer, would hug the tree, meaning branches from above are crashing down, avoid the "widow-maker." A tug on the back, and we pull out, swamper one way, sawyer opposite direction, abort, the tree is coming down the wrong way.

Amidst the action, I noticed that the Fox had left, replaced by boss man, Billy Joe. When BJ arrived, our so-called fire expert and boss, I thought, WTF, he should know better than anyone. I was involved with falling this tree. I didn't think anything of it, figuring he was boss man for a reason. Different from logging operations, falling trees on fire required a trained pair synchronistically working together. With the fire roaring, my chainsaw whirring, and intense heat surrounding me, my feet were burning, as I continued alternating one step to the other to keep my boots from melting. As a large part of the burning tree top came crashing down, I was oblivious to it until it landed next to me, breaking into smaller pieces. It was large enough in diameter that it would have seriously injured me if not killed me. As I turned to BJ to question a look, there was no one there. I was on my own. With intense adrenaline drive, I just fired up and finished that backcut in time to watch the tree go down in the flames. Threat over from that tree, now I had to get the hell out as I was quickly burning up, flames consuming my pants. Ken grabbed the saw from me as the crew hosed me down with the bladder bags of water. Not a fun experience looking back, too close a call. Now we really understood where we were with our new, so-called, "expert" fire manager boss, BJ. It was time to wonder where this guy came from, what was his background, and how did he get this job.

(Prof)- There was no one there to warn Buck of the fire burning tree top crashing down near him, missing him by inches. WTF! Ken ran in as the tree was finally falling into the burn. He quickly hustled Buck out of there as we doused him with the remaining water in our bladder bags, rag strands left for pants. He was on an adrenaline high, but the rest of us were wondering what happened to BJ? He apparently backed off from the intensity, staying outside our lines, and never informing Fox that Buck was independently falling that hazard tree, unbeknownst to him. So much for following the standard fire orders. And what about BJ, our new boss man, fearless leader, and role model? This wasn't the Longshot way. Once again, burned by incompetencey.

In his book, <u>Fire On the Mountain,</u> author, John Maclean investigates the tragedy of the deadly fire in 1994 in Colorado. He names an individual, *"...who held the top fire job...Fire Management Officer (FMO), had no fire experience. He had been placed in that post after his previous job in an unrelated field was eliminated by downsizing."* (page 25).

We had come to find out that BJ had been a ranger in another district. He was transferred for misconduct. He had some fire experience in the southeast, but we didn't know any of his qualifications. He was assigned this job with the intention of changing the way we handled fires in this new regime of park policy and wildfires. His expertise was spending long hours looking at computer models of fire behavior. That is what we found out. What we knew personally was that he was incompetent, untrusting, had personality issues, biggoted, and was drunk most of the time. Not good in any situation.

<u>(Prof) Quiet times</u>

"I went to the woods because I wished to live deliberately, to front only the essential facts of life, and see if I could not learn what it had to teach, and not, when I came to die, discover that I had not lived."

-Thoreau

It was a crisp morning in the beginning of summer as I crawled out of my sleeping bag. When it got too crowded in my skidrow palace, I headed out to my favorite spot for solitude, reflecting, and some poetry:

In the days of yore, upon a land called America, existed a magical kingdom called the North Rim

A seasonal people made their living there,

arriving when the snows melted from aspen lined meadows and asphalt road, leaving again when the snows fell.

This fable is about the group of men and women brought there by thunder and lightning,

Yes, this is about those that sought to tame the dragon,

Fire!

There were still some snow packs in the thick glades of spruce and fir. Aspen leaves were budding. The sun was warm on Marble Point, on the east rim of the Kaibab Plateau. I left my clothes off as the sun felt good in the crisp morning rays. Raising my hands in a solar salute, with all of Marble Canyon, Vermillion Cliffs, and Navajo Mountain at my feet, a sudden voice startled my solitude.
"I almost got arrested for driving like that down in Tucson."
I knew that voice, "Buck!" Turning around, there he was with coffee and bear claws. "Good morning, Mr. Canyon! Brought you your favorites from the V-T gas station on my way out. Two-can gives her regards too." with a shit-eating grin on his face.

Two can was so named for the two cans of Skoal she wore, one in each jean pant back pocket. She ran the concessionaire's gas station and small store just outside the park boundary on forest lands. It was a convenient stop for refueling on the long drive out plus the coffee was strong, the danishes fresh, and ice cream bars a treat when the craving hit. She was a large gal, very large, pale skinned, long stringy oily hair, wearing a ball cap, flannel and too tight jeans with her belly protruding. Her twangy, tough talk always revealing dip in her gums, lip, and teeth. But somehow, she was a fixture and we all greeted her kindly and shot the shit whenever there.

"She was asking what you've been up to, must really like that pirate look of yours Jim when you show up there wearing your bandana like a bad ass." a hooting Buck just bantering away.

"Well, mmmm, this mud is gooood!" quickly changing the subject as I was now in my favorite bandana.

It was to be a short lived good one too. We had been dispatched back for some protection needed as thunder cells moved overhead. Working our days off, but not complaining for we were to receive, "oats," or, "O-T" and for you all who are no comprende, that's overtime pay.

(Bucks)- Authentic Indian

"Be yourself; everyone else is already taken."
-Oscar Wilde

Often heard via radio traffic from the South Rim patrol staff was the stake outs, chases, and arrests of Native American bead sellers in parking lots, vista viewpoints, and anywhere around tourist congregations. The corporate concessionaire had the sole permit and authority to scalp the public with overpriced items in their shops in the parks. Meanwhile, poverty stricken Natives living outside the borders often turned to selling their wares in order to make some extra bucks. Thus, the most common practice was to blend in with other tourists and then, unscroll some handiwork and begin selling what they could. Rangers on the South Rim would make it a game of cat and mouse. Often undercover, disguised as tourists, they would go after these illegal "bead sellers." We often heard the radio transmissions when they were out of breath after a chase, tackle, and handcuff, with ranger extolling, "hhhhhhave one in, hhhhhh, custody, hhhh!"

Yaz, a Navajo, was a great hard working kid off the Rez that was trying to make a better life. He was with the maintenance division, but assisted us whenever the chance arose. As a kid out of high school, he was still feeling his Wheaties, and could work all day, and party as needed. Yaz, as we called him, was an entrepreneur. On his days off, he would head over to Flag, buy some tiny, plastic beads at the local Kmart, and string them together making necklaces (unlike many of his breathren who legitimately fashioned from real stones, precious metals, etc.). He made many of these. Then, he'd high tail it to the park's outer boundaries of the South Rim and set up shop along the road with his sign, "authentic Indian hand-made." His display of jewelry beads sold for fifty bucks a piece, and the Oriental tourists off the busses would buy him out. So I asked the Yaz one day how much it cost him to make a necklace, and he told me about 25 cents. YBH! (yeah boy howdy). He added that he was 100 per cent Navajo, and thus an honest Injun too, because he had hand made the necklaces. Case in point, capitalism at its' finest. The American way. Assimilation.

Once for our days off, he took me on some hikes only accessible with a Native guide in the Canyon De Chelly area in Navajo country. Driving out there we passed through Hopi lands. Following a truck, I noticed the bumper sticker, "Don't worry, Be Hopi!" Great perspective in this desolate place. It was a fascinating region and really sacred to him. I came to appreciate his heritage. I know it was different from mine. We came upon a juniper tree, and to clear our eyes from the dust, he pulled some berries to apply topically. As he removed them, he left some trail mix at the base. When I inquired, his reply was whenever we take (from his ancestors as the tree, a stream, etc.) we give back something in return. Hmmmm, novel concept.

(Native American) "...human beings believe everything is alive. Not only man and animals. But also water, earth, stone. But the white man, they believe EVERYTHING is dead. Stone, earth, animals. And people! Even their own people! If things keep trying to live, white man will rub them out. That is the difference."

-from a scene in, *Little Big Man*, 1970.

Reflecting back to my constant encounters with red tail hawks that season, I decided to ask this Native his thoughts and understanding since he was raised in a traditional, spiritual way. The Yaz took his time, calmly reflecting upon my inquiry, mulling it over and when I thought he was dismissing it, answered carefully, "When you encounter the hawk, it is a symbol that you need to take time to look around and observe the details that surround you."

Further elaborating, he slowly continued, "When you need direction and insight, call on the hawk as your spirit guide. Hawk's spirit teaches us to be observant and to pay attention to what we may overlook. The hawk has keen eyesight, it is about opening our eyes and seeing that which is there to guide us. Hawk spirit awakens vision and inspires us to a creative life purpose. Like the hawk, your spirit ability to soar high above to catch a glimpse of the bigger picture allows not only survival but to flourish as well. Look to the world around you for there are totem symbols buried in everything." With a final thought on the matter, the Yaz concluded by stating that many Native American tribes admire the hawk for its endurance, perseverance, and sharp eyesight.

It was different, but I appreciated his beliefs from another perspective. Being open and receptive made me thankful to him for also having his "clan" sisters over to make fry bread and mutton stew. I still crave those delicacies whenever I am traveling through. I attribute my love of canned peaches to this day in honor of the Yaz. He used to call it, "Navajo dessert."

(Bucks)- Sunset

I was thoroughly blessed in receiving one of the historic cabins along the Transept Canyon, a side canyon, with a huge picture window facing west along the chasm. Teddy Roosevelt era built, they were rustic, had been retrofitted and now had warm water, and electricity. A shower stall barely able to squeeze in, a light bulb dangling from the ceiling, an electric plate, and small frig, it was heaven on earth. Location, location, location! Ten steps away from the canyon's edge. I'd invite Boomer and the Fox over for cold ones and sometimes we'd barbecue real meat outside in my fire ring. His roomie, the Dove and many of our crew were vegetarian. They were phenomonal cooks and prepared delicious dishes, but ya know, sometimes ya just want some dead meat. So, we'd designate a certain night for dead meat eaters when we were in station for long periods (like more than a few days).

Gorgeous views of amazing sunsets. The chinking between the logs in my cabin left wide spaces for my wildlife viewing pleasure. From my bed, I could look out the cracks and see the moon on some nights, illuminating many of the mice posing and chowing away any morsels found on my floor from that day. To win the battle over my food, I stored everything in sealable tins. If I were in station, at home mellowing, I often encountered tourists pressing their noses and peering questionably into my picuture window cabin. Even as I strut about naked, I found the gawkers too numerous to deal with constantly. It was less than a mile along the rim to the lodge, and about a half mile the other way through forest to the cache and heliport. So, for evening peace, I discovered some rock outcroppings hidden by spruce and Ponderosa jutting out into the canyon. A few tricky shimmy's, a handhold and voila, I was free from the encroaching world of looky-lou's. And here I could sit and just take it in. A spiritual experience.

"Nature quiets the mind by engaging with an intelligence larger than our own."

-Terry Tempest Williams, <u>The Hour of Land,</u> p. 32.

There was so much to take in. An amazing display of colors as the sun set in dazzling orange with violet hues as the canyon rock layers highlighted their perspectives in cream, buff, rust, and on until it was darkness. Night skies were another experience of light shows with stars, constellations, and meteors just dancing around your every move of the eyes.

Up to this point, the many doors of my life, both open and closed and the various places that I hung my hat were more physical and cognitive in nature. I arrived at the canyon as an atheist, after a childhood of religion. These "nature" moments and the fires I were to experience would change my life forever, knowing that without a doubt there was a higher order out there. Beginning to stir my thoughts and feelings, I had touched God, or more likely, He had touched me.

"...the hills and groves were God's first temples, and the more they are cut down and hewn into cathedrals and churches, the farther off and dimmer seems the Lord. Every spritual lesson we need is subtly and spectacularly evident in nature."

-Chris Highland

(Prof) Zion Narrows

"The farther one gets into the wilderness, the greater is the attraction of its lonely freedom."
-Theodore Roosevelt

Campfires with friends under a milky way sky were epic. The moon just starting to cast a glow in the east over the plateau on the North Rim held many memories for me. Tonight however, Buck and I were up high in Zion country, specifically the Kolob Terrace off the North fork of the Virgin River. Tomorrow would be a "z' day, as in easy, a piece of cake as the backcountry ranger told us a week before when she found out we'd done Buckskin Gulch. Other than Buck's almost slime scum drowning, Buckskin had been a piece of cake. We hoisted a few Corona's. Cheers to another glorious evening under the stars. I began dozing off... "yeah, we had backpacks of food, wandering over hills, holes in barbwire fence, Romania in total starvation, being treated like saints, women wanted to marry me... and huh?"

"What Buck?" I came to.

Looking over at him, he was just shaking his head back and forth with that big Buck smile. When one's with true friends there doesn't always have to be words exchanged. Buck's a buck of a man. Me, I'm professor average behind the beard and hair. However, I can hike like a goat. Buck and I are both in our elements, alive and awake when our feet or our backs are on the rocks, sand, and soil of Mother Nature. Soon the stars tucked us into our sleeping bags, all warm with dreams of canyons and Mormon daughters keeping us company.

Awaking to a blue sky and coffee boiling over the fire, cowboy style, I pulled on a t-shirt and shorts. Pouring a cup for myself, Buck came out of the bushes with a grin and poured himself a cup.

"Want some orange granola?" spoke Buck.

"Sounds light and right." I rhymed.

"Ah, a poet awake."

"Aye matey." in my best pirate rendition.

"Aye then it is."

I raised my steaming mug and toasted, "To the trail."

"To the trail. May there be a lifetime of them."

"Our steps are not measured in miles but in the amount of time we are pulled forward by awe."

-Terry Tempest Williams (<u>The Hour of Land,</u> p.181)

The Buck and I were only on a one night stay yet we had full packs, with extra plastic bags to keep everything dry. Wading was a requirement as we were forewarned. Water level was posted as low yesterday at the Zion VC (that's visitor center, not Viet Cong). We skipped the mandatory backcountry permits. It was too late in the evening, the place was closed, and anyway, we were backcountry experts, we didn't need no stinking permits. Heading down the Virgin River watershed, cream colored walls in various time and water stained shades towered thousands of feet overhead. Too soon, the trail became the stream, an ankle tickler, amongst cool pines, silent walls, and feeders of trickling brooks. The gods called for reflection and sacrament. Depositing my pack on a boulder, I found my stone pipe, filled it with lime green sacred herb and facing the east I toasted, "To the sun, giver of light, the west, oh mother ocean of life, to the north, harbinger of many storms, snow filler of streams, to the south, the desert there to..."

"keep us honest." interjected Buck.

We laughed, I smoked another bowl and continued our canyon way, red eyed and bushy tailed.

Soon, thunder filled the canyon walls. Ominous clouds loomed overhead in our limited view in this slot canyon. We were also met by three major tributaries from above the Kolob Terrace. The Virgin River made a bend as Deep Creek, Kolob Creek and Goose Creek converged to put us in waist deep water with slippery stones underfoot as our hiking trail. We found temporary refuge on a sandbar, and together, "Falls!" we realized aloud in harmony.

It was a nice broad veil of water cascading over a cliff with an easy trail around it. The river veered here and a small, grassy, flat boulder sat atop the falls bathed in a sun drenched splattering. Lunch was decided upon immediately. A bonus was the natural jacuzzi formed by the side stream flows. Buck and I munched on French bread rolls, string cheese, and trail-gorp. The sun was inviting, but we vowed to put away a few more miles before dinner. By the next bend, four miles down, a good sized walking stick was required as a third leg for balance amongst the mossy stones and now raging waters. Various branches rushing by would have to make do. It was just a matter of snagging the right length of one.

"Piece of cake, huh, Buck?" I shouted amidst the pounding drums of water.

Three more miles of step by careful step of river walking and the Buck and I found a sand bar for the night's camp. A scrumptious dinner of what else: French bread, string cheese, and trail granola.

Afterwards, I broke out the bottle of brandy for medicinal purposes and the pipe was passed for spiritual remedies.

"So, what's up this winter, Buckster?" I inquired.
"Same thing as now, stars at night."
"Very sage-ee."
"Uh-huh, what about you?"
"Oh, I think I'll cut my hair, clean up my act, go work for an insurance company investigating peasants in the realm of the holy city of Tucson."
Howls of human laughter merged in the Virgins River song as canyon sirens sang with thunderous delight.
"Satirical wise ass." guffawed Buck and we chuckled our way into our bags below the shadowed cliffs. Flights of bats in the flickering star light above the canyon walls caught our attention and entertained us to sleep.

<u>**(Prof continues)**</u> <u>**Piece of Cake, huh?**</u>

Short-lived as it was, we were getting wet as the river was rising and swallowing up the sand bar. The stars were gone from overhead; it was now cloudy and dark. The dreaded flash floods of the southwest came to mind and became our reality. Trying to find dry ground amongst the canyon walls necessitated us to trek further downstream. After a mile of slow traverse using the walking stick branches to wedge in between the slippery stones among the rushing, swelling river, we came to a ravaging course of waterfalls, huge pools, and boulders. It was treacherous and tricky through the suds and foam and fierce grip of cool, swift water. I led cautiously, immersing myself into a big pool as torrents of water pounded me forcefully. The fast paced current and the pool now over my head, forced me to paddle along. I became disoriented in the swirling action, lost my footing and went completely under. My external frame backpack kept my head under. Without any solid footing, I couldn't lift my head up to catch a breath. I was drowning. I tried to maneuver over toward where I believed I came from. The fierce rushing action of water ripped the walking stick out of my hand. Feeling another branch and pulling with all my might I came up and out by a boulder. Buck had extended me his walking stick, pulling me out by sheer force.

(Buck's note)- Originally when Canyon went under I tried to swim out to retrieve him as I saw he was drowning. Swirling under the forceful, rushing river, he grabbed at what he could for a grip to right himself. As I got closer I got pulled under by him and now both of us were drowning. Reacting with my reflexes (and probably going back to my training as a lifeguard from my earlier youth) I broke the death grip and pushed away, back to the bank. Retrieving my walking stick, I swam out and tried again, this time successfully using the branch as a retrieving rod.

(Prof continues)- Gasping for breath I looked up and saw a cliff ledge rising above some of these "piece of cake pools" in the Narrows. Climbing up while slithering along with my pack some twenty, slippery, treacherous feet on a ledge (probably a bighorn trail) I quickly moved along and up to about forty feet above the river before reaching dead end. Behind me I saw Buck's footing give way and slide down as the rock ledge crumbled below him. Thirty feet of body bouncing down rock into a side pool. At this point, I was thinking of busted legs as I'd seen knee and rock collide. Scrambling, I maneuvered down to a boulder.
"Buck?" quizzically in a serious voice.
"Not good, Boomer." he grimaced testing his legs, shin bones exposed and bleeding profusely. Immersing his wounds in the cold water had a numbing and cleansing effect. In a short time the bleeding stopped and he was sore but trail wise.
"Whew!" I breathed in relief, adding, "How about some medicine, bottle or pipe?"
"Both." he grimaced.

I laughed, sat down, and took off my pack upon this heaven sent boulder. We would spend the rest of the night on this four by six foot boulder top as the raging stream flashed by us. Obviously the torrents of today's thunderstorm rains, somewhere far off but in the watershed were now washing down throughout here.

"Well Buck, it looks like I put on my pack and forgot to unfasten my waist strap. As soon as the water got over my head, I found myself like a turtle in a shell. I must have been in a stoned panic, I felt your walking stick thud on my pack, and I grabbed and pulled. Now we're both without our walking sticks."

After much consumption and a power bowl, we curled up as wet dogs around a stick fire on a cold night, and fretfully tried to sleep, while thoughts of a rising river toyed with our minds.

Sunlight through clouds overhead signified morning as we noticed the river wasn't rising anymore. It wasn't receding, but it wasn't rising, and that was good for us. Finding driftwood atop our boulder, we managed a campfire for cowboy coffee and instant apples n' cinnamon oatmeal. Mmmm, good. Along with some Tang orange mix, a pipe full of digestive aid herbage for me and, well, as someone has to say, "That's Livin.'"

Soon, it was time to pack up.

"You'd think we were off for a year adventure." Buck yelled over the swift current.

"Yeah, next time we pack inner tubes and daypacks." my loud reply.

"Or an air mattress." as the Buck hoisted his Lowe internal frame pack, while I put on my Kelty external.

Luck had us this morning; we found our walking sticks in an eddy behind our boulder. Thinking survival situation, we blew up some trash bags, inserted them into our backpacks and then lashed them to some branches. Now we could swim across the deep pools with our packs in front. Backpack ferryboats.

Some ravens laughed overhead.

Buck threaded our way over falls and rapids, boulders and pools. Finally, we came to a stretch of vertical walls where we could bobble along upright, waist straps unfastened, backs buoyed up by our garbage bag lined packs. A couple miles of this deposited us at a fern laden fresh water spring. Revitalized briefly, bobbing again some more miles, and then another treacherous stretch lay ahead.

I had to yell up, "How many holes you think we have left?" No answer.

"Is there any civilization around here?" Quite a stupid question, since our whole reason for our getaways were to leave development and people behind.

"How's your leg?"

"Healed by water." finally responding.

"Why the moaning?"

"Who's moaning?" Buck was now focused with attention ahead of us.

"You."

"What'd you say?" no reply as our voices were drowned out by the roaring water.
The rapids sang their song, while we slip-slided and bobbed our way along this "piece of cake" trek.

Another mile and the walls widened, dissipating the water frenzy and dropping levels back to our knees. It was here that we encountered a lone hiker coming up.
We felt like hugging him, just glad this flash flood fiasco was nearly over. The sun was out penetrating the shadowy depths. Then more and more hikers were seen coming up the river from the Zion Park trailhead. Many a camera laden tourist takes the mile up to the bend before heading back, carefully picking their footing, protecting huge investments around their necks. Bipeds of Homo-sapiens extraction, just walking and enjoying sights. Normally these are the tourons we try to avoid in our backcountry forays, but today, right now, we embraced them joyously, happy to have survived!

At the parking lot Buck's pickup stored a warm six pack. Now I guess it depends upon the situation but this piss warm beer actually tasted inviting. Slurp, slurp, slurp! Ahhh! Purchasing a cold sixer of Mormon 3.2 brew, we drove up to grab Bertha (my truck) from her trail head resting place (keys remembered this time). Then down the Kolob Terrace, back to pavement through the towering canyon walls of Zion National Park and into the town of Springdale to the Bit n' Spur Saloon. A Mexican restaurant with delectable delights. On the outside patio we hoisted ice cold, you guessed it, Corona's and feasted on chips and salsa, black beans, rice, chili rellano's, and more Corona's. The sun spun colors weaving purples and oranges along with pink and turquoise until flickers of stars emerged in deep indigo. Yes, a marvelous dinner was had. Dashed off to Kanab to the twenty-four hour market, Dove's, where you would get discounted if you had more than six in your family. Obviously, we didn't qualify here in Mormon country. Leaving the grocers with supplies in stow, it was a vehicle climb up the plateau. Maneuvering through deer alley, past the holy gates of the park's entrance, where the game was not only to dodge deer but law ranger alike until safely parked in front of the skid row palace, that island of sanctuary and home amongst the official trailers, pre-fab houses, and historic cabins. Ahh!

(Prof) A bit of trouble

"If a man walk in the woods for love of them half of each day, he is in danger of being regarded as a loafer; but if he spends his whole day as a speculator, shearing off those woods and making earth bald before his time, he is esteemed an industrious and enterprising citizen."

-Thoreau (Life without Principle)

Superintendent Pecker Track's office was the same as all those in power in the park system. Standby secretary situated outside the door to deflect the uninvited. Plush carpeting inside a wood paneled office with flags of the U.S. and Arizona standing in the corner with the customary photo of the president on one wall and a painting of the current park on another wall. Like a redneck pearl in an overstuffed shell, Billie Joe was seated across the abyss of a desk from Pecker Tracks. PT's grey eyes held firmly upon the unsightly bloodshot ones of Billie Joe, obviously from last nights binge.
"That crew is a bunch of prima donnas and I'd like to get rid of all of 'em next season damit." spewed BJ.
"Could you at least keep a handle on them?" in the authority voice acustomed with such a mucky muck.
"I'm tryin'. You know the North Rim though, it's another world. They won't even do what I tell them on fires."
"Hmmm, well..." now looking at Billie Joe and seeing the eagerness of his eyes. "If there's any safety issues involved... I want them out of the public's eye as much as possible for now. They are causing a bit of trouble by talking about our development goals and I'm starting to get letters here and so is D.C. We need to get a foothold of development beginning to really open up and expand the visitor experience. So keep those maverick's in line, I'll talk to you later." With these words of dismissal, PT picked up the phone as Billie Joe walked out. At his exit the dam burst.

BJ's temper was legendary. Slamming the door, the window glass reached breaking point and shattered, raining him with shards. Jamming in reverse out of his parking spot, BJ screeched over to the heliport by the maintenance garage. His neck veins bulged while barreling down the road purposely going for a squirrel out picking cones. A mortal disaster narrowly averted as the critter barely escaped the mad wheels of fire management officer Billie Joe Sagebrush's official government pick up.

Jack McGregor was already past retirement age, though his trim body and ever full of laughter eyes of blue hinted at eternal youth in an over sixty person. Jack was walking the canyon or rafting the river when time off hit him. He was in charge of the interpretive division at Grand Canyon. Jack was concerned about his home, the incredible miracle of nature called the canyon. He'd arrived there while in his 30's, when it was Fred Harvey concessions, back when it was just one gift shop, along with the Bright Angel Lodge and the El Tovar. Of course the North Rim had its Grand Lodge too back then. Now on the South Rim there was added a bank, post office, supermarket, gas station, Maswick Motor Lodge, and the Yavapai complex (referred to by locals as the Pit). There was an abominable addition to the Bright Angel right on the rim itself, a steakhouse, more gift shops, a kennel, jail, paved roads, busses, and an airport (the third busiest in Arizona, after Phoenix and Tucson). Meanwhile, the North Rim had only the Grand Lodge. My gang wanted to keep it that way. Let the one side, the year round open rim side, have all the development and tour-ons they could handle. Keep one side the way future generations should experience solemness, peace, tranquility, and where real (nature loving) people, and time stood still. Jack received a call from ol' Pecker Tracks, "I want your people to stop talking to the public about a motel we haven't even started yet." firmly admonishing his anger.

"They want to know what our plans are, and it's my job to communicate openly. So sit on it, okay? And goodbye." said the ever in control Jack, who laughed as he put down the receiver, picturing PT with a silent phone in his hand. Quoting Muir, he reiterated, "Nothing dollarable is safe."

"One simply does not challenge the NPS culture or its leadership or mention problems and make complaints outside of the internal agency structure. The image of the agency is paramount, and that's one reason why it so successfully garners public and political support."

-Paul D. Berkowitz (The Case of the Indian Trader, p. 62)

(Prof) A Forest Circus Dispatch

North Rim fire roads, both east and west side had been cleared, the cache was up to snuff, so it was time to get the lookout towers in shape. The one out west, Kanabownits, was the crew's get away. At the base was a small, two room cabin with 38 mysterious electric sockets hanging from the ceiling, testimony to by-gone generator days, when someone lived there all season long. It is a place I could call home, nestled on a forested ridge. There wasn't going to be a lot to do today other than some sweeping, storytelling, and as always, rim exploration. The Fox and I were paired in the green beast of an aging International 4x4 with three hundred gallons of water retrofitted as an ancient slip-on pump unit. We'd finished cleaning out the cabin and had found a nice rim spot when my radio crackled, "583, fire dispatch."

"583, go ahead." I duly replied as the Fox tore into his Dagwood sandwich.
"We've got a request for you to respond to a forest service fire on the boundary, ready to copy legal?"
"Affirmative."

Having given the township, range, and section, dispatch followed with, "take forest roads and follow the flagging. Also, see if you can locate the boundary, this may be ours, your contact is Steve Flambeau."
"583 copies, clear."
"Well, let's hit it!" laughed a sandwich devoured Fox, standing up from his pine needle seat. A raven flew into a branch above seeking stray lunch items.
"Let me eat first." I said, reaching for my paper bag of cheese, salami, sourdough bread, and orange.
"Eat on the road." demanded a now impatient lunch-less Fox.

"Go mellow out." I had to say as the raven glided to the needles ten feet from me.
"You damn laid back California hippie!" retorted the redneck Montana hippie-spirited
Fox.

"Go sit in the truck with the engine running and a hose from the exhaust into the cab, ya
redneck scum." my calm reply, while tearing off a hunk of sourdough and tossing it to
the raven. "AWWW." the raven grabbed it in its ebony beak and glided off to a perch.
"AWWW!" croaked the Fox, who smiled and sat down, mouth open. I tossed a hunk of
salami at his face. "AWWW!" was his response with a shit-eating grin. "Overtime,
hazard pay, excitement!" I replied to the Fox in my most serious, non-serious tone.

Finishing my lunch, Fox and I boogied down the road leaving the fatter raven behind.
We stopped but couldn't see nor smell smoke from the aspens and headed off the rutted
park roads into forest service graded, gravel roads. Heading down the North Kaibab
Forest roads, following directions and a map, past numbers upon marked numbers of
logging cuts, it was a veritable spider web complex of byways. Soon enough we came to
some forest service green engines and pickups. The Fox and I radioed dispatch and
headed down the flagging.

Upon our arrival, we found a slop over the size of a car garage, with flames the size of a
two year old running amuck. Putting down most of our gear, we went to work with
shovel and McCloud. One stroke from the edge of a shovel and needles went flying,
leaving nothing but bare earth. We went to hi-gear mode, racing the fire, which in this
case was not easy. Soon, the sweat was running off our noses. The Fox darted behind
flames and using his McCloud (combination large hoe and rake) grabbed up large hunks
of flaming needles, while I scooped up the rest with my shovel.
"Ya-hoo!" the Fox yelled flinging a rake of flaming needle back into the fire.
"Ha-ha!" I monstrously replied, slicing air scooping up needles. My nose was running,
shirt soaked, lips chapped and bleeding, yet in the fifteen minutes of kick ass intimacy
with Mother Nature's flaming glory, we were having fun. Another five minutes of fun
and spot fire number one was done. Onwards to spot fires' numbers two and three.
Where were those forest circus folks anyway? In an hour, the Fox and I rounded up six
hot spots and then decided to grab a bite. We had found an abandon forest service saw,
and laid our gear beside it. Plastic quart canteens were also strewn about. The water
in my canteen was lukewarm, despite freezing it overnight but this water was colder and
tasted good.
"Damn!" the Fox exclaimed, "Look down there."
I followed his eye down the line, ten or 12 chains, expecting to see another spot fire.
Instead, I saw what appeared to be Nomex-clad bodies lounging under some piss firs.

(A chain for those of you who are unaware is a linear unit of measurement used in the
woods. A chain being sixty-six feet long and measured in paces, which differs by
individuals according to their step. A pace being two steps. There's ten square chains per

acre, eighty chains to a mile and on and on and on…)

"Looks like our missing circus folks." I facetiously stated.
"Looks like a bunch of lazy assholes." the obvious stated by the Fox.
I remembered the radio with my gear, switched on the forest circus channel and called out, "Tipover IC, 583 Canyon, park service."
"Go ahead." a voice responded.
"Arrived on scene an hour ago and just finished containing some spots on the west flank."
"Copy, thanks, enroute now and I'll be there in five." in a weary sounding reply.
"Copy, we'll be here."

The Fox and I gobbled gorp and it wasn't long before Steve, a ripe, clean-cut Humboldt grad introduced himself as the IC (Incident Commander) and engine foreman out of the Deep Spring station. After a bit of chatter, I told him of the crew down below. I could see the bodies start to move now.

"Yeah, they've been kind of worthless. They're young locals and burned out from a previous fire at Zion the past week. Sorry, I'll get them up here to help mop these spots."
"Appreciate that."

The wind gave a good gust letting us know it was still June and storms were hanging around. Cumulous clouds were right around the bend, bringing some rain, lightning and thunder while blowing some fire embers into the air. It was spot patrol time just as the circus cavalry arrived, young and burned out. The Fox looked at me and grabbed his McCloud.
"Worthless as tits on a boar hog." he uttered and walked out into the Ponderosa's.
I walked over to a young Nomex clad individual. "Mind if I use your saw to buck a few logs out of our line?"
"Go ahead." he mumbled and walked up the line with a shovel in hand looking down at the glowing coals. He slowly bent over and proceeded to dice up the ember. I topped the gas and oil on the brand new Husquverna, put on my chaps, earplugs, shaded glasses and walked over to the first log, bucking it up, smooth as butter.

(Prof continues) Candy bar thieves

It was an afternoon of wind and spots, sweat and heat, before the westerly died down and we got a handle on four acres of burning pine needles and a few immature trees. By this time, dinners were ordered and ten more people were still en route. One of those arriving informed I.C. Steve and myself that the boundary markers were about a half mile back.
"Tag, you're it." Steve letting me know that this was now an official park fire rather than forest service.
"Yeah, boy." was my only response.

Soon, Larry the AFMO (assistant fire management officer for the forest service) arrived. He'd just flown recon an hour ago.

"So, did you see any smokes?" I asked.

"Nah, Jim."

Turning to Steve, I told him, "Once I feel safe, I'll cut your people loose as soon as I can get a couple of our folks out here to replace them."

"Sounds good, some of these folks need a sleep at home."

"Yeah, I got you."

Turning to Larry, I told him, "Keep those dinners coming too. I better get Buck on the air."

With a switch of the dial, I went from forest to park net, "582, 583."

"582." came the reply.

"Yeah, Buck, we've got a handle on this and I just learned this is a park fire. I'll be incident commander as of 1700, break."

"Copy."

"At around 1900, I'll be turning the forest troops loose, and I'd like you and Lisa to get geared up to stay out here tonight."

"Copy...I'll get ...back to you in a ...few."

"Hmmmm." I mumbled to myself, thinking what's up back there, sounds like Buck is a bit hesitant.

Larry reminded me, "Remember, Billie Joe was due over to the North Rim for interagency tree count training."

"Damn! That's it." I mustered.

Larry and Steve were smiling. The Fox laughed out loud. All glad we weren't dealing with the petty shit training back at base with BJ. Tools clanked back on the fire line. I looked up in the sky and saw a red tail hawk circling. What a majestic sight. I smiled. "583, 582." interrupting.

"582, go." I squawked.

"We'll be on our way."

"Copy, see ya Buck." Click, click, click, the radio answered (secret code for I can't talk now over the park waves).

The sun was in a southwesterly twilight phase. Fox and I were the only ones now amidst the fading smoke, along with the song of our tools extinguishing pine embers.

"583, 582." the radio blurted.

I walked over to my pack, switched the radio to local, off the repeater and answered Buck, "channel one."

"Hey Canyon, I'm at your engine, anything ya need?"

"Yeah, Eppler (as in Larry) left some dinners on the front seat."

"I've collected those, and…well, I'll tell ya when I see you out there."

"See ya." I finished while looking at the Fox.
"Maybe the beers are on Billie Joe tonight." the Fox joked.
"Hey, where's my candy bar?" I quipped to Fox.
"Mines gone too, damn lazy circus thieves." lamented the Fox.

The stars were starting their dance in the ever darkening night when I heard the clomp of boots, clank of shovel, Pulaski, and McCloud coming through the forest along with the bob of headlamps, "Professor!" the Buck yelped.
"Buck!" I yelped back, firedogs that we were.
"Fuck, Billie Joe is pissed. He thinks your crazy." Buck spat out.
Lisa was laughing beside him.
I wasn't laughing, "What the…"
Interrupting, Buck continued, "He wonders why you let all those circus folks go so soon after this fire was such a bitch."
"Shit, Buck, half of them were burned out candy bar thieves from Fredonia; I couldn't say they were worthless over the radio. Besides, I knew you wanted the time and it's our fire and oh…" Lisa was on the ground in stitches. What the fuck, I started laughing. Next thing, we were all sprawled in the needles roaring the insanity of our uptight FMO, ol' Sagebrush.

"Dinner!" Lisa yelled from the needles, after her convulsion had subsided.
We tore into our Houston Trails End dinners (not the typical MRE). Fried chicken, potatoes, salad, roll, pudding cup with a juice and soda, plus a mint.
Smiling over chow, the Fox had to reflect, "Doesn't get any better, does it?" as he pulled a swig from his canteen of now warm water.
"Just like a television commercial for real food." added Buck.
"Well, back to the real world of mop up." intervening sadly in my best type-A command voice.
"Slave driver!" laughed Buck as he got up, grabbed a shovel, and we all followed.

Mop up, that most glorious part of fire, NOT! Tool chipping at glowing embers on a piece of pine branch or log in duff. Chip, chip, chop, chop. If one has a five gallon piss pump (backpack water pump) it takes a couple of squirts of water, a scoop of earth, mix up the mud and exorcise the fire. On the North Rim, where water was precious, the (fire) engines far off, with backpack pumps cumbersome and leaky, some crewmembers resorted to using their urine to literally piss on hot spots (thanks Buck). Cold trailing was going through the burn area with the back of your ungloved hand, feeling for hot spots that need extinguishing. Dirty work. Tiring work. Bent over work. The time when most accidents occured. Guards were let down, exhaustion set in, but still there was plenty of hard grueling activity left to do. The dirt embedded in the lines of our fingers and palms while nostrils blowing black snot for days reminded us of the work we did.

About midnight, the Fox and I decided to leave Buck and Lis to finish and monitor. It took a twenty minute walk to the engine by headlamp and starlight with another forty minute drive to make it back to the cache. Within five minutes of that, I was naked, cold Corona in hand, hot showered, and content. Five more minutes and a bed never felt so good.

(Prof) Ego Tripper

"as soon as it is put into words, gets distorted a bit,...what is one man's treasure and wisdom always sounds like foolishness to another person."

-Herman Hesse (Siddhartha)

Morning sent me on a walk to the office. Mules cried for bales of hay, ravens shrieked for the same joy that I felt. As I entered the Pit, Billie Joe pushed by me with a, "Hi, Jim." I gave back a "Hi." and proceeded to search for the various government forms involved in doing a fire report. As I looked around the office, Ken came in saying, "Jim, I need to talk to you, sit down, please."
The tone in Ken's voice was strange, sort of half-hearted. I sat down quizzically.
"I'd like to know why you cut loose all those forest service folks so suddenly on a tough fire, and then stripped the North Rim of fire personnel?"
I looked at him, wondering about this line of questioning and approach. Then I saw Billie Joe's boots barely peeking through the open door. I nodded at the door and Ken shook his head acknowledging, yeah, I guessed right (following orders from above).

"Well, there were a few problems with keeping some of the forest crew folks. Most of their people just spent two weeks detailed on fires and were pretty bushed and useless. One crewmember gave Steve, the original fire boss, and myself problems. Hey they even stole from our lunches. Those things are better left unsaid over the air waves. That all occurred when it was spotting and responsive action was needed. As far as stripping the rim of personnel, I only requested two fresh people since we'd gotten most of the hot spots by then. I also asked (AFMO) Larry, who flew after the storms if we had any other smokes, which he affirmed we did not. I got in at midnight knowing that you and Tex would be on duty this morning. It was a fire in our boundary. My decisions were based upon those events." Thus defending myself to the footwear outside the door, which had strolled in at this point.

"That's good enough." the shoe bearing culprit responded and left.

Ken muttered something in his own tongue and apologetically offered, "Sorry Jim, I trust your judgment."

"That's okay. No need to apologize for that shit."

I did my fire report then joined the Fox in the Zen of tool sharpening. The Fox inquired of my unusual quietness. I informed him of the shoes encounter.

"You know I heard he just cancelled tree counting and was leaving."

Just then the radio buzzed, "506, vehicle enroute to the South Rim."

"Fire dispatch copies."

"You must have pissed him off Canyon, but good. Thanks bud, and good bye Billie Baby."

I laughed and missed my file stroke on the tool putting a nice slice through my glove tip and barely missing ye olde finger.

"Close encounters of the finger kind." the Fox commented.

A raven laughed. Mules brayed. I breathed a sigh of relief.

Billie Joe raced through the entrance station without stopping. Veins in his neck bulging, red faced and cursing, he swore, "Know-it-alls, think they're experts, and don't need to consult me for every fire. I'll shit can or destroy every last one of 'em, goddamit." He swerved abruptly off the pavement and onto a logging road, where he stopped, reached in his cooler and pulled out a 12 ounce beer, "This Bud's for me." He took a gulp, belched, turned the government car around and got back on the highway. Stopping at Jacob Lake to eat, he leered at the pretty, young Mormon girls, working their summer away at slave labor. Bishop Jacob ran a tight ship, the latter day saintly way.

"Eying little girls with bad intent,

Snot running down his nose,

Greasy fingers smearing shabby clothes,

hey Aqualung."

-Jethro Tull (*Aqualung*)

(Bucks)-Nankoweap

"The trail puts you in harmony with the universe."
-Enos Mills.

Prof had another hike planned on our off days for a wonderful inner canyon experience. Nankoweap Creek flowing into the Colorado River with Anasazi granaries above on the canyon walls was our 14 plus mile hike. Contouring down was a joy. Meditative walking with sensory input abounding. Breaking me out of my trance first was the red tail hawk's cry and then the steady cadence to songs as Jim loved to sing to pass the time. Keeping in tune, he belted out words to some of the latest music he had bought on cassettes. *"Money for nothing and your chicks for free..."* as he began with Dire Straights along our route traipsing journey. Gorgeous redwalls in this marble canyon area, we quickly made camp and set to catching our dinner (trout from the creek). In my haste, I nonchalantly threw down my sleeping bag over some rocks. A great hike, exploring ancient sites, fresh fish for dinner, and now it was time to settle back for the nightly entertainment, the star show.

Propping my head over the pile of rocks behind my bag, I was in my ritual mode of reading a book by headlamp. A stir from between my legs caught my attention. With lamplight shining down, I noticed a small, maybe 18 inch long rattler that was coming out from under my bag between my legs. As I stood, I watched it slither down to the river, apparently thirsty and then return almost in its same tracks back. When it reached my bag, it disappeared underneath. I lifted my bag and noticed it went into the crevice of rocks that I was using as a back support to read. With light directed into the hole, I quickly saw a whole den of rattlers, the infamous, Grand Canyon pink rattlers. The color was more like a washed out rose, blending in naturally with the eroded rocks and sandy beach that we were on. Not needing much more excitement, I diligently moved to an area of sand, nice and soft, under a tree away from snake alley.

Tempting as it was, I had previously learned not to dig around in the soft sand with my hands and toes. This was a desert and the infamous scorpion had taken its sting on many a victim down here. I was informed it was the smaller ones that had the more serious venom. Didn't want to find out, although I witnessed several incidents from others less fortunate. Turning onto my belly, propped upon arms, I whipped out my novel to aid me to sleep. Once again reading by headlamp, just inches from my face I watched as a small two inch sized, translucent scorpion skirted by, tail up in familiar fashion. Hmmm, time to avoid nice small tree overhangs and rocky boulders for my privacy and skooted a few feet back into a more open area for precautionary sake. Still, it was nature in its own terms, we were just passing through lightly on the land, enjoying the magical aura of all of it. Live and learn.

(Prof) Polar opposites

Of all the fables of North Rim romances, surely that of Patrick and Lisa is the most endearing. Pat was the youngest of three brothers, originally from Phoenix and now at the rim. He'd been raised a park brat. Without a mule, raft or helicopter, he never set foot in the canyon unless it was an EMS response or a search and rescue mission. Blonde, blue-eyed with a big toothy grin, he was a "pretty-boy" as Lisa put it, and that she said was his salvation. I always felt that Pat should have gotten a booth on the South Rim to tell his famous stories while paying public would plop down their money as he wrapped them up in his yarns. He was a bullshitter with the women at the saloon too. Dangling a cigarette from his lips, "Bogart-style," and informing any senorita that his boat was moored down on Lake Powell usually had a throng surrounding him, salivating for some fun with this amigo. He'd do some crazy shit for the lust of women. At the entrance gate of the park, after several weeks of snow melt, a seasonal pond had formed, several acres in size. Along the shores an embankment of snow was still several feet high. The pond itself only a few feet in depth. Anyway, Pat's idea to attract some live ones coming in to the park was for him and Buck to float around the pond in only their swim trunks toasting brews to the newcomers. He had some tractor inner tubes blown up and they both hopped on baring the cold snow melt pond water. Even with the sun shining, it was a cool 50 degree day, and obviously freezing cold water from the snows. They were out there for about thirty minutes, shivering, shaking, and hoisting a "welcome" sign as well as raising their beers in toast fashion. So when I asked him how many girls he met, his answer was typical Pat, "Boomer, we had fun. Several cars honked as we cheered and welcomed them." I pressed further about anyone stopping, to which he replied, "Nah, Buck and I were freezing our huevos off. We ended up shivering so badly that we couldn't talk straight, so we cranked the heat in my car and headed back. But hey, it was fun!"

Another time that I will never forget is when Pat arrived to my place shaking and stuttering, scared shitless. "Boomer, ya never gonna believe this..." and he preceeded to tell me about an encounter he had with a waitress from the lodge. She invited him back to her place as her roomies were gone for the night. She lit some candles and he thought how romantic. As they undressed, she took out a mantle and began lighting dozens and dozens of more candles, to the point where it felt eery. The whole place was lit up and an alter set up with even more candles. "Boomer, there must have been a hundred candles, man. Freaky!" He went on to say that she began chanting something about a sacrifice and that's when he bolted. "I didn't know if she wanted to sacrifice a cat or me. She was some kind of demon or witch worshipper, it was scary man!" I inquired what he was going to do when he saw her again, as she was a local TW employee. "I'm not eating at the lodge when she's waitressing, that's for sure." Interesting enough, another similar story emanated from a romeo ranger's encounter with this same gal. She was attractive, but man, literally an "evil woman."

Pat did give up the playboy ways when Lisa paid him attention and entered his life. She was the only one that could hold his interest. He was a John Wayne type with a few hippie habits. Lisa was not a John Wayne fan at all. But then, I always told her, it looks like the times are a changing. Lisa was a liberal punk rocker of evergreens, water, and snow from up Washington way. Pat called Washington, "Green Hell." As far as music tastes, Pat liked country, Lisa hated "twang." Pat voted for Ronnie, while Lisa thought he should be hung like a rustler. Two dichotomous opposites. Yet, it was an endearing romance, and indeed this was their third summer on the rim together. Pat remained in Arizona each winter, while Lisa spent a couple working in Antarctica, where she was on the search and rescue team. While there, she also managed to run a marathon and illegally climb a mountain before some Frenchman later ascended the same and claimed fame with legal documentation. One off season took her back home to the peninsula with her winter boyfriend, Mongo. Much to Pat's chagrin, they were pretty tight. I kidded Pat that perhaps a ring would change her mind. He grinned and told me that he had one picked out. He often mentioned that one day he was going to marry that girl.

<u>**(Prof) Meanwhile back at the rim and beyond**</u>

We met at the pit Thursday evening in mid June. Thursday being the only day that all six of us Longshots were on duty together.

Ken began, "We all got memo's from the superintendent to quiet down about impending development and he's especially upset at us for telling people to write. I heard that he came down hard on interp for ending their shows with development news."

"Anyone fired yet?" asked Lisa.

"No, but he's coming over for a chat tomorrow."

"Good, Buck and I are outa here tonight." I cheerily added.

"Ya-hoo!" echoed a smiling Buck.

"Lucky you." moaned Lisa.

"Well, I'm saloon bound." voiced a departing Fox.

"Let's boogie." said Tex, and we all did.

My roomie, the Dove, was putting away his dishes from a pesto feed, while Jake (the Snake) was lounging on the couch nursing a glass of red. Robbins, our staff geologist and resident gay cultural director was exchanging recipes. I could smell sacred herb from my room and Bennies laugh while the ' Dead were singing,

"...there's a dragon with matches.
that's loose on the town
take a whole pail of water
just to cool him down

Fire, fire on the mountain

I went into the backroom and started boogie-n' to the music while packing until Bennie tapped me and handed me his ceremonial pipe. I sat down alongside him, and we lost ourselves amongst the clouds and music and the gods did smile.

The gods were not smiling on Pecker Tracks for the moment though. Enough letters had been written mentioning the development that a congress member or two was coming over with an inspection team. Still, the road was being widened while power lines went underground. Plans were in for a concession to have year round yurts at the Kaibab Lodge (just outside park boundary) the only thing for fifty miles between the North Rim and Jacob Lake on scenic highway 67. Uranium mining claims all around the canyon rims, noise encroachment from the thousands of scenic flights over the canyon and air quality worsened from cars, construction dust, and smog from as far away as Vegas, and L.A., it was Californication! Hey, I know, I lived there, and now here.

"The tree which moves some to tears of joy is, in the eyes of others, only a green thing which stands in the way."

-William Blake

Buck and I showed up at work after our days off. Nothing much, just a quick jaunt up some trail in Zion, where we met two honeys. They were headed down, as we arrived at the summit, stopping to ask us,"Where's happy hour boys?"
To which we promptly replied, "Bit n' Spur, in about two hours, hold some seats for us." Low and behold, we had ourselves two jack Mormoms (intentionally mispelled) with margs in hand. Yeah boy howdy!

Back at the rim we began a two day orgy of cleaning up roadside brush piles left by a visiting hot shot crew. Why two days? Well, we had the seventh annual North Rim 10K fun run to do and the mucky mucks wanted the course to be pretty and pile free. Going ridiculously far, they even wanted any visible saw marks on a tree or branch to be smeared with dirt covering up any fresh cuts. And yet development was slated as a natural progression for this park. False front western boom towns came to my mind. After the first night, Buck and I ended up at the saloon pounding tequila with the infamous Spider woman, Monique (who managed the reservations desk). Why spider woman? Her famed dark eyes burned holes of desire into men's souls. Of course Buck managed to get spun in her web of evil desires that night, a tequila one, as I remember. Buck was in bad shape the next day and whining about me slave driving him with mindless work and no water breaks. I escaped with every dump truck load, which took about forty minutes each, leaving him stranded single-handedly of course, on a hot, sunny day, parched. Character building.
"Slave driver!" he cursed as he sweat from his eyeballs.
"I'm only conditioning you for the run this afternoon." I replied sheepishly grinning.

Finally, work over, it was race time. There were sixty runners, men and women, with a South Rim press rank there. Neil, the maintenance division running master, won the male event, while Lisa was edged out by Katy, a South Rim interp. After the race in which Buck placed ninth, just behind the long legs of Tex, he disappeared (to puke and crash). The rest of us were all affectionately toasted and roasted. Meanwhile, I ate chili beans, salad, rice, rolls, with burgers, steak, chicken, and any other kind of carcass you would want to devour. I also treated myself to the Corona's packed in ice with wedges of lime. To avert lethargy like a feasting lion, there was dancing at the basketball court, where Otis had his stereo out. Otis was a former TW employee who now worked the park's entrance station as a fee collector. This fall he was determined to attend Santa Rosa Community College for nine weeks of seasonal law enforcement training to become a patrol ranger next year. After eating and some dancing, I walked home after plucking one more Corona. With monsoon season almost here in the North Rim pines, I might need some rest. Nobody home, one hot shower downing an ice cold one, reading book in hand, and it was dreamland. It's a tough life!

What was I reading? A popular novel passed around that summer, <u>The Haunted Mesa.</u>
"Each of us has a vision of the world that belongs to him alone, and when he dies that

world dies with him. Others may share in some parts of it, but none will see it exactly he does, nor will all experience it in the same way, for they are living with their own vision of reality. Each man's vision of reality is based upon his life experience, the influences of people, places, books, dreams, work, all the various aspects of his existence that go to make up him, or her."

-Louis L'Amour (p.245)

Part Three-
Going Up In Smoke

"How hard it is to hide the sparks of nature!

-William Shakespeare

(Prof) Lancelot Lasagna Dispatch

"...you can't start a fire without a spark..."

- from a Bruce Springsteen song

Park Service reports state that on Thursday, June 26, 1630 hours (4:30 P.M.) a forest service recon plane spotted a light, white organic smoke of moderate volume about a half acre in size in heavy timber and being blown over on the North Rim.
Piece of cake!
At 1900 hours (7 P.M.) the report notes Engine 6 (of North Rim, Grand Canyon) was dispatched to Kanabownits tower.

It was into the twilights last gleaming that Buck and I departed. Buck with a full tray of lasagna taken from the kitchen of Tamara, assured me, she wouldn't mind. We had just pulled a full day shift and were dispatched in the middle of our happy hour imbibing. Our assignment was to go out, confirm the report and be ready to size this up the next day by being the closest resource available.

At 2200 (10 P.M.) Buck and I climbed the steps of the lookout. As we watched the far off flames from the Ponderosa candles lick the night sky, a feeling came over me, and I chuckled slyly, "This one will be a campaigner, a real hull-a-ba-loo! A fire for our graybeard stories." Priorities in order, Buck's response was, "Oh, yeah...well I hear lasagna calling me." As he started down the stairs, I looked back at an estimated 2-3 acre fire. Following along I shouted in glee, "To camping out."
"To borrowed lasagna." cried Buck.
"Yeah boy howdy." I mumbled to myself.

We consumed the whole pan of lasagna while our campfire settled into glowing coals. Buck and I set up cots for a few hours until we would be given the go ahead for our initial attack. My last toast as I finished sipping my canteen was, "To the glow under the stars." While I lay in my cot and looked up at the infinity of suns in the night sky, I thought of all the myriads of souls that have gone before me,
"Maybe each star is a soul from earth." I said as much to Buck.
"Then with black holes the universe is shit out of luck." was Bucks reply.
In the ensuing laughter, we fell asleep.

(Prof continues) To the fire

At 0500 (5 A.M.) we were back on the clock brewing up a pot of coffee on the Coleman stove and eating chunks of leftover Italian bread. Half an hour later, and we were up in the lookout, plotting the legal location according to township, range, and section. Every fire has its legal location as does every law-abiding citizen. How else is the government to keep track of us?
"Well Buck, looks like we got ourselves a new legal. This one puts it out by Lancelot Point instead of Galahad. Probably the tank commando road will get us there."
"Yeah, looks like it on the map, Professor Canyon."

The tank commando road was a locust tree choked old fire road through the backcountry that we hadn't cleared in a few years for lack of use. There were a couple of downed logs, and a five foot diameter Douglass fir, however by careful maneuvering, and lots of experience in our rig, we were quickly around this downfall. We wanted to beat Billie Joe's flight scehduled for 0800 and now was not the time for road clearing. It was mostly clear but slow going. To the south of us, the area named Shinumo Amphitheater, a vista greeted our eye. On the Holy Grail along these named points were: King Arthur and Guinnevere Castles looming up out of the colorful abyss. Indeed, as the legendary points surrounded us, we felt as knights of old and the last true heroes going to battle with Pulaski's and chainsaws to slay the fire dragon on Lancelot.

Approximately 0700 hours our arrival at road's end welcomed us amongst giant Ponderosa's and the faint smell of smoke, miles away. Within minutes, Buck and I had our I.A.(initial attack) gear on, with a full set of tools and five gallons of water in a "piss pump" to sling over our packs. Leaving behind our sleeping bags and all the benefits that this engine carried, we set out on foot to contour to our fire, hoofing close to 60 pounds each. After all, we can always come back was our thoughts.

Getting to a fire is never a quick matter when hiking cross country, no matter how easy the terrain. But this was rather mild trekking in Ponderosa glades, traversing between shallow, spiny locust filled drainages interspersed with aspen and fern groves. While I scouted the route, Buck flagged behind. The radio cackled and pilot Dana's voice declared, "Dispatch, 210 in service to fire at Lancelot Point."

"Damn, Billie Joe's enroute!"
"Easy, Buck, we'll get there."

Twenty minutes later we heard the Beating Beast and the ship (the Bell Jet Ranger helicopter) pass over. I could still hear Buck cussing behind me.

(Prof) At the scene

It was at 0800 according to park records that Buck and Canyon arrived and met with incident commander Billie Joe Sagebrush at a helispot. (Fires were now being referred to as "incidents" and fire bosses now were called "incident commanders" according to official government jargon).
"Hey Canyon, Buck, my plan is to stay here until noon or so and based on your suggestions and my observations, I'll instruct you on the objectives I'd like you to accomplish. When I leave, you'll be the designated 'I-C' and Buck, you'll be the monitor," discharged Billie Joe in formal government speak.

"Looks like about 5 acres currently with a nice 80% slope and a blow down on it." I stated.
"Sounds like saw work to me." added Buck eagerly looking at me.
"Right now I'd like you two to hike the fire and come up with some plans of action." commanded Billie Joe.
Overhead, a raven cackled and a Kaibab squirrel answered from nearby as a crashing sound issued from inside the fire with the roar of a Mack truck. A dense black cloud mixed with 100 foot flames shot up from the forest. I looked over at Buck and encountered a shit-eating grin with the light in his eyes, signifying this is what we live for. Looking back at Billie Joe, who appeared a bit nervous, I said, " Time for a nature walk, see ya in a bit." as we left to scout.
"Have fun!" Bob (BJ's assistant) smiling, spoke and added, " You'll wish for some corks on that slope."

Corks, the spike boots of loggers and fallers, would be a godsend, but our Vibram soles would have to do. Taking the plunge going into Big Spring drainage, the downed trees were a labyrinth of criss-crossed logs under a young canopy of piss firs (white fir or abies concolor). Every step would have to be placed carefully.

Fire elves danced in delight, feasting on fallen needles, twigs and greedily gobbling young firs that had taken advantage of fires absence and sprouted. On the north flank we came upon the rim dropping steeply away, 80 degrees from the edge.

"Yeah boy howdy, doesn't look like the fire's slopped too far down yet, Professor." Buck proclaimed.
"Well, let's go look see, Buck-ster."
After traversing the slop over, Buck echoed my thought aloud, saying, "If we had our

whole crew and began now, we can catch it."
"Let's go find Billie Joe?"

Billie Joe and company were still under the Ponderosa's munching candy bars when we
arrived back. Buck and I had been gone a half hour.
"Well, what do ya think?" asked Billie Joe.

"I think if we don't take care of that slop over soon, we'll be in trouble. We could jump
on this with the whole crew and catch it before it takes off."
"Did you find any fuel breaks?"
"Not from the road to the fire."
"What about down in the drainage?"
"We didn't go all the way down, we just traversed the fire."
"Well, go check it out again!" Bill Joe commanded.
I turned to Buck, "Well, you heard the man."
Buck picked up his shovel and started walking to the rim. I followed along, really glad
that Buck, for once, didn't say what was really on his mind. I could hear one of the ever
present ravens doing his best turkey imitations.

We jumped over the foot high frolicking flames into the warm gray ash and cut across
the fire, keeping an eye out for widow making branches which could crash down on us
from burning trees to these two smoke bums below. It didn't take long to cross the fire
and jump back out of the flames into the green. We followed for about a quarter mile
along the rims edge from the fire to a small drainage.
"This looks like a bit of a break, huh Buck, no down timber, a few big pines and some
Doug firs waving below."
"Let's get on down, I'll take the flagging you ol' scout."
Yeah boy and down we went for forty chains (half a mile) a scramble into...
"Hey Buck, there's a beautiful creek down here with nice cool spring water to slake the
thirst of a god or at least a hot smoke bum."
Buck's face popped over the edge of the cliff, a big smile beaming, "This is what it's all
about professor, just gettin' lost in the beauty of nowhere."
I didn't have to say a thing as I cupped my hands, knelt down to the water's edge, dipped
and drank deeply. Ahhh, fresh, cold, clear...Obscenely, the radio on my belt came to life
with a voice, "Canyon, Sagebrush." Quickly, once again the electronic squeal amongst
the laughing waters, "Canyon, Saaage----brush."
"Sounds like that fire must be heating his asshole." commented Buck.
"We couldn't be so lucky." I uttered and our laughter joined the creeks.
"Caaannnyon-----Saaaagebrush!" obviously angered.
"Damn, Buck!" I squealed and twisted the radio off its swivel and calmly, in my best
radio voice, said, "Sagebrush, Canyon."
"Status?" the radio questioned.

"We've found a creek here at the bottom and are now proceeding downstream to look for an easier way back up and a better fuel break."
"Copy, ETA back to the rim?"
"About half hour,"
"Copy-Sagebrush clear."
"Canyon clear."

"Well, let's go and see if this might offer a future route down into the drainage." Such hopes were soon shattered when Buck and I came to a fifteen foot ledge, followed by another, and more ledges on down. The clear deep pool beckoned, but up on the rim a fire called.

Up on the rim, the flames had been enjoying our absence. Under the open Ponderosa glades of previously golden needle carpets now lay gray smoldering ash. Pines were being ravaged as flames climbed up in flickering spirals of light, spewing black, smoky belches with the fuel consumed. The young white firs turned into candles for a moment, their needles baked, and smoke hissing from the skeletons of former trees. Buck and I were transfixed in a gaze. Rainbows of rock lay spread open in front of us: Sagittarius Ridge, Hatauta, Moradnock, and Castor Temples, Mescalero and Mimbreno Points all at our feet in the abyss below. The holy grail, a sword of stone beckoning the gods to come forth.

(Prof) Dry Tinder

"I never had a policy that I could always apply. I've simply attempted to do what made the greatest amount of sense at the moment."

-Abe Lincoln

I looked at Buck, whose sight was still in the canyon.
"Have you got a plan yet?" inquired BJ.
"Well, Buck and I came up with three on the way up. One, could be full suppression starting now with our whole squad. We could clip it possibly under 40 acres. Two, there's a decent fuel break down at the creek. Improve on that and we cut a line across the point letting it burn the point. That would be about 160 acres and take one 20 person hand crew, starting 'em right now. Or, option three, we could back off to the fire road, flanking and sealing it off then just monitoring and burning out from the road, if needed. " Approximately 3,200 acres of fuel reduction." interjected a smiling Buck.

"In any moment of decision the best thing you can do is the right thing, the next best thing is the wrong thing, and the worst thing you can do is nothing.

-Theodore Roosevelt

Indecision flickered across Billie Joe's face, like a flame seeking dry tinder. The fire was beginning to pick up intensity as the morning sun blazed its warmth upon the southern aspect of this jutting point of Ponderosa forest. The park fire manager was taking his time, and Buck was antsy to get going. In just two hours, the fire had easily doubled in size from the 5 acre estimate to nearing 10 acres with flame length picking up as it engulfed the dead and down. This area had been suppressed before, keeping fires down to a few acres in the past. However, over the decades, the forest had grown stagnant, with an accumulation of several feet of dead fuels. An unhealthy forest and overloaded, ripe for a major conflagration.

"In firefighting, decisions are based on probabilities, on the best information at hand, and they're made quickly, very quickly."

-Fernanda Santos, <u>The Fire Line,</u> p. 221.

Back at the ship (helicopter) Billie Joe decided to get a squad of five more people in, but first he wandered off walking the fire again for himself. The official log, according to Martha (in NPS dispatch) states that on Friday at 1130 hours, a helicopter shuttle begins from the South Rim.

So we cleared a better helispot, and five people flew in two separate flights (ship capacity of 3 people plus gear) with the Bell Jet Ranger taking 45 minutes per round trip from Grand Canyon Heliport to Lancelot helispot.

A few good friends were among the firefighters arriving: such as the infamous dancing Poleski, Len the "Wad." What a relief to have his experience out here. The word out amongst the female delighters was that this good looking guy was taken. In fact, his future wife to be was on that ship. Everyone was happy to see Jinny, one of the best huggers and law dogs I have known. Guys loved her but yeah...also taken! It was good to see the Wad in love again with such a wonderful gal in Jinny. Previously, he had been singing an old John Conlee song, Rose Colored Glasses,

"But those rose colored glasses

That I'm looking through

Show only the beauty

'Cause they hide all the truth."

It was good to see him wearing his see through goggles again. In Jinny, he not only had beauty but integrity as well this time.

Also on the other ride was Slim Tim, a good bro' and old smoke bum. Steve, a very competent ranger and Tack, a female backcountry cutie arrived too (we'd get to know her better on fires later on in the season). Hugs all around. We broke for lunch of some good old government' "beenie n' weenies." No sooner was the lid of our C-rats opened via our P-38's (government issue field can opener) than a raven landed on a Ponderosa above; a scene of smoke bum gluttony and laughter. Billie Joe was down under a fir and he wasn't laughing. Meanwhile the fire elves continued to dance.

After lunch, the ravens picked at the empty containers down by the fire packs in the dirt and needles. Buck and I walked over to Billie Joe under the piss fir.
"So, what's up Billie J?" I asked.
"I'm going to scout the northeast end again, don't do anything until I get back."
"Okay," I acknowledged. Buck was looking really antsy at the light gray smoke column from down rim as Billie Joe strode off once again.

"There are three kinds of people in the world: those who make things happen; those who watch things happen; and those who stand around and say, "What happened?"

-Tommy Lasorda

The radio cackled and 210 called from the air; Dana, the pilot, wanted a snag by the helispot removed. Of course Tim proceeded to get the saw stuck, for which he suffered verbal harangue unmercifully. It took us an hour of Pulaski and wedge work to get the saw free again. I tried to get Billie Joe on the radio with no success.

"Fuck Buck, where's ol Billie-baby?" I chuckled.
"Guess he got lost in the woods somewhere down below."
"That, or ran for his life the chicken shit little bastard." now mumbling my wishes.
"We gave him our plans, but the damn bureaucratic ticket puncher wants a look for himself again. How many times does he have to walk this?" Still no Billie Joe.

For an hour and a half or more, Billie Joe had disappeared. Thoughts of a widow-maker falling on him, or BJ falling 1,000 feet, or maybe the fangs of a rattlesnake drawn from the depths of the gorge striking quickly to help rid the cause of government incompetence came to mind.
Finally at 1500 hours (3 P.M.) the radio came to life, "Canyon, Sagebrush."
Cackling back, "Sagebrush, Canyon."
"Meet me on the south flank with Buck."
"Aaafirm."
"Sagebrush, out."

The elves were dancing with glee as a good gust of wind blew, pine needles crackling in the fire. Coincidentally, a flora of sagebrush whooshed into oily flames, blue and red with a black puff of smoke to finalize combustion.

The log states that at 1500, BJ gives the word for a full suppression response. FINALLY! It only took him seven hours to decide (from 8 A.M. until 3 P.M.).

Billy Joe's veins stood out blue against his red neck, in his yellow Nomex shirt with green pants. He pulled out his radio and called to have another squad sent over. BJ further instructed us, "Jim, I'm going to have Buck take over as I.C. (incident commander) and you will be lead monitor."

"OK," I stated and looked over at Buck, his face flushing red as his ground pounding fun was now replaced with overhead responsibilities tied to BJ mired in his petty bureaucracy.

"Any problems?" asked BJ as his lips twitched.

"Nope." swallowed Buck quickly and affirmitively.

I smiled a (shit-eating) grin at Buck, who didn't smile back. A tree crashed like thunder somewhere in the burn, making Billie Joe jerk his head and glance into the fire. I laughed encountering Buck's solemness and Billie Joe's stone cold eyes. We walked back to the helispot, voices silent, smelling the dry pine smoke, listening to the snap, crackle and pop of talking flames.

"Billie J, did you ever consider any of our suggestions or the contingency plans?" Buck interjected.

"No!"

"Okayyy... boss, how soon before we can get our Longshot crew out here, and we'd consulted with the Wad earlier and concurred that a hotshot crew should begin work down on that 80% slope."

"Denied. As soon as I head back on the park helicopter, we'll begin mobilizing for this fire. I estimate it's about 20 acres now."

(Buck's interjection)- Damn! With the park's helicopter traveling at 140 mph, it would still take laboriously long to amass a (put together park) crew of 20 and their gear out here. Five members already present, it was still fifteen more folks required at forty-five minutes a shuttle carrying only three plus gear. That was five more flights. At forty-five minute intervals plus time for a twenty minute refuel after three shuttles, I was looking at 245 minutes or just over four hours before assembling a full crew. The hotshots were typically requested for such hazardous and difficult assignments as an 80% slope. Putting a make up crew together of various park personnel from the various divisions and asking them to perform such a task was possibly endangering safety. But when you're taking orders from above, incompetents that think they know more and have to prove it, your hands are tied. What a game!

(Prof continues)- On the next ship out at 1530, Billie Baby (a.k.a.-Billie Joe Sagebrush) left us there taking his assistant Bob with him. His final orders were that we were to take an indirect attack, away from the fire. Indirectly, this led us to our own ideas of direction such as safeguarding the helispot, now our safety zone, which was the Wads main concern. Based on his experience as past leader of the Longshots, the Wad became crew boss, I became the line scout, and Buck remained the fire boss (er...incident commander). I set off to flag our route while the Wad set the squad of five assembled to scrape line and give us an anchor point from the helispot, a future sleeping area/dining room with a view.

(Prof) Down the Hotline

With the changing of the day to darkness, the shadows crept across the buttes, pinnacles, and fantasyland of rock. Cool air flows from above battled with the ongoing hot oven below of the inner gorge, both vying for dominance. The fire elves grew from children to adults. Closer and closer to my flagging followed the Wad and his gang of knights entering the fray. I gave Tim a hand by swamping brush while he wielded the Stihl, sawing a swath through the thick timber for Wad's squad. Lots of small diameter, ten to thirty foot firs had to be removed by the lone saw. Slow going. The elves chuckled at our progress.

Frantically working, people sweating, Ranger Steve Stoic called for a hand as the flames jumped the line behind him. A young fir was quickly devoured in a loud crackling, red flame eruption, billowing black smoke. Tim and I heard a bounding noise only to look up and see a basketball sized rock heading our way. Dropping the saw, Tim leaped doing the splits. The rock rolled between his legs and down the slope. We both uttered, "Fuckn'-A" in unison. Ranger Stoic and the others were having a tough time after only two and a half hours, but for that matter, so were the rest of us. The Wad, looking at Tim and I and thinking of the other three rangers, expressed his concern for safety. Working the 80% slope with downed logs to straddle, and dodging rocks all night long in the dark was too great a risk for the spot duty rangers.
"Let's call it a night, improve the helispot, eat some beanies, and call it another day in paradise." Len proclaimed with finality that Tim and I agreed on. "Come on Steve, Jinny, Tack, let's pack it up. Relief should be coming soon." were the orders to the already charcoal faces.

I remembered the sleeping bags Buck and I left on the engine. It would be a dog curling night on the ground. The elves chuckled, a raven cackled, and the moonlight glowed eerily overhead. I've spent many a night on fires in my life. The first night of the Lancelot fire is the jewel in my crown of night fires. With a candle seemingly lit in the great abyss, the fire on this Great Thumb Mesa grew, consuming 100 year old pinyon-juniper groves in flickering gulps. Behind me Ponderosa's blazed away burning from the tap roots sending heat up the hundred foot trunks and baking the needles to a tender brown crisp. While many survived, a few met their doom as we witnessed balls of fire and thunderous crashes. Those that fell turned night into day. Buck and I, without our bags, stayed on the clock monitoring and making instant coffee in empty combat-ration cans. Soon enough, the glow of Ponderosa's burning was replaced by the sun's rising in the east. Along with it, came the radio blaring.
"Lancelot IC, fire dispatch."
"Lancelot."
"Your request for a type 1 hotshot crew denied again."
"Reasoning?" inquired Buck.

"Sagebrush says that you should be able to handle this with the park employees."
"Copy." came the reply in a dejected voice.
"Also, breakfast will be flown in at 0900 hours and we should have the resources to you for a full park crew." (The rest of the park personnel to make up a 20 person crew that were supposed to arrive the previous evening).
"Copy."
"Any needs?"
(Yeah but WTF, Billie J. won't acknowledge anything but what he wants, so instead...)
"Negative" said the frustrated, tired voice of Buck acting official like.

"Fire dispatch out."
"Lancelot out." said Buck, eyes now twinkling again at the beauty of morning.
"Damn, continuosly denies our request to fight this fire with what we need. We consulted and mutually agreed on our resource requests and plan of action and yet what the hell is he doing? He's hidden his sorry ass so long, how would he know what resources are needed."
"Calm down, Buck, ya know the game. Incompetents rise to places of authority to make decisions for those of us in the seasonal ranks. It flavors our fires and gives us great stories to tell." I mocked to the now type A-Buck. A canyon wren sang its melody and I smiled, lost in the magic of fire, of living in the present and not having to deal with the Billie Joe factor.

"Well Buck, maybe I better take a walk around this fire while you boil some more water and baby-sit the radio until everyone wakes up."
"Dispatch, Lancelot IC."
"Go ahead, Lancelot IC."
"Yeah, I'm going to need some Marie's over here to take care of us this afternoon."

"Lancelot IC, re-phrase that. That's bordering sexual harassment."
"Okay, let's make this clear as possible, Meals-Ready-to-eat, M-R-E's."
"Dispatch copies, we'll send you the MRE's (marie's), how many cases do you need?"
"Two for now, have a good day."

"I'm puttin' us on at 0500, professor."
"Sounds good, I'll call ya if anything exciting happens." I went and grabbed my Pulaski and flagging. As I approached the fire's edge, I was caught in the cool air of morning rushing to greet the coals of heat. The fire had grown by leaps and bounds and soon I was confronted by line to cut to prevent further encroachment over the rim and into more vegetation. I pulled the radio off my hip and put it to my lips, "Buck, Canyon."
"Go ahead."
"She's gonna need some work out here Buck, better roust the gang and have 'em tool up."

"Copy prof."
"I'll tie in with them in 15."
"Gotcha."
Click, click.

Most of that morning it was my Pulaski, the fire, and my thoughts. I became one with the tool and the fire. As primal as it gets. I felt sorry for Buck, chained to the radio (monitoring updates, weather reports, communicating with us and the asshole boss). Organic matter was scraped from the forest floor as sweat poured off of foreheads. Voices, some in laughter, some in the seriousness of orders, carried on in the light breeze under the Ponderosa's. Every now and then, a two hundred year old Ponderosa would meet the end of its mortal reign in the forest. Each time I heard, saw, or felt a tree fall, I thought of my short time on this planet. In retrospect, my thoughts went back to these trees as seedlings and as my mind wandered I contemplated this forest back then.

Park records show that at 1340, ship 210 landing at Lancelot with passengers: Stahs, Boman, and Dumachet. For this lone canyon wanderer, it would turn out to be a major event. The log also states that a red flag warning for high winds was issued for northwest Arizona, canceling any further flights with crewmembers.

The media caught wind of this fire. Channel 2 news out of Phoenix arrived. The air quality was being further jeopardized in the park and thus city slickers trying to escape urban smog as well as foreigners coming to see prime U.S. grade "A" property were being denied their views. The whitewater business down below us was getting smoked out by the nightly drown-drafts. Thus our river rat friends working for peanuts for corporate ventures weren't catering to the whims of their paying customers for a Grand experience. The media had a hey day. IC Buck had re-requested a type 1-shot crew. BJ sent him a desk jockey to monitor weather and spy. This guy did nothing of much use while there except his one alert to us over radio to, "Note the Lenticulars," as in the pancake shaped clouds forming overhead as an indication of turbulent air. For his two days there, this guy was off by himself and said nor did anything else except that one broadcast of the flying saucer-like clouds. It became a standing joke amongst us, "copy the lenticulars," and would be added to our other sayings on the crew. With media exposure, Sagebrush had to finally concede that his desire to keep this all in his park was not going to happen and thus the Flagstaff Hotshots were on their way via crew carriers.

At 1530, the Flagstaff Hotshots arrived, with Tex leading them in.
Chowing down and finished by 1630 at the helispot, the shots tooled up to catch the fire where it had slopped over the rim. Their other objective was to tie into the line that Wad's crew scraped.

Eighty chains of line (a mile) were cut on top of the Kaibab Plateau that day by the (still incomplete) park crew. Forty more ass kicking son of a steep slope chains (a half mile) were cut by the shots. One hundred twenty chains of line total (mile and a half). A hot dinner was flown in. Mashed potatoes, string beans, and roast beef all in their tin containers while the salad arrived in a garbage bag, complete with paper plates and plastic silverware. The raven population around the spike camp was picking up. The magic of the fire elves dancing with stars burning in the night was always my favorite time.

After dinner that evening the new park crew's job was just beginning. Improving and patrolling the line were in order. Another 40 more chains of shot line on steep slope would be constructed. At 0100, the shots completed their task emerging back on the rim. I continued as scout, and true to my calling, I noticed a pair of bright blues on a dark haired mini fighter that evening. The next morning would bring those eyes into this lone smoke bums life, at least for awhile. This gal was having boot problems. Her soles had melted away from the intense heat that she withstood on the burning ground. She had the brightest blue eyes and a good spark of life!
"Hey, I was hoping that you could help me with this talking boot of mine." she inquired, with a grin.
"I think my 1,000 mile tape should help." I replied, returning her grin.
Naturally, I proceeded to wrap her boots and find out her name (Janice) and where she worked (Desert View district) as well as what days off she had. When I found out she was free the same days as I (sorry Buck) and had nothing scheduled, I asked, "Maybe we could do nothing together, somewhere?"
"Sounds like something to me." She smiled.
"Maybe we better go find that fire now that you've stopped my boot from talking."
"Let's go do nothing instead." I jokingly stated.
"Come on." She laughed and off to the fire we went.

For breakfast, the Wad had heated the tins of roast beast and smashed mush as the animals fed among the burning flames. The Lancelot fire was contained (encircled) for the time being, fifty-eight and one half hours and 60 acres of sweat later.

Billie Joe called and asked if there was anything we needed.
"Breakfast!" Buck retorted.
"Okay," BJ said, adding, "don't take things so personally."
"Copy." Biting his lips from replying further, the words hung in the heated air.

Finally, Buck and I headed to our sleeping bags that Tex had hiked in. As we reached our camp, I walked up to Buck reassuring him by saying, "Hey, glad we made it." I laughed, Buck laughed, and we hugged. As I crawled into my bag, I remembered the blue eyes of a young filly and smiled. Sleep came fast; the bed of earth felt good.

(Prof) Containment (fire encircled)

"Job stress is defined as harmful physical and emotional responses that occur when the requirements of the job do not match the capabilities, resources, or needs of the worker."

-unknown

210, the helicopter arrived in the morning bringing Ken instead of the hot breakfast we were expecting. "So where's breakfast?" I queried as the ship descended down into the abyss and back to the South Rim.
"Billie Joe forgot to get the order in, he also wants me to take over as IC. He thinks you all aren't organized over here." Ken stoically emphasized.
"Grrreat" rasped a relieved Buck, smiling. Buck's vocal cords were singed and hoarse, due to the excessive heated smoke while forced into wearing too many hats: trying to command and organize while keeping up with Billie Joe's constant requests/denials over the radio, monitoring weather, posting as lookout, cutting line, and communicating with the crews and the media. "Sorry, Buck, it looks like you've got a smooth show going here to me. I'm just gonna have to call ol' Billie Joe and tell him you're still bossing this puppy." A smile crept over Ken's dark face.
"That's bullshit!" stammered Buck (not wanting to deal with BJ anymore).
"Yeah, but a good one." laughed Ken.
Slim, Wad, and myself rolled on the ground while Buck strode away hot and frustrated.

(Buck's interjection)-I had many other IC experiences before and after this incident. Normally, I welcomed the opportunity as it was a challenge that was my passion, wildfire. However with the new management in Billie Joe, dealing with his ineptitude, untrusting character, and lack of support, it was difficult to "play the game." Many times I found myself holding back anger and animosity towards his unprofessional approach and self-serving egotistical nature. He really wasn't on "our team," to deal with the fire(s) at hand in the best possible way as we had been trained. Communication was essential and that was always lacking from him, making for all of us an unsafe situation. On this specific fire at Lancelot Point an added element not mentioned previously was at play. We were forewarned by the forest service to keep the fire out of the continuous fuels to the north (the steep slope area) as it could transfer to their lands. The forest service was preparing the site adjacent to us for a logging sale, to harvest the timber. It equated to their different land management policy (timber, grazing, mining, watershed, and recreation) versus the park policy (preservation and protection for future generations) thus my constant request for the hotshots. I witnessed many of the put together park crew (from rangers to desk jockeys) as good people, however inexperienced in a fire of this magnitude and intensity, dealing with the hazardous conditions present. For many that were sent out, it was their first fire. I felt a personal connection to their safety and as IC was adamant about that above all else. Finally, my leadership style is "hands-on," and I felt the need to assist these hard working folks under my direct command. I offered help whenever I could free myself from the radio and monitoring of activity as I noticed many were struggling physically with the arduous job of line construction, safety zone improvement, and escape routes. This was not a fire for first timers, at least not so many "newbie's" together making up a crew (and partial one at that). Given the job, they performed admirably, stepped up to the plate, and gave it their all. I was thankful for having good, hard working people sent. However, their lack of situational awareness caused me constant worry. Watching the inexperienced among the many hazards was difficult.

(Prof continues)- After finally encircling the fire (containment) we were to begin mop up operations working to "control" it. In the evolving fire management policy of the park service in the '80's, mop up began to change and was now different from the forest service. The park service's new policy was to leave the fire to mop itself up as much as possible ("letting the natural process of fire to combust fuels to organic matter for nutrient rich replenishment," as the official jargon went to the public). We were instructed with, "Light hand on the land." That meant preserving most snags (dead standing trees) as wildlife trees. We also dug line around some bird nesting sites to protect them for propagation of species. The hard fought handline constructed around the fire's perimeter was always maintained and anything close to it or a possible threat of going or blowing over was safely extinguished or removed. Otherwise we let nature take its course and consume the interior. Our old policy and the other agencies, had mop up around the perimeter working in towards the center making sure all embers, flames, smolders, were out. Depending upon the differing conditions it varied as to how far we worked towards the center putting everthing out (i.e.- vegetation height and type, slope, wind, fuel moisture,etc.).

Mop up went fast. Buck came and grabbed me for lunch. He promptly informed me that when he left this afternoon, that I would get IC status.
"Whoopee! You might as well get hiking so you can get out, huh?" I teased.
"Just eat your lunch." said Buck as he choked down a ham sandwich.

That evening, instead of 35 gladiators battling the fire knights of Lancelot, there were just seven smoke bums, the burning forest interior and the stars overhead. Billie Joe had demobilized the shots for another destination and returned the park crew to their respective duties as law enforcement, interpretation, trails, etc. for the effectiveness of running a place like Grand Canyon National Park to the public. This Lancelot fire was now a far off venture and finally out of the public news.
"I'd say this calls for a toast." bloated Slim.
"Here, here!" we all saluted as we downed our canteens. As I walked the line, embers winked like glowing eyes from the forest floor while the crackling songs of flame kept me company.

Day 5 for me began at 0800 with leftover fruit, coffee, and the usual mop up patrol. It wasn't until 1430 that any excitement occurred. I was walking back up to the helispot when I encountered a spot fire that was growing fast. It took five of us to catch it and I ended up melting my web gear (straps holding fire shelter and water bottles) in the process. At 1800, I cut Slim and the three other South Rimmers home (as directed by BJ) while the Fox and one other hiked in so I could get the heck out! This fire was now controlled. Handlines had been widened and improved and mop up continued moving from the handline in towards the center. Normally we would maintain a much larger presence on a fire this size, but our resources were running low and exhausted. BJ was still managing from his office and always monitoring radio traffic. As I saw the Fox on my way out he joked to me (prophetically) I'd be back tomorrow for the "real fire." "The only fire I'm going to right now is in a bowl of hot chili, bro." I replied. Famous last words.

(Prof) The real fire

Tuesday morning and I was feeling good after a real nights sleep on a mattress, a hot shower, and a cup of coffee. I saw Ken with a cup of smile outside the (fire) pit.
"Any word from the Lancelot front?"
"All's quiet."
"Guess I'll start on fire reports."
"Sounds like a plan."
The radio squelched alive, "Fire dispatch, Fox."
"Fire dispatch."
"I've got a spot on the northeast side, prepare to copy size up." Click.
"Oh shit!" we responded in harmony.
"Fox-Dispatch, go ahead with size up."
"I've got a one acre spot on the northeast side down the 80% slope below the line, torching and running...break."
"Jim, grab Lisa in the cache, and take 210 on a flight. I'll gather Buck and we'll drive and hike in. Take over from Fox until I get there." sternly commanded foreman Ken.
"Gotcha."
"Copy-go ahead." Clicked dispatch to Fox.
"I'll need additional personnel to contain this, I'm going back down to cut line now."
"Copy, fire dispatch out."
"This is Ken, I'd like 210 dispatched to North Rim to pick up Canyon plus one, he'll assume I.C., break."
"Copy, we've notified 210, break."
"Buck and myself will be heading out in engine 5 on the fire roads."
"Copy."
"Longshots, clear."
"Fire dispatch copies."

"210 off the ground."
"Copy Dana." I radioed.
"See ya dare."
Click, click, click, click. Someone was shooting off, radio happy.

The Bell Jet Ranger (210) with fearless "curly red" as we nicknamed Dana our main
pilot, for the obvious locks on his head, settled down at North Rim heliport. I sat up next
to him, put the headset on, buckled my seat belt, and nodded, O.K.
"She's puttin' up a good column, looks like fun."
As soon as we got above the trees, I could see the 3,000 foot plume.
"Yeah boy!" my only comment.
He nodded. I flicked on the radio switch, "Fire dispatch-Canyon."
"Go ahead." fire dispatch replied.
"The Lancelot spot is putting up a 3,000 foot column, white, straight up. I'd like to have
a 20 person crew mobilized and also an air tanker stand by."
"Dispatch copies, we'll get back to you."
"Thanks much, over."
As we circled the spot, I tried calling the Fox and getting his people out of the hole so I
could nail it with bomber slurry, while it was still small. If the fire makes a run up the
hill, we're fucked, I thought.
"Fox-Canyon."
Pause.
"Fox-Canyon"
No answer.
"Well, Dana might as well put us down."
"Fire dispatch-Canyon."
"Dispatch." Billie Joe's voice had replaced the original dispatcher.
"We're landing at the Lancelot helispot, I'm going to try and get the Fox out of the hole
and then I'd like to hit this spot with a bomber, break."
"Yeah, well... I'll get back to you on that. 210 return to South Rim."
"210 copies, off Lancelot en route South Rim." replied Dana, waving to me as he
ventured over the abyss, yawning.

"Well Lisa, let's go down in the hole and find the Fox."
"Okay Jim, maybe I should stay up here for radio relays."
"Good idea." and down I went. The shadow of a raven passed by me, a Kaibab squirrel
scolded me, and I laughed back at it.
As the Kaibab squirrel went up a white fir, I went down that all familiar 80% slope.
More line, I thought, oughta just let it burn.

(Prof) With a Macleod stuck up your aspen

The Fox had a big grin on his face, the McCloud in his hands keeping a steady rhythm. Huge clouds of duff and needles flew around his smile.
"We've got this one." the Fox had spoken.
"Ha!" my Pulaski felt like a magic wand as four to six inches of mineral earth appeared, becoming a scratch line. Sweat poured off my nose, flames crackled and then fell silent upon meeting soil.
Working diligently until I heard a familiar voice, "Yeah-boy, get on that steed and ride!" Buck suddenly shouted from above. Reinforcements. Longshots. Ya-hoo!

At 1115, we were on the verge of triumph in suppression.

At 1130, BJ showed up and went down in the hole. He looked worried as Ken looked dejected without his usual smile in place.
"Jim." Ken said as he motioned me to come over.
"Yeah."
"I'm taking over. Billie Joe wants to put in those original contingency lines when we get two crews here."
"Hey, it'll be too late by the time that happens." Shaking my tool I reiterated, "We've almost caught this."

"When angry, count four; when very angry, swear.
-Mark Twain

"Damn!" yelled the red-faced Fox. "That chicken-shit-piece of wasted human flesh!"
"Come on, let's give it a try." I asked again.
"I'd like to Boomer, but we have to play his game. He's the boss and if he screws up it's his butt." Buck with hand on Pulaski, tossed it into the trees and walked up the line without saying a word. Ken went after Buck. I grabbed the Pulaski as the Fox and I went back to cutting line. Let Donnie baby roust us was my thought. Five minutes later, turnip red-faced and breathing hard, he showed up.

"Canyon, Fox, get out of there. You couldn't hold it if you caught it. Look at that snag that's burning."
"It'll stay in the burn, I've looked. Come on, Sagebrush, give us a chance."
"Get out now!" Billie Joe interrupted then turned his back on us and left.
"That scum-sucking geek!" scowled the Fox while heaving his Macleod skyward. It came resting in some aspen branches about twenty feet up.

As the flames crackled I vacated the line with the Fox following. A raven landed nearby and just perched. Somewhere I heard a laugh from the fire, or maybe just the forest talking.

Up top, the Fox and I joined Buck already under a Ponderosa. Billie Joe, Ken, and Gussie (the chief ranger) were over by the helispot. Gussie kept quiet. He was out to personally observe this fire now that he had the task of keeping the media informed. "BJ wants three helicopters to ferry troops, but he's not even gonna attempt to hit the fire with some bombers." informed Buck.
The Fox and I sat down next to Buck and proceeded to gobble down some gorp and Gatorade.
"So, Buck, what did Ken say to you?" I cautiously inquired.
Just then, the ever present black winged voice of the canyon, cackled, "AWWW!"
A smile spread across Buck's Hungarian features. "He said next time put that Pulaski where it counts. So I asked him, Where's that? and he chuckled, 'in Billie Joe's ranger hat.'"
"Ha AwwwHAHAAWWWW!"

Ken walked over to us collapsed on the ground rolling with laughter and told us that ol' BJ's plan (recorded in fire history notes at 1245) called for the old contingency lines. The same ones that Buck and I had suggested back in the beginning of this fire!
"Well, I gotta go meet with BJ and Gussie." Ken informed us.
"Have fun." one of us muttered.
"Yeah." sighed Ken.
So, we sat around on the rim, waiting...Once again...

Ken managed to order one slurry bomber.

At 1400, a second crew was ordered from the Kaibab National Forest. The fire was running and torching, having a naturally good time. Someone reported the spot fires at seven acres. The forest was tinder dry, especially in the canopy from the preheating. The danger now was the possibility of the fire getting into the dried out canopy and crowning over the rim below into consistent fuels or even over a crew itself. A classic re-burn.

Buck had radioed this very concern to BJ earlier (when he was IC) predicting a crown fire possibility. He witnessed several torching runs and noted the consistency of canopy supported the very liklihood of crowning. BJ's response was that after checking the computer for fuel model types of Ponderosa forests, it was non-existent for a crown fire to occur. Typical government bureaucrat far removed from the field of reality. All he could see was the end of his nose in the mire of his shit passed on as leadership mismanagement. Crown fires in Ponderosa forests would be well documented in the future by knowledgable experts (Dr. Merrill Kaufman comes to mind with Colorado fires like the Hayman).

"It ain't what you don't know that gets you into trouble. It's what you know for sure that just ain't so."

-Mark Twain

At 1515, three tankers arrived instead of the one promised. Government efficiency in action.

Ken came over the radio, "Fox, Jim, I'd like you guys to go down in the hole where you feel it's safe and see if this slurry is going to slow it down."
"Ken, you've got to hit the fire. With all those crisscrossed logs stacked on top of each other, only a crew and chainsaws will do anything effective."
"Boomer, I know, I'm just tired of arguing with that asshole, Billie Joe. Let him screw up, I just don't want anybody hurt."
"Okay, sorry about that."
"I'll take care of the ying-yang if you want." said a serious Fox.
"Uh, I'll see you guys. Be safe."
"Sure, Ken."
"Well Foxy, which end do you want?"
"I'll take the east."
"In that case, I'll take the west."
Overhead, the sound of the air tankers filled Shinumo Creek and Lancelot drainages.
Soon, a fine red mist started raining down, covering bits of foliage and ground. Working the steep slope was not an easy drop. The slurry covered only the tops of the logs (while the elves were dancing underneath and happily licking the bottoms with hot tongues).
After the last of the drops, I went to see if the fire was close to rounding the bend. It was only a chain away.

Buck, now designated as crew boss was leading a new put together park crew assembled by BJ.
I transmitted to Ken via radio, "You'd better send Buck's crew down here fast, it's close to hooking this bottom east corner."
"Copy, but BJ wants the other side as our priority."
"If it hooks here, it'll be heading to the helispot, our safety zone, and as of now it's only a chain away."
"Copy, I'll relay and see but BJ's got Buck's crew already committed."
"Copy, Canyon clear." Hell! I shouted as I felt like flinging my radio. Clusterfuck!

At 1600, as North Rim notes depict, a Kaibab (type-2) crew arrived with Rodriguez as their crew boss.

At 1630, the spot fire was 7 acres with the entire fire now at 120 acres. Ken (hands-tied) and F.M.O. Sagebrush were the two bosses for this incident. With Buck as the designated NPS crew boss, Rodriguez as the USFS crew boss, I became the task force leader (overseeing the two). "Hit the beaches!" echoed in my mind.

At 1630, Buck's crew was finally approved to working the east line.

Daylight had turned to night as the smoke filled and surrounded our presence. As I walked through the center of the burn, I heard a roar. Scurrying into a clearing, I saw the fire coming towards me. The crown run stopped at the edge of the clearing.
"Fox-Canyon."
"Go ahead, prof."
"Yeah, I got cut off here, I'm going back up."
"Copy."
"Don't cut across, the dry canopy is getting nasty, torching and running.
"Copy, I'll go around and meet ya." Click, click.

Flames were now four to six feet racing up the 80% slope.
"No way now." I voiced my thoughts aloud.
"No f-ing way now." the Fox firmly seconded.
"Canyon-Sagebrush."
"Go ahead."
"I'm going to send this forest crew down."
"Negative, this fire just rounded the bend into a head fire, traveling upslope, intense fire behavior, moving at 6 chains an hour."
"I copy Canyon, we'll hold that crew here." Ken's voice responded.
"Ken, you might want to get busy cutting a bigger safety zone at the helispot and camp."
"Copy, we'll get on it. Any estimate of how soon this run might get here."
"Around an hour."
"Copy."
"Canyon clear."

Suddenly, with the noise of a freight train, the fire was running through the treetops to our east.
"We better get Buck out of that hole." the Foxes words rang out.
I already had my finger on the transmit button, "Buck-Canyon, the fire is making some runs at you."
Buck could hear the train, but not see the flames through the darkness. He'd already stopped line construction and had the crew together when the radio cackled. "Yeah, I can hear it, I'm trying to find a safer escape route now." as he scanned his options. With a

momentary pause, the line looking straight up was clear for an escape. Ascending the 80% slope was the safest way out in this thicket of crisscrossed downed trees stacked up three feet high. The roar of flames and clouds of thick smoke filled the air like a gray blizzard with orange embers flying by, and gave Buck's words credence, "Let's get out of this hellhole. Up the line, now! Go on," ordered Buck to his crew of mixed NPS personnel. Once again some first timers were on the crew. The crew darted up the slope. Yellow Nomex clad mountain goats. Buck counted as the bodies shot by him. One of the crewmembers, a regular dispatcher on the South Rim during non-fire times, started clutching her chest and collapsed. Buck dropped his saw, picked up this gal and continued up the steep slope, climbing stairs of fire line constructed earlier. Each persons step was about three feet to the next step above on this extreme slope. Now, it was a dire emergency. Human lives were on the line. Crewmember Pat came to check on the gal. Buck just shot out, "Let's hightail it out of here. I need you to be in the lead and get us through the fire, quickly."
"You got it Buck." Pat's boots didn't seem to touch ground as he disappeared up the line.

The young gal came to, said she was exhausted, but was adamant that she could move on her own. She was true to her word. It was her first fire. Buck, chainsaw back in hand, followed as the embers flew around him. He kept looking for the crown fire, as he heard the train roaring.

Finally reaching the rim top with crew huddled, he looked around, and quickly barked out, "We're going through the burn. The flames are fierce, but once we're through the flaming front, we've got black. I don't see any other way. We can't outrun this. The fuel loading is intense all around us. This is too hot. We've got a re-burn going on in the treetops, a crown fire supported by high winds coming our way. Pat, you lead us back to camp, I'll bring up the rear. Let's go!"
"Yes sir." saluted Pat.

"In wildfires people live by embracing death. The blackened earth-land that the fire has already burned-is often the only place where a person can escape the flames."

- Michael Kodas (<u>Megafire,</u> p. 52.)

As the crew made their run through flames into the blackened forest, they realized how close they came to being crispy-crittered, and relief set in when they appeared back at the safety zone. Pat still had that mock seriousness about him but a smile in his eyes. Buck was in awe at the fearsome power of the crowning fire overhead, rushing like a freight train, devouring trees in its' path as a force of nature that can only be admired and revered but not tamed. He swore at the stupidity of this incompetent BJ running the fire show, a supposed expert for Grand Canyon, as they stomped on ashes and climbed over burned logs, while intense heat from the flames traveled overhead.

"...you could be overrun by a fire or overcome by smoke. You could be crushed by falling trees, rolling boulders, explosions. A firestorm could suck all the oxygen from the valley. A crown fire, leaping from treetop to treetop, can reach 2,000 degrees Fahrenheit, releasing the energy of an atomic bomb every fifteen minutes."

-Colleen Morton Busch (Fire Monks, p.144)

(Prof) Backfire

Fox and I found Billie Joe at the safety zone.

"We better fire up all the saws and put a canopy break in that fuel or she's gonna run right over us." the Fox blurted with his red face gleaming.

"You can take shelter in the burn, I don't want any trees cut." BJ admonished firmly.

"You're talking about 50 peoples' lives here." I added.

"There's nothing to worry about." BJ firmly stated.

"Maybe you ought to get your ass down in the hole to see." Fox blurted out.

"You shhhit." Billie Joe stuttered and took off to a waiting helicopter.

"Good riddance." as I breathed a sigh of relief.

"Where's the saw?" Fox asked. I grabbed some wedges and a falling axe following him. Soon, the air was filled with the sounds of saw work.

We had fallen many trees to break up the consistency of fuels overhead and created a highway swath of clearing.

"Good job on those trees, I think the four of us should go see what's happening with this fire." Ken seriously intoned, saw in hand.

"Sure, boss." Buck picked up a shovel (the tool of his liking) while I grabbed a Pulaski (my tool of choice). The Fox spotted a Macleod, his preference, and off we went toward the rim. Presently 40 people were at the improved helispot. Records indicate the time to be 1915 on this Tuesday. The rest of the souls at the helispot seemed to be awaiting divine direction from these mere mortal smoke bums.

A freight train of fire came roaring over the rim where Buck's crew was previously. Embers filled the sky, our faces shined in the excitement, awe and fear of nature's force. Another roar of flames ensued.

Ken turned around, his ever present smile now replaced by concern burning in his dark eyes, yet the calm in his voice underscored the moment, "We better get back to camp, I have a plan." Twilight was beginning.

"Canyon, get the forest crew folks together. Buck, get the park people. I think we need to get ready to go the backfire route, what do you guys think?" solicited Ken.

"That sounds good." I proclaimed.

"I have some torches ready." smiled the Fox.

"Let's get moving." stated Buck.

"Okay, have everybody meet here in five minutes. Let's put everything non-essential in a clearing, except our PPE (personal protective equipment) in case we have to evacuate. We've already improved upon our escape route. Everyone is to travel light."

Five minutes later we were all gathered.
Ken started, "I wanted to inform you all and make sure we all understand. This is serious shit! I hope there are enough angels in heaven tonight. Canyon, Fox and myself will set a backfire. If it holds, we stay." We all nervously laughed while the fire sang its primal song and the embers danced in the air. A rolling thunder of flames was moving aggressively through the treetops consuming massive acreage of timber. A Kaibab squirrel scolded us from a nearby Ponderosa. Ken continued, "Buck, I'd like you to hold the line and have some experienced folks patrolling for spots. If we have to escape, you lead the crew out of here. Ya got it?" (as Buck acknowledged) and Ken finalized, "If this doesn't work, and we have to evacuate, I've got (ranger) Wit and some others waiting to pick us up at the end of the W-6 fire road a few miles away. They can take us back to North Rim. If we have to deploy, this is our safety zone, it's been cleared out" Let's do it now."

Ken's voice thundered and I wondered about his ancestors' battles of the past, indeed, my own ancestry and their battles. To each his own, in his own lifetime. "We're going to try and back fire off the line. With nature's help, we'll spend the night here. I want you all in groups of four, radio's, water, fire shelters ready. Travel light with night gear and tool. Go grab a bite if you want. Okay, any questions, then get ready, 15 minutes."
I stood there with the Fox, Buck, Lisa, and Tex, signaling to grab a bite. Ken smiled knowing we were ready. The roast beast wasn't the usual stringy rope of sinew. The spuds were instant, but mashed and mixed with canned peas and warmed, we scarfed it down while everyone else scrambled with their webbing, not very hungry. The fire roared in the background.

At 2030, I was sixty feet in from the hand line toward the fire. The others firing off with me were spread out in a wide diagonal back to the line spaced every ten feet apart. I gave the word and started laying a strip of fire down from my drip torch (a canister of gas/diesel mix ignited from a spout). As my fire line met with the next person, ten feet away, they would lay down another fire strip. Soon, the six of us had lit a sixty foot strip of fire along the line for a quarter mile buildup. If the fire coming towards us would draw our flames (that we set) into it, our fires would roar to life. As our fires would roar to life, they would rob the fuels needed by the flaming front while being sucked into the main wall of fire. The resulting fire would peter out and die down. If this didn't work we certainly wouldn't be able to run from this train. Shortly after our lighting, the main fire came up out of the hole and met our backing fire. Ponderosa trees were crowning as flames 150 feet high towered like giant dragons belching smoke and embers. For two hours, we chased fire brands falling into unburned forest ahead, causing spot fires. None of the spots got out of hand. The only worry now was if the fire burned under the rim into the continuous, brushy fuels that encircled Lancelot Point, where our helispot and safety zone were, we'd be surrounded.

At 2300, Ken put the NPS crew to rest, except for the Longshots. Most of us were scattered beyond the helispot on spot fire patrol. Only one other small spot fire was found, and it was kept at campfire size within minutes after discovery. The crown run was abated. The backfire worked. However, other trees were still torching, illuminating the canyon wall opposite us over a mile and a half away. We didn't get any sleep that night. Ken told us that he was turning it over to a class two team (of experts). Exhausted, we all needed a break.

"...have a mind that is open to everything and attached to nothing."
-10th century scholar Tilopa (India)

(Prof) Demobed

"Life is too short for grief. Or regret. Or bullshit."
-Edward Abbey

At 1030 the next day, Buck and I walked out with the rest of the Longshots following us. Ken had to fly to the South Rim for debriefing. Lancelot was over for us, for now. (It would be fought and battled by other crews for another month).

The Fox and I decided to hit the North Rim saloon when we got back and stay 'till closing. We needed an outlet to escape this insanity and ineptitude that we just came from. Buck was supposedly to disappear in his pick up to deal with it in his own way, solitude. Lisa disappeared with Pat. Tex joined us briefly at the saloon. Frankie the bartender had an excess shipment of liquor lying around just sitting there all lonesome. The Fox and I were only too happy to help him out. Let's see, there were the usual Corona's. But when we told Frankie of our intent to stay 'til the last round, in a streak of viciousness, he started serving us "practice" Long Island ice tea's. By evening we had ordered prawn shrimp dinners at the bar to swim around the massive amounts of liquor being consumed by ourselves. The only movement about us was the occasional swinging of the doors to go to the Grand Lodge bathroom as we had to "drain the lizard" in the Fox's terms. Eventually, Frankie switched us to gin and tonic with bitters. The clock on the wall showed 9 P.M. The Fox now resembled a toad who mumbled things in between sucking on his cocktail straw, or was it catching flies on his tongue? It was the usual North Rim saloon crowd that was corralled that night: a few wranglers still wearing their chaps and spurs, some dudes and dude-ettes off the mule rides, a sprinkling of European tourists, and some local TW and NPS folks. One gal came in with some friends, a real beauty, with the effect of having Fox's eyeballs bugged out. However, the Fox and I floundered on the shores of our ice teas and gin while Frankie smiled maliciously behind the bar.

"Your turns coming." I leered back at Frankie.

"Ashily, that's a wunnerful." the toad in Fox drooled.

A freshly showered Buck appeared and soon disappeared out to the veranda (with a starry night view of the canyon) along with the beautiful gal and her friends. The clock on the wall said 10:45.

(Prof) Tequila Amnesia

"When we drink, we get drunk. When we get drunk, we fall asleep. When we fall asleep, we commit no sin. When we commit no sin, we go to heaven."
-George Bernard Shaw

"Last call." announced Frankie. A wave of desperate drinkers descended upon the beach of his bar, including the Fox and myself. After the waves subsided, Frankie brought us some tall desserts. They had chocolate for sure, but the vodka, Kahlua, Baileys, crème de menthe, amongst other unknown liquors added to the decadency. As tradition dictated, we gave him a five dollar tip. He marked up $1.25 total on our tab for a draught beer. Ah, yes, local economics and who you know!

Soon, the local Mountie Pete flushed everyone from their beverage and jukebox reverie. We grabbed a ride from the TW shuttle to the "ghetto" (the local employees housing). From there, we wandered to rim's edge and stumbled along the Ancient's (Anasazi) path in the moonlight over to park service housing and my skid row palace. My roomie, Dove, was awake and playin' the blues. Alongside him were other North Rim friends and neighbors: Jake (the snake), Pat, Lisa, and Cathy, a TW waitress of renown stature. Jake had his head in a position trying to merge with Cathy's. Ron, the Dove, was singing a Howlin' Wolf classic, *"I got a little red rooster, too lazy to crow for day."*
I grabbed my harp, and joined the play. We went right into Carl Perkin's, *"Honey don't."* The door opened and Monique with another waitress showed up carrying a bottle of tequila. Oh My! We played on leading into, *"Gloria,"* and everybody hopped up on the beds and began dancing. At 4 A.M., I awoke with Monique on top of me, with thunder and lightning filling the picture window above. There I was, caught with my pants down, a woman's dress up, and a case of tequila amnesia. She stirred and I kissed her, might as well make it real. Lightning filled the room and thunder shook the bed.

Part Four-
Live and Let Burn

(Prof) As the rim turns

"I am the master of my fate, I am the captain of my soul."
-William Earnest Henry

Pecker Tracks picked up the phone dialing the North Rim and laid in immediately with, "Gussie, you've got to get those people to tone it down. I heard where that Indian employee of yours has been trying to unite all the tribes around the canyon into one coalition with the environmentalists. This stuff has got to stop or our jobs will be on the honey wagon." (park maintenance term for the job of suctioning out the port-a-potties). The chalkboards on the surrounding walls were filled with North Rim projects ranging from trailer parks, new picnic areas, trail paving, information signs, plan A survey, and on and on. "Everyone must be productive here on the edge of canyon bliss. The public needs serving, the taxpayer needs to see their dollar wisely spent."
Coming out of his trance, Gussie responded to ol' Pecker Tracks, "I'll look into it," knowing that he was tied to his bosses demands as a permanant employee with a heavy heart. The phone clicked. Ol' PT was furious.

"...there is all the more reason to be alarmed over the disproportionate levels of power wielded within the" (NPS) *"agency by those individuals and groups that truly are dishonest and unscrupulous. Their accepted presence and influence within the agency, often at its highest levels, has an intimidating as well as demoralizing effect on the balance of the workforce, signaling for many the futility of trying to do the right thing and play by the rules."*

-Paul D. Berkowitz (<u>The Case of the Indian Trader,</u> p. 82)

I was headed out for a long date on my off days. When not venturing forth with Buck, I was a reclusive poet hiding my life away amongst streams, mountains and canyons, so I took it as another adventure. Recovered from a night of intoxication and wanton lust with a dark eyed maiden, now I'd be off with a blue eyed patrol ranger, not the naturalist person I thought she was. "Busted!" I found and tried to piece the Ray Charles tape together as I headed down the mountain through House Rock Valley, Vermillion Cliffs and over the Navajo Bridge with the cold, green Colorado River below.

Continuing on through the Res(ervation) markers to gage my time: Bitter Springs, Cedar Ridge, the Gap, and Cameron Trading Post, where a Navajo taco and ice tea were

always beckoning. I ate every last bite of that monstrous plate of fry bread, beans, cheese, lettuce and salsa and headed down highway 89 another half mile to the Desert View, South Rim turn off. Finally, I made it to Janice's government trailer, unit number 5, around 1200 park time, high noon to a cowpoke. She was just finishing a tuna sandwich and apologized for not waiting, "I was hungry."
To which I smilingly replied, "I just finished a taco in Cameron, note the distended belly." as I puffed myself out and we both laughed, tension broken.

Grabbing a pop, but without much further ado, we were off to Flagstaff for an afternoon of urban frolicking. First, we took in a ho-hum Redford-Hannah flick, followed by a better Mexican dinner, and topped it off filling an ice chest with camping goodies. I had to take her to my favorite quick lake getaway just outside Flag. (My last time here Buck and I tore one up in town and headed to this place to sleep it off. We both woke up laying in the middle of the dirt road with the screeching tires of a truck nearly running us over. Thankfully, it was Tex and his gal with their animal entourage).

There's a big marsh, surrounded by tall Ponderosa's, lots of birds cackling and the San Francisco Peaks outlined in the background. We also did our share of cackling and conversing into the early morning hours of moonlight when it happened, we kissed goodnight.

Morning light brought kisses and binoculars with the Peterson field book and laughing disagreements over identification. A craving of espresso took us back to town, then down into the Verde Valley for a hike up Wet Beaver Creek. About a mile into the hike, a thunderstorm of gigantic bolts and raindrops kept us and an inchworm huddled together under a boulder for a couple of hours.

Thunderstorms are truly fantastic in the southwestern pinion deserts. They give life, and for me, a joining of souls. Denise, myself and the worm inching its way upon my leg to hers, were as timeless as the cliff dwellers huddled together in shelters before the passing glory of discovery. As the storm subsided and blue skies appeared, we left our companion under the rock and headed back. Along the way we were diverted at a large drop pool, and did what everyone does after a storm. We went skinny dipping and frolicked liked otters in Wet Beaver Creek. Continuing on down to the Verde River, we stopped for an ice chest feast, a few brews, some words, kissing and dreamland. The next day was a flash. I was in love. Again. Departing was hard. Plans were made for a future hike on the North Rim.

The drive back through the desert was lonely as the landscape. Naturally, I stopped at Cliff Dwellers, for a cold couple of Corona's and bummed a "fatty" from the waitress that I knew there. I would take it easy as I climbed up the Kaibab Plateau through deer alley. Tonight there were two or three carcasses along the shoulder. Excessive speed usually was the culprit. With the road being widened and the curves straightened new land records would be attained. Just mount spikes on your fossil fuel beast between the headlights, and voila, fast food at road kill café.

I walked into the usual house of revelry, with the Snake, Monique, and Dove playing Neil, *"Old man look in my eyes…"*

Pat came up to me, hugged me, and sobbed, "Man, I screwed up!"

"What?" I didn't understand as I handed him a Corona along with the one I just opened. Pat began to tell me of the Independance Day parade and mule polo game along with the encounters of the lawdog kind at the corral.

"God, it was a beautiful day Boomer. I dressed up as a clown for the parade. We had the two wildland engines, the structural brigade fire truck, all with water shows, the TW bread truck decorated as a Budweiser can, ranger cars with lights chasing it, the wranglers all duded up on their mules, and man were they awesome. Silver spurs, silk scarves, ten gallon Stetsons, all sparkling. Trail crew natives dressed as Indians, complete with squirt guns and toy bow and arrows. Last but not least was me, Pat the clown, on big Hank, the coal black sixteen hand mule prince."
"Quite the parade." I responded.
"Well, afterwards we high tailed it to the ball field despite Gussie's decry of 'No mule polo.' Word gets around in this small place."

"What was thought of as fun by some, became a question of liability and illegality to others. It was Tex, Mike, Bernie, Larry, Randy and I against the wranglers. It was a grand game. Hank and I got the parks only two goals. The wranglers got five, but hey it was fun." pleaded Pat.
"Hey, I believe ya, sorry I missed it. How did Tex do?"
"Ha, his mule kept going in circles."
"It figures." I had to chuckle.
"Anyway after the game, we high tailed up to the corrals while dropping our mules off at the trail crew barn. Not a ranger saw us during the game or after. Anyway, we're up at the wranglers place, sittin' on the fence, passing the bottle, when up pulls the patrol car and miss ranger bitch comes struttin' up." (Pat was referring to new ranger Crystal, who had badge fever as bad as any macho testosterone figure).

"She walks up to us with a demanding voice, 'What's going on?' Well, I just blew. I jumped down and grabbed her by the shirt collar and told her we had some fun and that's all you need to know. Then I pushed her away and told her to go fuck herself and while she was at it, Pecker Tracks too. I finished by yelling, 'screw the park service'."

I looked at Pat in disbelief, he'd been a fixture here for years. Pat's only goal was to work for the park service permanantly one day. I asked, "So, what do you think will happen?"
"Heck, if Pecker Tracks gets a hold of this, I'm history." prophesied Pat.

Ranger Dimwit had Crystal write in her report verbatim what Pat said to her. She had come by earlier and apologized to Pat for her strong demeanor. He was surprised and grateful but also disheartened by news of the report. Word had come back down from the large desk in the coffee room at the North Rim administration trailer.

Gussie was there while Pat's supervisor Dennis read the memo aloud stating,
"I see no other course of action than to terminate Patrick from the park service in light of his views. Let the termination be final, two weeks from today, at the end of the pay period.
Sincerely,
Peter Tracks."
"Sorry Pat." continued Dennis.
"Can't I apologize? It was the whiskey talking." pleaded Pat.
"You can try." answered Dennis, who looked over at Gussie, nodding approval.
With eyes cold, "Write a letter Pat... and I'll see what I can do." stammered Dennis.
Pat did write the letter. Delivered it in person (on the South Rim) to the desk of the superintendent with an instant reply of, "No, sorry, now leave, please."
Pat started smoking again and Lisa was pissed. Lisa went off rock climbing with her off season beau, much to Pat's dismay.

Buck and I along with some others ended up for the next couple of days on the Fox's five acre Emerald fire. It was a fun one being in the sage and open pines out on the Rainbow Plateau, a side canyon west of Lancelot. Had splendid views of the isle of Powell in the sea of Grand. Perhaps the Emerald fire is of note to me because of a future partnership that would be formed there with a Dean Ralck, commonly referred to as "Deano." I actually met him earlier that year at the prescribed burn boss class. Deano had performed his fire famous stunt, hanging with one hand from a branch, while pissing on a hot spot in a snag. Unlike some overhead stiffs, Deano was no drag. It was good to reunite with him there. Otherwise, it was a pretty straight forward fire.

(Prof) Why?

Another week gone by and finally Janice showed up. Yeah boy howdy. We spent the next couple of days lounging on the rim exploring waterfalls and Anasazi rock gardens deep in the heart of Arizona's spectacle of time unearthed. It was good to have two days of laughter and love. Goodbyes are always hard. Feeling melancholy I went and contemplated love on the rim's edge till the morning hours, getting back in time for my gear. My shift was about to begin, 0700 that morning.

Ranger Dimwit walked in. He appeared nervous, but I took it as the usual government façade coinciding with facial features hiding the truth within.
"Jim, I've got bad news. Lisa fell climbing Friday night and is in serious condition at

Flagstaff Hospital." Pausing a moment (I detected moisture in his eyes) he continued,"Sorry Jim, I've got to go." as he walked out. I couldn't move, stunned, and silent. I've got to find Buck was all I could think. From the palace and into the blue skies, I shuffled over to the "pit," Tex greeted me, not with words, just a big hug. Fox, alongside him, said, "Brother." and gave me a hug too.

"We tried to find you." said Tex.

"Yea, I spent last night out at Marble View. Dim caught me at the palace this morning. It's hard to believe this. Does Buck know?" I asked, tears starting to well up. No one had seen him since it was his new days off.

Mules were quiet, and even the raucous raven perched above on the Ponderosa was silent.

"I've got to go see Lisa." I declared.

There on the rim outside of Buck, Lisa and I had become more than friends, though not lovers. I had fallen in love with her sister Lina, on a visit a few years earlier, even spending Christmas with them one year, when I was on another ill fated journey of the heart.

Rhoda, Witt's wonderful wife came by to say how sorry she was and if there was anything that she could do.

Aloud, I thought, "Yeah, I need a hundred dollars to get to Flag."

Rhoda opened her purse and gave me one hundred twenty dollars. I was speechless, other than, "Thanks."

"Well take it and get out of here." commanded the Fox.

Waking me out of my dream state, I took the money, hugged Rhoda, yelled adios, grabbed my toothbrush and fired up Bertha. On the road I settled in with a hooter, a Corona and some comforting rock n' roll tunes, trying to make myself feel better.

At Marble Canyon I saw Buck's truck and pulled in. Buck had a plate of taco's and a cup of coffee in front of him. A pretty Navajo waitress by the name of Marell came to the table.

"Pitcher of beer, please." I ordered.

Buck stopped eating, put down his fork and asked, "Aren't you supposed to be working today?"

Marell brought the beer. I hadn't been able to say anything yet. Buck took the beer and looked me in the eye.

"What's wrong?" he realized aloud.

Lisa, she's in serious condition in Flag."

"What!" Buck put down the beer spilling half. I took a big gulp of draft.

"Let's go!" said Buck and laid down a ten dollar bill on the table.

"I'll drive, you're all messed up." demanded Buck.

I grabbed my, ahem, shit, from Bertha and got in Buck's truck.

Miles rolled by and not much was said, only the tunes from Mellancamp's latest, *"Scarecrow."* Reflections of Lisa came to our minds. She was an animal as far as fitness goes, had a try out with the U.S. Olympic team as a marathoner. Her vegetarian lifestyle was unique. At steak cookouts she would ask for the fat trimmings, so that she could suck on them, said she craved them, lacking body fat herself. She was a tough cookie amongst the fire dog males she hung with. She could dish it out as best as the rest. We'd laugh at her nomex shirt from her days up in the great Northwet with printed logo, "you light 'em, we fight 'em." Once, playing volleyball at our sand courts she was sandwiched while going for the ball which gave her a bloody nose. As soon as she recognized her own blood she passed out. Maybe her only weakness.

No fruit to declare at the Ag inspection stop. No taco's at Cameron this time. W did stop to refuel though. While I pumped gas, Buck asked if I wanted a beer. I adamantly stated only one! He said same for him, too. True to his word, he came out of the store with only two beers. Of course they were 36 ounce monster cans of brew. Sluuuurp!

A couple of hours later and we arrived at the hospital in Flagstaff, going directly to the intensive care unit. She had gotten out of surgery a few hours before. Pat was already there. Her barely recognizable face broke into a smile at the sight of us. She grabbed my hand in one of hers and said proudly, "Canyon, I didn't faint."
I smiled, and said, "You'll do anything to get out of a little work."
She laughed. I cried. Buck stood there, mute. We all stood silent for awhile looking at the tubes and high tech machinery.
Buck broke the silence, "Lisa, what happened?"
"Well, it was this useless slimey ex-friend of mine, Mongy." She turned a bit red from her legendary temper. "He talked me into one more climb if I'd anchor him. So I tied off, or so I thought." she paused for a moment. "I'll have some juice." I handed her a paper cup with orange contents. She drank, we sat, and then, handing me back the cup, "Thanks."
"No problem." came my reply.
"I thought I clipped my anchor line off to my harness, instead, I hastily clipped to an equipment loop and not the belt. Then when Mongy fell, the loop tore off from my harness." Lisa closed her eyes. "Damn!" she breathed. None of us said anything for awhile. Pat went to the bathroom, a nurse came by to monitor vital signs.

She continued, "Mong fell another thirty feet, and I'm told I fell a hundred twenty. The rope caught on some rocks and I bounced along the cliff suddenly stopping. I felt snapped in two. I did stay conscious. Two guys came by, a miracle. A climber and paramedic, they…they saved me." Tears came from her eyes as well as Buck's and mine. She went on to tell us that it took a search and rescue team three hours to get her off the cliff with generators, floodlights, and a Lifeflight helicopter ride to the hospital.

"I had to help or they couldn't have gotten me off that cliff, and the blood…" she faded.
At this point Jason came in, the one who helped Lisa, "She has to be one of the strongest people I know. The paramedic onboard the ship couldn't get a pulse, nothing. She was as close to death as one can get."
When we finally came to, Buck said, "I gotta go have a bite."
"Yeah." I agreed.
Lisa quietly said, "Thanks boys."
"We'll be here all week, unless a big one breaks." I said.
She smiled as Buck and I walked out to the truck.
"Now I need a beer." exclaimed Buck.
"There's a sports bar just down the hill." I remembered aloud with the blue sky beaming down. We got drunk on pitchers watching some game, irrelevant now. As Buck and I left the bar, the blue skies were gone and replaced with stars in the night.
"Should we grab a few sandwiches and head out to the lake, Buck?"
"Sounds good."

Once at the lake, turkey sandwiches in our bellies, Corona's in hand, and stars overhead, we laid out our bags and in silence fell asleep.

The sun took the chill out of the morning air bringing the marsh to life with the songs of habitants. It also got Buck and I out of our bags into the truck which delivered us to the warm confines of Macy's Coffeehouse. Soon double cappuccino's stirred the brain into a functioning mechanism. Buck was in a hurry this morning as I could see the lightning quickness of his dark, brown eyes. He drained his cup and was out the door. I walked to Martans Mexican restaurant and had a chorizo con huevo with frijoles y aroz, more coffee, a newspaper and walked up the hill to the hospital, just as Flag was getting ready for its day. A raven crouched by the side of the road, feasting on the slight remains of an emaciated, run over dog. The sun rose higher and heat waves shimmered off the blacktop.

Later that afternoon Buck arrived at Charley's Pub in the Old Weatherford Hotel as previously discussed. I greeted him with an ice cold Anchor Steam draught.
A blues band was jamming and the bar was packed. We had a little table against the wall, listening quietly while the music played and people swayed.
Breaking silence I spoke. "All Pat talked about today was him and her getting married."
"What about Lisa?"
"That's the sad news. She may be paralyzed from the waist down for the rest of her life." I took a drink of my beer to keep the tear at bay. It was hard to think of her living in a chair. Her life had been running marathons, climbing mountains, dancing…and I had to take another sip of beer.
"She told me she's not sure she wants to live."
"I can empathize." solemnly Buck acknowledged.

"Well they call it stormy Monday, but Tuesday's just the same." echoed the lyrics from the song. Buck braved the throng of humanity in quest of another pitcher of Anchor. He came back with two pitchers plus Slim (Tim) and a couple of women who turned out to be waitresses at the El Tovar on the South Rim. Appearing at our table we were further surprised by seeing Jake and the Dove. Several rounds, comforting friends, and the next thing we were all up and dancing. 'Dem blues just kept playin' and playin' until at least two A.M. I struggled joyously on my way with the Snake, Dove, and local friends to their house for the night. Buck, Slim and the waitresses took off to other parts…

We spent the rest of the week visiting Lisa daily, at least until Thursday, when the call came that we were needed back. They had some lightning that evening on the North Rim. Timing was good because Lisa's dad and sister Lina were arriving soon to assist her mom that arrived that first night.
"Buck we better get up there and hit those lightning strikes."
"Should we grab some Corona's for the Res crossing?" asked Buck as he pulled into a Circle K on the northeast side of town.
"Can't dance." was all I could muster and went in spending my last five dollars on cold ones. Buck spent his last ten on gas and we were overtime plus hazard pay bound.

(Prof) Back at the rim

I arrived first to the office the next morning so I started the gallon coffee pot up. The phone rang.
"Fire pit." I answered.
"This is Billie Joe."
"Yeah, this is Canyon."
"I'm sending a couple of new hires over this week."
"Okay."
"Good. I want you all to work your off days until they arrive."
Moaning internally, thinking of missing my Petrified Forest trip, I figured I'd clear it with Buck and responded, "Yeah." to BJ.
"BJ, any legals on smokes from yesterday?"
"Not yet."
"Well, I've got to get some stuff ready."
"Ok."
"Bye." I mustered and hung up quickly.

As soon as Buck arrived, I told him of Billie Joe's call and added, "Hey Buck, I wanna take off to Pefo" (park acronym for Petrified Forest) "on my days off."
"Hot date?" he smiled at me.
"At least for now. She's headed back to school soon."
"So soon?"
"Actually in three weeks."

"We better get to work now and get a shift in." he said. The smile on his face verified what I knew he would say, "If nothing shows up, take off, we'll cover."

"Music is my home. When I'm trying to find my inner peace, I put music in my ears."
-unknown

Buck, Tex, Fox and I spent all day sharpening saws, shovels, Pulaski's, and joking a lot to the tunes of: Beat Farmers, Dylan, Grateful Dead, Talking Heads, Toots and the Maytals and Neil Young. The ribbing was part of the bonding experience. What else is one to do when one's confronted with how thin the thread between life and death is. Every helicopter ride, every tree one may have to fall, every bolt of lightning in the storm above you may have your earthly name.

"Shit happens, and if we just want to restrict ourselves to things where shit can't happen...we're not going to do anything very interesting."

-Laurence Gonzales in <u>Deep Survival,</u> p.113.

(Buck) Mat the "Hoss" boy faller

"I think I don't regret a single excess of my responsive youth-I only regret, in my chilled age, certain occasions and possibilities I didn't embrace."
-Henry James

One of BJ's new hires was a young stud logger from Idaho. He'd learned from his family roots over the years to harvest trees for a living. Being only 20, devout, bigoted, and bias, he took a job with us as an emergency hire to stash some extra savings while awaiting his appointment into the military. It fell to me to train this young whipper-snapper kid into Longshot shape. We all were open and respectful of each other's differences, life experiences, beliefs, etc., yet we were not willing to compromise when it came to safety. Young Mat alienated himself immediately with us, by his put downs, negative comments, and harsh behavior exhibited to others around us. He further excluded himself from team dynamics and any social interactions, not that we didn't try.

The call came in for a fire out on the Widforss Point. So, I took young Mat thinking the best training is experiential. A tall tree was burning with some ground fire. As incident commander, I gave my size up, and then proceeded to scratch out a line to contain the flames and an area to drop the tree in safely. Young "hoss" wouldn't budge. He was pissed off. He complained. He refused to do anything but what he liked to do, and that was to saw trees. Well I explained the difference of fires and falling versus logging operations without fires and falling for timber production. No dice, young stud was adamant he was not going to wait around for size ups and then he refused to swamp for me. I had to fall the tree individually without a safety spotter. Finally getting him to work a tool so we could get back quicker, we mopped up and the next day returned to base.

Upon seeing the crew, I gave my cheery, smiling, we're back greeting. Young "hoss" just dashed out wildly from the cab of the engine, running to his residence. Jim helped me wash the engine, and put gear away while hearing the story unfold. Immediately afterwards he gave a call to Ken (away off district) about the situation.

Ken arrived the next day dismissing young Mat, since he didn't follow orders, didn't fit in, and was unsafe. Never heard back from him and often wondered how he did in the military. In his place, Ken hired Tack.

(Prof) Blue Mesa

"Drink wine, it's what remains of the harvest of youth-
the season of roses and wine and drunken friends. Be happy for this moment,
this moment is your life."

Translated, loosely, *"Make whoopee while the sun shines. With me. Right now."*
-The Rubiyat of Omar Khayyam:

This was one time that I was glad when 6 P.M. rolled around and no smokes were found. By seven o'clock Bertha was packed and by 7:01, in the first throes of sunset, I was rockn' and rollin' down the hill. Crossing the park boundary line, I loaded up my pipe of sacred herbs and blessing my journey toasted it with a Corona.

The morning sun rose as I entered the visitor's center in Pefo. There I reclined on cement benches and watched cottontails hiding in the landscaped oasis of the pavillion. Coming out of a trance I heard Janice waking me from an impromptu morning nap. "Hey sleeping goofball, daylights a-waisting away."
"Pardon me, do I know you?" joking back at her.

A kiss brought me to my feet and off we headed in "Jeanie" her Toyota hatchback for a magic carpet tour of the petrified remains of a once upon a time forest in the Triassic age. We made all the official tour stops and then took one that wasn't on tourist brochures. A hike to a prehistoric bridge of a tree. As I was trying to take a picture, the camera was thrust on my head, and off she ran. Flashing a pic, I smiled and ran after the blue eyed life-filled energy force I was with now. In my arms and down to the desert floor our love fell, for the first and last time. Down and down through the small dark forest with pink pastels in a tight slot canyon. It was a place oozing with delight. Next stop, Blue Mesa. We skipped our way back to the Toyota. Awww, love.

We sang songs and pulled over for the sunset until the sky brazed away unto glittering stars. Dining on guacamole and chips, washing it down with Gewirtzeimmer, a dreamy sleep overcame us in the warm desert night.

Sunday morning brought us to the Holbrook dog pound on our way back to Flag. Janice had talked me into a dog. It had been four years since my last one. My heart was broken as I couldn't make a choice of one out of twenty. Caravanning now in separate mobiles, I became very distraught with my failure to pick and save one. Arriving at Flag, I told her of my problems. A hug and Chinese dinner made me feel better. Then it was goodbye once more as she returned to Desert View while I trekked two hundred more miles to my side of the rim.

Arriving to the skid row palace, I remembered that the second annual fiesta was being held the next day. Smiling, I crawled into my bed around midnight and for once, nobody was up. But I couldn't get to sleep. One of the curses of seasonal life was upon me again, smitten with love. It seems in these modern times that we can become a gypsy of sorts; our dreams, jobs, and mobile lives make love and being together difficult, at least that's what I found in my seasonal life. Here I was in love once more, but she was headed away to school. I still had a job to do and smoke to find. Tossing and turning, I knew that I was really gone this time. Another curse that I have to say I seem to repeat. Why is it? Is it fate? Is it my own doing subconsciously? Or is it just these days when our lives are run to the beat of the clock and not the rhythm of the sun, when our jobs are of machines and metal, not of the earth and soil. Is it not a wonder that love is something hard to find. Mental exhaustion finally overtook my mind until I felt someone shaking me. It was Buck with a big smile and a cup of 'jo as the sun was pouring in the window.

(Prof) Signing In

"Get up old man." he joked.
"And to what do I owe this honor?"
"The call came in last night, fires in Oregon, Nevada, and Idaho. We might send out a crew and Billie Joe wants you to go."

I got my Nomex pants on, cotton t-shirt and socks, laced up my boots and grabbed my cup. Sipped a mouthful and left the palace for the pit. The mules brayed and crazy Randy, Mike, Bernie and the rest of trail crew came down to the pit and joined us for some mud.
"Hey Jim, we're sorry about Lisa." Randy gave me a hug and the next thing you know, hugs were going all around like a Grateful Dead show or something. Coffee made the rounds along with park gossip and finally goodbyes were said. The trail crew hopped on their mules and headed down the North Kaibab Trail, the only maintained inner gorge path off the North Rim. We hopped into our four wheel drive engines, Tex, Fox, and Tack (remember her from Lancelot?) in the green bomb, while Buck and I took the white beast. Ken stayed back to see what was up paper wise and to monitor the interagency requests for fire resources in the big bust out far west.

Buck was silent until we got to the basin. I kept my eyes on the road and woods. The basin is the largest meadow on the north side. It is a wildflower paradise with an assortment of colors along with: deer, coyote, hawk, turkey, and even antelope have been spotted there. Tucked away in one corner was Robbers Roost, one of the few topside springs that flowed into an old log, hollowed into a trough way back at the turn of the century. The basin had been used in those days by rustlers who stole horses and cattle to sell one here, one there, the American way. Pure spring water loomed as a treat and it sounded good, so I asked Buck, "Want to check out the spring source?"

"Nah, let's go sign in at Tipover, instead. We haven't done it this year yet. Then we can do the loop and finish with an ice cream at the Kaibab Store."
"Sounds good." and we kept on going past the basin into the pines and firs, spruce and aspen forests. Soon, we were at the junction with the Sublime Road, but not our destination today, so we continued past Kanabownits tower and cabin, ball bearing hill, the tank commando road (out to Lancelot) finally going up to Crescent Ridge and down into the meandering long narrow meadow by Tipover. We found the green bomb with Tex, Fox, and Tack there as well.

"Yeah boy howdy!" cheered Buck.
"Spring water and signing in." chimed Tex, empty gallon canteens in hand.
"Read our minds or just overheard us?" as I was caught up in the coincidence.
"Crew karma." joked the Fox and got us all to laugh.
"Still havin' Mexican feast tonight?" inquired Tex as we made our way to the tank.

"You bet. We need it more than ever." I joyously answered.
"Amen!" sang out Buck.
"Strange that we haven't made it here 'till now," I thought, "this is supposed to be an annual early summer tradition." Thinking aloud, I echoed, "This has been a strange season and traditions need to be broken."
"Revolutionary thoughts for broken down smoke bums." added the Fox.
"Speak for yourself in the broken down department, bro"
"I ain't your brother."
"And I'm no smoke bum." added Tex.
"Smarter than I am." I quipped back to Tex.
"I learned from your ten seasons in my two." smiled back Tex.
Tex, what a guy! A saint and like the Hopi's, never said anything bad about anyone, ever. Another thing about him was his ability to keep things in perspective at all times. A stellar guy. I smiled at him glad to be friends and colleagues.

And then there was the old water tank in all of its broken down glory. Names of Longshots from summer's past, penciled and etched in the rusting metal resevoir sitting amongst the tall grasses, wildflowers, and surrounded by forest a long way from anything.

The Fox put the last flurry to his signature, Tex filled empty canteens from the still flowing cool water, Buck ate his lunch, and I looked at the aspens on the hillside. Tack, a backcountry ranger gal that had been filling in with us since Lisa's fall was doing admirably. She was originally there at Lancelot. Cute, five foot-two, blue-eyed blonde, who chewed Copenhagen and was a hiking fool from Bisbee, Arizona. When not working backcountry patrols, she hiked around the canyon for her days off. She fit right in with us and was highly amused by the Fox's constant attempts at seduction.
"Come with me sweet sister to the Kona coast after our layoff and I'll show you such sites…"
"I'm not your sweet sister!" Tack replied spitting out her chaw with such a smile that the Fox was cut off at the pass.

A Kaibab squirrel scolded us for intrusion into its domain.
"We'll be gone in a little bit." I chuckled to the Kaibab and sat down next to Buck with my bandana pirate look on.
"I see you packed another winner." commented Buck, tearing into a yogurt cup after his turkey sandwich and chips.
"I don't have waitresses to bring me lunch sacks every morning." I shot back jostling him verbally.
"The fruits of love and a sandwich too, professor."
"Yeah, but if you weren't so ugly…" laughed the Fox, as he munched on an apple.
"Can I help it my love is away." I defended.
"And getting further away." witted the Fox.
"Be nice." I had to say, the truth causing me a bit of pain.
"Sorry," contritely voiced the Fox, and with open eyes, "I was just kidding."
"I know." and smiled painfully.

We ate our lunches, joined by a pair of ravens, who heard the chomping mandibles or maybe wiffed the Fox's liverwurst sandwich. He tossed most of it to the shiny black beaked partners scavenging.
Buck turned to Fox and Tex, "So, what are you guys up to this afternoon?"
"The basin for a scout, and then into the cache." Tex managed while chugging down water.
"And you?"
"Kaibab store for ice cream and climb up Abbey tower for a look. Got to make sure the roads are always open, in case of fire." answered Buck in mock seriousness.
"Yessiree!" echoed the Fox.
Back to the trucks, goodbye springwater, and I picked up my now full canteen. We set off leaving our names, a gurgling spring, and two liverwurst chomping ravens along with a Kaibab squirrel in a ponderosa tree.

<u>**(Prof) Why Not?**</u>

"If life gives you limes, make Margaritas"
-Jimmy Buffett

The poster read, "Hola Green-go's, breeng a Mexican main deesh and some cerveza, por favor to the Skeed Row Palace, si, Monday noches at 7. Garbage can margarita's, Tee-kee-ya, wild muzeek, macho senores y bonita senorita's. Te Vere Alla."

The Dove got back from the Page Big Pig market just as I got off work.
"Do you think a case of tequila will do?"
"I hope so." I laughed.
"Could be a hundred people."
"Tis true, ah for now though, a Corona will do." waxing poetic, I opened the refrigerator and asked, "how 'bout you?"
"Ah romeo, si a cerveza, oh poet of skid row renown. And a lime"
"But of course." and our words gave way to the sound of two bottles being opened with laughter.

Guests started showing, otherwise known as the rimmers, in various garb.
Buck arrived with Molly, resplendent both in Bermuda shorts, Hawaiian shirts, straw hats, and a case of Corona's in his hands, while Molly showed up with an opened bottle of tequila. Both had big grins.
"Is this the Mexican luowwwl?" Molly slurred with her blue eyes sailing in my heart, which was such an easy beast to slay.
"No, this is the Hawaiian fiesta." was my smartass answer.

Molly set the bottle down and gave me a big hug and nice smooch, while Buck did the same minus the smooch, which I planted stealthily to his whiskered cheek. Buck got a little red, Molly laughed, which caused him to chuckle as well. I picked up the case.
"To the ice." as I dashed off to the back coolers.

Tex and Kathan with the Fox showed up in serapes, Corona's and more tequila.
"Senor," el Fox whispered, "mota, el gordo numero." showing me a big fat joint.
"Si." I smiled, never one to decline jah spirit of god. "Let me make the first batch of margarita's, and shall we then sojourn to Senor Mota?"

The Dove and I had assembled some new trash cans with liners for our margarita's. Into these I poured bottles of tequila, triple sec, and filled the rest with lemonade and ice. The backyard of our skid row palace faced west across a side canyon known as Transept, known for spectacular sunsets. Between the rickety wood steps of my bedroom, the Dove had placed two stereo speakers from which Dylan was now singing, *"When you're down in Juarez, and it's Easter time too and gravity fails and leaves you naked howling at the moon…"* I owned the lyrics as I sang along.

Around our fire circle, we now had four giant picnic tables, two trash cans of margaritas and coolers of beer. Beyond our tables, toward the rim, was a grove of aspens and ferns with tall grass through which the Fox and I walked. Threading through the trees, descending to a finger of limestone bluff, we emerged on a vista, cliff rose blowing in the breeze, white petals adding fragrance to the scented smoke pouring out of our lungs. I took a hit and let the clouds settle behind my eyes, with the sun starting to fall in the western horizon.
"Pretty good mota, bro." is all I could chokingly reply.
"Indoor grower friend from Missoula just sent me a care package."
We smoked in silence, letting the canyon also take hold of us in the open eyes of jah spirit. Soon, we were red eyed and bushy tailed.
"Fiesta!" I shouted.

"Ol-e!" yodeled el Fox and back to the palace we headed.

The party was starting to go full swing by the time we got back. Margerite greeted me with a long kiss, "Howdy stranger, can I give you this fresh mug of…me?"
"Why sure Margerite, you are delicious."
Laurel, Gussie's fiance came up to us, "Hi Jim, Margerite, how are you guys?"
"Good." replied Margerite, "Where's Gussie?"
"He should be back from Tucson later. He left today for a conference." Laurel smiled, her blue eyes simmering through me.

While Laurel and Marg chatted, I thought of a time in the saloon where Gussie had described his first days with the park service in the early seventies.
"Yeah Jim, when I first showed up I looked like you and they ran me all around my first week. After that, I went and got my hair cut, trimmed my beard neatly and the next thing I knew, I had quarters and gained respect. Even though we shouldn't judge books by their covers, people do and that's a fact."
"Yeah," I added, " a sad fact that has to be changed."
"A dream." said Gussie.
"Not to me." was my reply and strongly held belief. I went off in a trance like stupor recalling that incident.

"Hey, wake up amigo." laughed Margerite.
I smiled and said, "mota coma ala Fox."
She could only comment, "I should have known." And we moseyed over to join Laurel conversing with the Snake and Robbins, for some naturalists' insight and sangria.

"Ninety percent of my salary I'll spend on good times, women, and Irish whiskey. The other ten percent I'll probably waste."
-Tug McGraw

<u>**(Prof) The Iter**</u>

Chuck Berry was blasting from the speakers, *"Maybelline, why can't you be true?"* An assortment of plates, bowls, and containers were filled with a variety of pot luck dishes: frijoles, enchilada's, quesadilla's, taco's, salads, chili rellano's, burros, rice, cookies, cakes, even a half gallon of Ben & Jerry's Cherry Garcia flavor had made the feast.
"Check it out." I expressed to the Dove.
"My other contribution." he replied, as he heaped his plate with the veggie dishes.
"Silly me not to have guessed from such a Dead Head." as I scooped rellano's onto my plate.
"Silly you."
"Where should we sit?" Margerite nudging me.
"At the fire table." looking over to see the gang in a congregation at this outdoor eating extravaganza.

As the Dove, Margerite and I went to sit down, Buck stood up and announced in a voice that commanded all's attention.
"Gringo's, join me in raising our drinks to the Skeed Row Palace and the Dove and Professor Canyone."
"Ole!" everyone raised beverages and a hundred margarita's were downed at once, causing a human jam at the trash cans.
At the fire circle, Buck passed everyone cold Corona's from strategically placed coolers. I rose to toast, "To the Dove, who really did the work as I've been…"
"Worthless as tits on a boar hog!" in unison, the whole fire crew harmonized on the old smoke bum's saying.
"As usual." the Dove added.
Only sounds of gastronomical feats were to be heard in between the necessary words such as, "Salsa please." or "Another Corona, por favor."

As I finished the last of the frijoles on my plate, the Fox caught my eye with a nod to the point. I winked back in acknowledgement while the Dove elbowed me, and Buck announced, "Smoke alert." in a subtle tone. The fire table was in procession to the point. Ranger Dimwit had noticed us. However, his full glass of tequila demanded his utmost attention, two fisting it. "So, the Dim is cutting loose tonight, good." I thought.
Margerite gained my attention and asked, "How was your weekend?" and further, "I do hope all is well, ok, always."
"Thanks. Lisa is still in serious condition and Janice is leaving in a week or two. Hard to believe everything so suddenly."
"WE'RE ALWAYS ON THE EDGE!" she gasped.
(Words ringing truth with our location and lives) "Yeah, so true." and leaning over, kissed her cheek.

Finally out at the point, I sat down next to Tex and Kathan.

"Jim, I forgot to tell you." Kathan suddenly burst.

"What?" I burst back. Kathan's enthusiasm with life was far more powerful than the doobie I toked.

"Last night coming across the Mesa's, I found something I thought you might love."

"What?" mystified response with joint to my lips.

"Well, you'll have to come over to our cabin and find out." a smile lighting up her facial features, leaving me further in mystery.

"After-we-finish theeese, senorita."

"Si senor."

The party was starting to really lift off. The Talking Heads were singing something about, *"Burning down the house."* As I got into Kathan's VW, the Dove called out to me, "Let's jam when you get back."

"It'll take you that long to tune up." was my holler back as I got in.

"So tell me what's the surprise?" I begged in mockery.

"I want it to be a surprise." and we headed out of skid row down to the end cabins next to the ghetto. Pulling into Tex's, we were greeted outside by Ahnee, Kathan's golden retriever, and Echo, Tex's old faithful hound dog.

As Kathan opened the door to the cabin, there stood a white furry head with half floppy ears, and small, dark brown eyes. Venturing into the unknown, the eyes looked up and smiled. I smiled at the four legs about a foot tall with a plume of a tail coming towards me. A look of love were in those eyes. She sat down next to me. My hand itched her ears and stroked her silky, furry body.

"Looks like I've got a new companion." I truly admitted.

"100% Res mutt puppy, she's a girl, too."

The moist nose sniffed my hand, and the three of us climbed into the VW, back to the fiesta.

"What are you going to name her?" she asked.

"Iter." I replied.

"How did you come about with that name?"

"When I was with Janice, I bought her a stuffed toy dog. She found a label attached that had the word, 'item' on it. She put it up to my face, playing around and said, '(b)ite 'em,' so, I took it and playing back, replied, '(b)iter, as in bite her instead. This dog will always be my love and a fond reminder of it.

Iter didn't hesitate to enter the palace. Just inside the door was the kitchen, where the Dove was seated, amp at his feet, sky blue guitar in his lap, mic with cord laying on the table, harp in one hand and holding a margarita mug with the other. Besides the Dove, the front room was now empty with all revelers out back. He looked up, saw the Iter, and asked, "What's this?"

"That's the Iter. She's my new love."

"Best looking four legged girl that I've ever seen. Come here girl."

She hesitated for a moment, then came over and consented to petting. I sat down and picked up my "D" harp. Dove stopped stroking the dog switching over to his guitar. Outside, we could hear the 'Stones', *"Country Honk."* We resisted the temptation to join the masses. Instead, we jazzed it up for awhile inside, launching into *"Susie-Q."* In no time at all we had a crowd. Continuing, we did a bit of, *"For what it's worth,"* changing the beat and filling the hallways with tequila mad rimmers.

As twilight descended on the canyon, the skidrow palace entered the zone. Flushed faces everywhere. I saw Gussie and Laurel in the corner by the frig chatting with that lost in love look. Buck had a lampshade on his head and was bouncing like a pogo from bed to bed. The Fox was with a young Hopi woman named Redtail. Tex, Kathan, and a bunch of other folk were clapping their hands. The Dove started the chords to, *"Gloria."* I made up the words until the *G-L-O-R-I-A* part, and the palace was a rockin'. Literally, the place was bouncing, old wooden floors creaking. Fifteen minute rendition later and Margerite grabbed the mic, *"I want to tell you all a story…"* she was standing on the chair that I was sitting on. Ron picked up on it while I grabbed an extra mic, and with a harp we all rocked to *J-U-L-I-O* for another fifteen minutes. The palace was awash in a smell of sweat and tequila. Looking up from my harp I saw the now shirtless Buck dancing with a tall, sexy, TW employee. Come to think of it, he disappeared shortly after that.

When the music ended, I found Margerite drawing me into my bed. I noticed my new friend following. "First Margerite, I want you to meet my other woman." and introduced her to the Iter. I went and filled a bowl with water. Iter sniffed it and then lay down by the bed. Margerite grabbed my hand and we went off and made love. I dreamed of Mexico for some reason.

(Prof) Breakfast

Awakened not by the sun streaming through the eastern window, but by a cold nose on my dangling hand. "You need outside Iter?" as a lick to the hand confirmed that thought. Disentangling myself carefully so as not to awaken Margerite, knowing that she had the dinner shift tonight, I noticed my clock, 7:30. "Damn, time to get up anyway." as I let Iter out in the back and noticed that someone had already cleaned up from last night. A plate of scraps lay beside the steps, obviously for the dog. Heading to the bathroom, I splashed cold water on my face, put on a t-shirt, Nomex, and boots. Kissed Margerite, let the dog in and checked her water, food scraps and then noticed a five pound sack of dog cereal with a note, "Here's some to get ya started, Love, T & K." Smiling, I headed to the pit in a zombie state of mind, thinking only of coffee and aspirin.

Walking over to the (fire) pit, Crazy Randy and the rest of the trail crew at the mule corral gave me a big, "Ya-Hooo!" acknowledging the good time last night.

Just as I reached for the door it opened to Buck, who had a cup of coffee in hand and offered it to me with a smile. His smile took my hangover away.
"Let's go have breakfast at the Lodge and then go out to Fire Point making sure there's no trees blocking the road. Maybe even head over to Monument Point too."
"Sounds good." came my reply.
I smiled back and went outside, loading up the saws, and stuffing our gear into the green bomb. We went down to the Lodge for breakfast and cured the hunger blues.

(Prof) Bigger not better in the Bureau of Land Mismanagement

August loomed hot for fires. Storms of dry lightning started the month out striking parched timber in Nevada, California, Idaho, and Oregon. Before I could say my goodbye to Janice, or Iter, I was bound for Nevada with Tex. We went as heliport managers. Packed on a charter for Winnemucca, Nevada to fight the dust bowl killers (as we called the high desert fires) we arrived that night after a dinner in a Nomex filled casino. Subsequently, we shipped out to a dust bound fire camp, thanks to the mining operation we were located next to.

We spent the next two and a half days loading Nevada state inmate crews onto ships to spend their days mopping up around rocks in 110 degree heat.

These big campaign fires bring in the best teams around, class one level. Typically, you wait around for a briefing on the day's objectives, the fire status, behavior, yesterday's news, weather, and a host of other pertinent info. On this project fire, our day went like this:
Wake up at 0430, wait in line for breakfast in the dark. Geared up, scanning the plans for assignments and waiting around for transportation with much anticipation. Another hour or two waiting for a ride or flight. In our case, it was a school bus drop off at the heliport, as ground pounders continued on, finally hitting the line around 0900. Work 'til the busses showed up and took you back to camp by midnight, only to start up at 0430 again and again.

Note that type one crews, like hotshots, don't spend everyday coming back to camp; they spike out on the line, and have provisions and water flown or parachuted to them and thus stay out for days or weeks at a time.

As heliport managers we were far from the action. Even the always positive Tex put it more bluntly, "What a fucking waste, our fire isn't even in view."

For two and a half days, Tex and I ate our breakfasts, loaded cons, ate lunches, loaded more cons, ate dinners, drank anything in site and went to our sleeping bags every night, trying to sleep while generators hummed. Because of all the b.s., we mostly prayed to be demobed (demobilized) to more glorious assignments, overtime plus hazard pay on some other fires. At the end of our shift on the third day, we were sent back to Winnemucca for dinner. Waiting to demobe to... somewhere, anywhere but here.

"Let's try and scam a motel room. With room service. Swimming pool. I'll see what I can do."

"You old smoke bum, I know ya caaan do it." drawled Tex.

"He who asks a question is a fool for five minutes; he who does not ask a question remains a fool forever."
-Chinese proverb

We pulled into the demobe trailer outside the high school gym. The guy at the desk had a Lassen National Forest shirt with a name tag, Gary Donobedian pinned on. He had the thickest forested mustache that I'd ever seen, illuminating a dark face with brown lights dancing as eyes.

"Hi Gary!" I greeted.

"Just call me Stash, how you doing?" issued forth.

"Fine. Canyon. Grand Canyon. North Rim helitack, old Plumas engine slug." (Plumas bordering Lassen National Forest on the north side).

"Glad to meet you."

I reached out as he did and we shook hands, discussed some fires in the past that both of us had been on with our respective units.

"That's Dave, better known as Tex."

"Obliged." smiled Tex, and held forth his sinewy mitt.

"Could get mine lost in that web." laughed Stash.

"Don't tempt me unless you want to find us room and grub for the night." smirked Tex.

"Why, I think that can be arranged."

"Pretty good for a rookie." I whispered chidingly to Tex.

"If you weren't so worthless as tits on a boar hog."

Within half an hour, we were enjoying a swim before dinner in the Winnemucca Motor Lodge.

After dinner, we headed back to the motel. Unable to find any Corona's, we settled for local domestic, split a sixer, had another swim and was off to bed with the boob tube, like the rest of America.

As we walked back to the demobe area after breakfast under a pale blue washed out sky, it was already 90 degrees. Breakfast had been a hardy one: Wonderbread French toast, synthetic hash browns, plastic filler disguised as sausage, and plenty of burnt coffee.

"Well, we're back on the clock." I informed Tex. Back at demobe, we were told that our status was in limbo, the current name of the game. That meant one thing, take out our novels (for me it was Vonnegut's <u>Breakfast of Champions).</u> We donned shorts and camped out on the lawn beside the auditorium, waiting.

"I'd sooner be home than making all this easy money. Keep us together now professor."

"Gotcha." I knew Tex was a homesick pup.

It was all about, hurry up and wait. And wait, we did.

The morning crawled along. At noon we were in the shade of the gym stretched on cots, picking out the best parts of our delivered lunches. I lucked out and got deli turkey on rye with Swiss. Tex got the dreaded ham.

"How about a trade, two snickers and two lemonades for the turk?"

"Bucky, you don't eat meat." I had to remind Tex.

"Turkey is an exception, but how about your apple then?"

"Here." I handed the apple to the veggie (still turkey-less) Tex, keeping my orange and popping a Pepsi, while taking a bite of my sandwich.

After lunch, we napped and waited. Around 1700 (five o'clock) we heard our names.

Tex and I walked over to demobe, and Gary was grinning, "Grab your stuff, you're on a charter to Boise for reassignment, sign this."

With a thanks, we were off to the Winnemucca Airport, where we boarded a deluxe turbo prop. A Robert Redford look alike was our pilot. A showgirl type was his assistant. They were known as Charles and Sherry. We were the only passengers. By the way they acted, I'd say they'd both caught the martini special before we arrived.

"Buckle up gentlemen, and once we're in the air, help yourself to our bar." Sherry smiled.

"Why thanks, maam." a grinning Tex acknowledged.

"My pleasure."

She put on some headphones and we proceeded to lift off as Charlie manually flew the craft while juggling maps on his lap.

Once we leveled off, our seatbelts became undone, and grinning at each other, we helped ourselves. I poured a shot of bourbon and chased it with an ice cold Little Kings Ale. Tex poured a healthy slug of vodka. Looking for juice, but settling instead for a can of pre-fab screwdriver for a mixer.

"A double, huh?"

"Never did like having my feet off the ground unless my head was too." Tex chuckled. I guffawed, and we were back at our seats, smiling.

"We've got to stop in Reno and pick up some other folks." Sherry informed us.

We had our drinks, landed and disembarked, bled our lizards, and re-boarded with two others. We immediately made ourselves new drinks. Joining us was a Lassen engine foreman on an overhead assignment, along with a trim and proper, immaculate woman as a timekeeper. She had a wine cooler, the foreman a beer, while Tex switched to Little Kings, and I stayed consistent.

It was 10:30 P.M. before we landed in Boise, feeling no pain. By 11:30, we were in a Denny's with an eighteen dollar per person meal allowance ticket. Tex and I went whole hog. Mozzarella sticks and fried clams for appetizers, soup and salad, and as high a price dinner as we could get. The immaculate timekeeper looked on in disgust, finally commenting, "That's the taxpayer's money, you know?"

"Do you know what it's like to be on the line for 36 hours straight with flames licking your asshole, smoke so thick that you puke up the ham sandwich on stale Wonderbread that you've been eating for the last three meals, with an occasional MRE (meals, rarely eaten)? That's where we're maybe headed, and that's what we've experienced in the past, so as far as I'm concerned, this is the LAST SUPPER!" I somewhat calmly yet emphatically responded between bites of prawn and fries.

She remained in silence, and studied her Jell-O salad. I ordered two Corona's at our own expense. The foreman joined us and the last supper was consumed. At 0100, we were checked into separate rooms at the Holiday Inn with wakeup call at 0600. Turning on the tube, I found several men and women undressed and being lewd and lascivious. A sign flashed on my television. If you wish to view this, press the red button and your room will be properly billed. Laughing to myself and thinking of Uncle Sam footing the bill for porno, I pressed red, and uh, went to sleep with the telly on. At 0600, the phone rang, taking my fantasy away from the television set which was still smoldering away. Jumping in the shower, dressed and ready took about fifteen minutes. From the hotel it was BIFC (Boise Interagency Fire Center) bound via a government van.

(Prof) Deadwood

Arriving at the military command post of wildfire, Tex and I hung around the coffee machine and coolers of juice for five hours. Finally, we were vanned out on a three hour drive to the Deadwood (Fire) Complex. We arrived for the tail end of lunch, warm meat loaf sandwiches. However, it was the only thing warm as I heard the fires were living up to their name. We were in standby until evening. Making camp in the woods nearby a stream, nap came easy until dinner. After pork chops, baked tators, with salad and carrot cake, we found we weren't needed for the night shift.

"A smoke bum could get fat up here in Idaho."

"Carnivorous scum." muttered Tex, while he chomped on a carrot.

"Well, that carrot was alive until some machine or humanoid yanked it from its peaceful existence in harmony with earth."

Tex took another bite of his carrot, "Get ya another cup of chocolate?"

"Can't dance."

While the generators hummed and the fire generals made their plans of people and smoke, Tex and I sat at our picnic table and watched the stars glow in the clear Idaho night.

It was back to loading crews in ships. There were a few hot spots in our complex, but not many. To perk us up, I was told by an old smoke bum from Yellowstone/Tetons that future flame fun awaited us down the road. Smoke from the other fires soon started settling in our valley for the evening. After a week of much feasting, working fourteen hours a day of heliport duty, Tex was drafted as camp medical officer due to his EMT status. I was sent to BIFC for re-assignment. I wanted more oats (overtime).

Most of the rest of the folks wanted home. Without a word take a guess who was sent packing first? That's right. The next thing that I knew, I was homeward bound in a four seater, with a tired pilot, supposedly able to get me to the South Rim. Dodging thunderstorms through Idaho and Nevada, we pulled into Cedar City, Utah with a couple of hours of twilight left. This was the pilot's hometown, and he didn't want to take me back until morning. The local circus folks refused to get me a room. So, I hustled a seat with a southbound plane to the rim. One of the most terrifying and yet beautiful rides I've ever experienced. As we crossed the inner gorge of the canyon over the esplanade, two billowing cumulonimbus lay in our flight path. Thunder and lightning roared and flashed from the heavens. Instead of going around, we shot the gap. Below us, I watched as lightning bolts were born and thunder roared in my ears. When we touched ground in Tusayan, on the South Rim, my immediate thoughts were, "It's good to be back home on earth." I got a ride from Slim to the barracks there, showered, put on jeans, t-shirt, brushed my long hair, and went to the Bright Angel. Slim was there for the music and women, myself, a Corona and a celebration of life seemed in order. As the first round arrived, I toasted, "To life!" We clinked bottles and the music was playing, *Fire on the mountain.*

(Buck) A mystery

While Tex was away on his adventures, his woman Kat was having some of her own. During her summer break to keep busy, she had organized a co-op of fresh veggies as well as handled the association's book store. Watching diligently the animals of their herd there on the edge of Transept Canyon, she heard a wailing cry one night. Startled, the posse all quivered as the brave Kat went out to investigate. A continued, crying, wailing sound emanated from some spruce at the edge of the canyon. Further inspection revealed a pale woman in an old fashioned white dress. Still partially hidden by some distance and the trees, Kat inquired if help was needed. The woman continued to cry out, moaning, and moving toward the precipice, Kat following closer. What appeared to Kat next was shakingly repeated to us later. This woman-figure, had walked out from the spruce onto and past the rocky ledge somehow into thin air. A ghostly apparition? What was the meaning? Trying to uncover the mystery, it was found to be reported by others in the past. Stories were mentioned of the wailing woman and her search for someone. Tales of murder/suicide in the cabins from long ago were reported... And so, the mystery continues...

At 0800, I hopped on 210. Pilot Dana greeted me at the South Rim heliport, "So, how was the tropics of Nevada and Idaho or wherever it was?"
"Other than the flight back, BORING! Didn't even see a flame other than the evening campfire."
"What?"
"Not even any H" (hazard duty pay).
"Understood, well I'll give ya a fun ride. We've got a stop at Phantom and then Roaring Springs before I kick ya out."
"Got any mud made?"
"Ya know where it's at."
While Dana did the morning check, I poured a cup and made the manifest. Food and other goodies were slated for the Phantom ranch folk, and a canvas for inner gorge artist, Bruce Aiken. What a sort. Bruce, when he arrived from the Midwest was just another longhair blowing along on his Harley to the wind. Now Bruce had become reborn, while his paintings became world renowned. His paintings held people in their visual grip, just as the canyon walls held the Aiken family down at Roaring Springs. Roaring Springs is just off Bright Angel Creek, and gushes its life giving waters out of the limestone. All water used on both rims comes from Roaring Springs and is piped and pumped up from the bottom depths.

Soon, I had the ship loaded and Dana had her cranked up. We were strapped in our seats, wired up to our headset helmets, and off to the wild blue yonder, then down, down into the abyss. Scanning for mules before landing was our next focus. Wouldn't want to spook a tour-on off their wilderness experience. I unloaded the cargo to a smiling and welcoming Vern and Patti at Phantom Ranch.

Off again, headed up the gorge to the spring. Took care of business there as the next step was now finding the morning updraft (where the sun meets the rock) to climb the invisible elevator and soon, we were looking down on aspens and ponderosa's of the North Rim.
"210, North Rim heliport." went a voice that I recognized as Ken's.
"210, go ahead." Dana answered.
"Winds from the southwest at two to five."
"Copy, thanks Ken."
"See ya in a few with some hot jo."
"Click, click." went the radio, acknowledging.
I was on the ground and back home. Ken handed Dana a cup to refill his, unloaded, and watched as 210 took off to the South Rim. I gave Ken a big hug as he greeted me, "Hey, welcome back Boomer."
"How ya doing?" I asked, curious for home news.

"Great!"

"Any excitement?"

"Well, we sent Buck and the Fox out to Idaho with a mixed park and forest crew. They should be back this Sunday or so."

"Need me this weekend?"

"Yeah, it's just me and whomever I can round up. Slim, Bob, and BJ are it on the south."

"How's the old BJ?"

"Well, I haven't gotten any late night phone calls." he laughed.

"Any strikes?"

"Not a one."

"Well, let me get unpacked and say hello to my dog."

"She's with Kathan at Tex's. The mutt wouldn't come out from under your bed when I tried to feed her the first night you were gone. Just growled."

I laughed, "So I owe Kathan."

"Yeah!"

August flew by under the blue skies up on top of the mountain laying down. Monsoons, thunder, lightning, hazard pay, overtime. No idle time for this warped mind. I did receive a bill from the government. While they paid for my motel room in Boise, they didn't pick up the tab for the, uh-hummm, extra television viewing pleasure. Damn!

(Buck) Heroes

The Fox, Wad, and myself were sent out to Boise. Eventually ending up on the Oregon-Idaho border above the Snake River, where they used wet burlap bags and the few flappers available (like a truck's mud flap attached to a handle) to smother out range grass fires. From there, we were bussed to Weiser, Idaho for town safety. As fires burned all around the small ranch/farm community, embers were threatening the structures and outlying homes. The Wad had t-shirts made up for the assignment: Weiser Hotshots. Housed in a local motel, meals were provided by the various restaurants, with an open invitation to the local grocer for snacks. Government paid a per diem for each firefighter, but the townsfolk and business owners informed us that whatever was wanted, was "on the house."

And we took to that town, the hospitality, the genuine appreciation felt was reciprocated by our diligence in keeping them safe, and not taking advantage of the situation (as hard as that was with the local honeys worshipping us as rock stars). Our departing farewell was a town parade with us as the honored guests.

Our next assignment was down to Phoenix, where we waited, and waited. Hurry up and wait, the all too common saying in fire and military. The result was that we were finally demobilized back to our bases. As Fox and I arrived on the South Rim, we were picked up by a forest service crew that needed resources. The Wad stayed to return to his regular position in the park.

I was assigned a squad boss position, and we were enroute to Silver City, New Mexico. The twin otter fixed wing aircraft that was flying our 20 person crew had to circle a dirt mesa top several times to scare off the cattle grazing there. It was a hairy, rough landing, barely making the taxi only feet before plunging off the mesa. Needless to say, we were all holding brown bags, several in use as we became religious during braking maneuvers. The fire was a pretty straight forward operation: saw work on trees and line construction. We were in a strike team with another crew. Together we kicked it out, containing and controlling it within two days. Off for an "R&R" to Silver Sity. Had time for a brew, walked the town, and headed back onto busses for our next assignment, Arizona.

The Hulapai Reservation, was just west of the South Rim, Grand Canyon. What struck me here was the allowed use of bulldozers, as the forests and rangelands allow, but is forbidden in parks and wilderness areas (different land management uses). We followed a D-9 cat (a very wide bladed bulldozer). Our job was improving the line constructed by removing any organic combustible material that remained upon its' track. We battled this Ponderosa blaze for three days. The Hulapai put up a local fire camp for us. The ladies hand rolled burritos with stewed mutton, chiles, and all the fixin's. They even wrapped some for our lunches. Wow! It was much appreciated and went far in our energy reserves. After this one, Fox went back to the North Rim, while I went on temporary assignment to a hotshot crew.

(Buck)-Getting down and dirty with the shots

The hotshot fire crew was a good place to work out the anger from Lancelot. Assigned to southern California meant a lot of time in chaparral using the bow bar. Pretty much one fire after another, flying here, flying there, out of state, back to base, living in the woods along the fire lines that we constructed to hold the fire at bay. Working, working, working. It was good, physical grunt labor. Just what I needed. Being with the 'shots meant that they were available for fires anywhere, at anytime. Thus they traveled and were mobile in crew carriers (like convict transports) and were located near an airstrip for longer destination assignments.

One evening while awaiting the next detail, a bunch of us headed out to the local lodge bar. Like Spider woman at the North Rim, this lodge had their version of the beautiful, sultry, young, aspiring, future business woman seeking opportunistic fortune at all costs. Rose, with her thorns had a number of suitors trying to lure the fair maiden into their dominion. Many failed. Miserably. Yet she loved it. Mind games. It was entertaining to watch. Mr. Mojo was rising and with Attila the Hun instinct, a nonchalant attitude, a so-called bad boy image and this Pandora was flirting with the idea of another one about to bite the dust. Wham, bam, thank you, m'aaam! Mutually beneficial. That helped ease the pain, somewhat.

Then the call for Hawaii came in. A strike team of two shot crews were requested. With my training and certifications (rated as an air safety manager as all the Longshots were) I drew an overhead air assignment as the rest of the crew battled it out in the trenches. Actually that rating allowed us as a crew to snag the assignment to Hawaii, and for me to pick up with the management team. Volcano flows caused the forests to burn with vengeance. Once controlled, the locals threw a big lua and hailed the 'shots as heroes. A day of R& R was earned and we were sent out to the coast at Kona. I almost missed the flight back. One beautiful wahine, an enchantress named Patty, with golden flowing locks almost convinced me to be her first mate on a sightseeing boat operation. Barely made the plane door closing as a Van Morrison song came to mind,

"Well it's down the road I go
And I hear those gypsy voices
Calling me
Way on down the road"

Back at the mainland station, word got out that the, "bad boys" were back in town. For some reason, many women are attracted to these so-called "bad boys." Something about the free spirit (or maybe it's just the commando look, whatever). The wild, adventurous, and fun loving person was typically sought out. We actually had "groupies," young, college-aged, and immature, but so many gaining valuable experience that summer. Yeah boy howdy! Baaaad to the bone! Brief encounters of the torrid kind... cowgirl in the sand, dandy candy, Humboldt honey, Southern belle, and yakkety-yak (don't come back). As the fire conquests numbered that season, other types lessened, due to more times spent away. Money racked up. My hips deteriorated. Shit happened.

On a training day while on rescue and rope practice, we were preparing to rappel off a 70' cliff. I was belayed by a sleepy, half-assed incompetent. An unexplained, uneasy feeling came over me. Untrusting this fuck up, I asked a second time to check the belay ropes, only this time, another member came by to verify. Sure enough, a coiled rope with no anchor. It would have been a 70' plunge off the vertical, landing on boulders below. Thanks to gut feelings and knowing people. Who to trust, who not to. I was surely missing my trusted crew the Longshots.

But there was the promotion. Wayne had his chainsaw ricochet off the ground with the effect of cutting part of his face off. He was medi-vac'd and lived through it. I got his slot, moving up to the number one saw team. Wayne eventually came back to visit, his season over. Had a new face, surgically reconstructed. He even looked better than before. Except for the suture marks. Frankenstein came to mind.

Being on the first saw team led to some serious falling in big timbers of Northern Cal. One such complex fire had the boss boasting to the locals of his crew's ability to put down trees anywhere desired. One such cedar beast around 100 feet tall, with a five foot dbh (diameter at breast height) was a leaner on a slope. Only problem was that the lean was away from the slope and our boss man proclaimed his team could fall it back down the slope (against its' natural inclination). Why did he do this? The locals wouldn't. Maybe pride and arrogance won out. As low men on the totem pole, we took orders.

I was swamping as my partner Mike was sawing in steps at the base to reach the trunk and then begin the front cuts. Upon the back cut, even before placing in the wedges, a high breeze caught the tops of the trees in the forest, causing a swaying action to occur. This tree began to fall, sitting back with its natural lean. Mike had time to kill the saw, remove it, and bolt to his safety path to the right, as I was moving in the opposite direction for my designated safety route. Catching my foot upon the brambles of poison oak we were standing in resulted in my backward fall. Sliding down the slope, helmet coming off, and life in peril as this tree was following the same path coming towards me. Couldn't do much maneuvering while sliding downhill on my back, head first, even as I tried to swim and squirm with my body. Every year while on fires or in the forests, people get "pancaked," part of the nature of this hazardous duty (along with the fire, rolling logs, boulders, etc.). Miraculously, the tree missed me by only a few feet. Bouncing upon impact, it richocheted but missed again. Wasn't my time I guess. Whew! Brief moment to steady my racing heart and it was move on. Our boss man was disappointed in us and let the crew know.

Going into another fire somewhere in the High Sierra's of California, we drove our rigs to the designated site. Wanting to get started immediately and shave some time off hiking in several miles, our boss man decided to drive up the old mining jeep road. Only our crew carriers were double axle wide rigs not meant for the narrow historic mining trails designed long ago for mules and widened by military jeeps. It was slow going and four wheeling for sure but then we came upon a cliffside eroded embankment where the road had slid partially off. A good place to stop, but no, boss man was adamant we should go on (of course he wasn't in the rigs as he was walking beside them). I saw this as a possible safety concern and raised the question as well as proposed that only the (two) drivers maneuver the slide. Sure enough, I was tagged as the lead driver now and was to proceed on my own. If I made it across safely without plunging the thousands of feet below, then they'd send the next rig across as the crew walked behind following. Inching my way in a vehicle that I hadn't been trained in was precarious. It consisted of a split shift transmission, which I'd used only once before, so I really was focused upon the task at hand, my safety. The only factor shielding me from further fear was nightfall. All I knew at the time as I hugged the cliff wall and looked out with my door cracked is that I was about three inches from going over the edge on soft pack dirt and rocks. I knew it was a far way down. Death for sure if I didn't make it. So I am writing this letting you know that I did make it, and we did our fire job admirably. Upon returning in daylight, I was once again in the lead as the crews filed out for this hairy cliffside funeral procession. All I could do now is hug the rock wall (with my mirror retracted) and listen to the voices as they called out my distance from the edge... "6 inches, 4 inches, wait, no, 3 inches, I think you got it now, okay, keep going straight" (no shit what else can I do, would you mind shaving some of the cliff off, was going through my mind at these comments). Getting out to inspect during the daytime, I veered over the edge once done, Whew! Ass pucker factor was a 10! Sheer drop off of over a thousand feet below. After this assignment, I was designated another "official driver" for the crew and could add this to my red card of qualifications (split shift transmissions).

Rocking and rolling along, we had another night assignment (so typical of 'shots) for a range fire in the foothills of California. It was burning several thousands of acres by the time we arrived and our detail was to back off (from the fire) one hill and burn out from above (on the next hill over). At night, with cooling downdraft breezes, it would carry our set fires (from fusees) off our line down the slope and create a wider, blackened line from our dug handline so that the fire would be robbed of fuels. Thus was the plan. A con(vict) crew was below us on the other side in the dark. No communication existed between the crews and no one had spotted them in their bright orange jumpsuits setting fire to the tall grasses below us. Successful with our scratch line operations, we were waiting for the nightly downdrafts to begin our burn out. However, we looked down behind us to see a fast moving flaming front about three feet high racing right towards us while the original fire was ahead of us. We were trapped. The command was to jump the flames below us as we ran to safety on the other side. Wearing 45 lbs. of gear plus tool weight while running downhill and jumping over flames ready to scorch our balls was a real "rush." Hooping and hollering, we sounded like we were on a warpath. When the excitement wore off, the question of safety, once again, came up. How could they, the supervised convict crew, light a fire below the hill we were on? Did they not see us or know we were there? How come communications were lacking and who was overseeing these operations (both ours and theirs)? And on it went. Interestingly enough, several of the cons told us aside that they saw us above, but they lit their fusees anyway, since the command was given. Hmmm! Reminded me of a fire camp we had and the cons were serving the food. Orders were given for one steak and a scoop of scrambled eggs. The guy in front of me asked the server for another steak (making two). The con looked around for roaming eyes, and seeing no one watching, forked another one on his plate saying, "I sure didn't get here by being honest..." And so it was.

On another assignment, it was an eery feeling awaiting a fire that surrounded us while stuck on a knoll top with nowhere to go. A pit of the stomach feel. Everyone on the crew ready to rip open and cast out their shake and bakes (fire shelters). We awaited word to deploy, no options left. The fire had encircled us on all sides from below (where was the lookout?). Fortunately, the winds shifted, and a tanker had bombed an escape route with slurry. A breath of relief, even for adrenaline junkie hotshots.

Fitness was paramount of importance on the shots. The more line your crew constructed in the least amount of time, the better the rating amongst the shot crews went. We were always the top or next to it, depending upon the week of fires. Competitive edge, bragging rights, whatever, asinine decisions continued to percolate down from above. Case in point was our return from a mountaintop fire. Several cat lines had been bulldozed leaving foot high trenches along slopeside hills. As we exited the forest our strike team of two hotshot crews were to hike back to the crew carriers. Donning headlamps for the nightfall, and filing out singly in orderly fashion, we descended the mountain. Boss man sensing that his crew had to prove it was always the best, commanded us to run back to our vehicles in the dark, down the slope while hoofing our 45 lb. packs plus tools. Some of us, like me, had to also lug the chain saw over a shoulder and carry the extra gear and fuel needed (about 15 lbs. worth) while others carried torches, hose, and an assortment of supplementals. It was hairy going over the mounds of earth and into the trenches while running downhill carrying all our stuff in the dark so that we could brag about how "bad ass" we were to the others whom we beat. Luckily, no one twisted an ankle, knee or worse.

My impression of the crew was one of admiration. Physically fit specimens, hard-working grunts, endured tremendously, persevered through all conditions, yet most were of the mindset to just follow orders. Not ones to question. Which was good to an extent. When safety was compromised, I always questioned (a Longshot trait that the Wad instilled and Ken practiced) and thus I was thrust into becoming the safety boss. Nice title to keep me busy filing papers, and shutting my mouth. But safety was compromised on many occasions without addressing the needs to any satisfaction. Several times on assignments as a crewmember, I was clueless as to what was going on. We had been left out of valuable information for our situational awareness (how the fuels, weather and topography had been affecting the fire). Sure I could see and experience all around me what was happening and make myself aware, but where was the safety zone and our escape routes, etc. When I inquired, I would be told to keep working. Shut up and fall in line. Edginess prevailed when we were indirect and working in heavy fuels with no sight nor sound of any (fire) activity only smoke filled air. Where was our lookout? This shot crew was a finely run paramilitary organization with an ego-driven leader (ala BJ). A replay of another selfish hedonist out to make a name for themselves disregarding the crews' safety at times. In the game of fire, safety is not to be compromised, ever!

"... federal inquiry into the Esperanza fatalities" (fire in San Bernardino NF in 2006 killing 5 USFS firefighters) "concluded that a lapse in situational awareness played a destructive role. Firefighters need to know what is going on around them, be able to perceive the potential for change, and be willing to modulate those perceptions based on what is actually happening on the ground."
-Colleen Morton Busch (Fire Monks, p.63)

My final assignment came on a Sierra fire as I was designated IC (incident commander). Nothing but a small log fire on a slope. Two of us went in to initial attack. As the helicopter set us down yards from the fire, I gave the initial size up as my partner, Rex, an experienced BLM shot, went to work with the saw. No sooner than finishing radio transmission, and giving a hand to swamp the brush surrounding the base of the log, some fire transferred to a new type of vegetation that I was unfamiliar with at the time. It was manzanita, with a volatile waxy substance within that ignites rapidly. Thus, a blow up occurred, that fast, racing up the entire hillside and spilling over into the next valley. Originally standing out as a single 30 foot juniper tree in a field of brush, lightning struck knocking ten feet out of the top sending it to the ground. Flames consuming this log on the ground came into contact with the consistent fuels surrounding the hillside. The scrubby, chapperal of manzanita bushes had the effect of a full blow up. Slurry bombers were called, two full crews arrived, and I turned over the management to a more experienced, local team. Took two days to control it. The worst was that they were told to contain all these "small" fires to less than an acre, as resources were spread thin. I felt pretty bad about all the money spent and resources required for this one and wished I had been briefed about these "new" volatile fuels that were unbenownst to me at the time. Interestingly enough, Rex, the experienced BLM shot assigned to me was very versed with manzanita. When I found out later from him about his experiences in such brush, he responded by stating that he was trained to get started with the line construction, in this case, saw work and not say a thing. Never mind that upon arrival we could have switched tactics and begin saw work cutting off contact with the fuels above. It would impact my decision making in the future. It was time to come home.

(Prof)-Oh Well and Circles of joy

The park records state that we were to paid twenty dollars each in per diem for the trip to the South Rim and the, uh-hum, Lancelot Fire critique. How the critique even came about, I can't tell you. I do know that as a crew, we felt we had an axe to grind with Billie Joe for his indecision and incompetence, in not caring about the safety of fifty people as the REAL fire was threatening to overrun us at the helispot. The Fox and I had been disregarded concerning our size up of the fire's behavior after our scouting mission following the air tanker's futile drops. Buck, as IC, had also been ignored several times for observations and our crew's insight as well as dismissed several times for resource requests.

*"A 1997 NPS review team identified a longstanding problem in the North Rim forests: an accumulation of litter, such as fallen trees, branches, leaves, and needles. Combined with an invasion of spruce and fir, which provided fuel ladders that **could lead to enormously destructive crown fires**, this set up a potentially dangerous situation. **The problem first had been recognized on the North Rim in 1981 by regional plant/fire ecologist Kathleen Davis...**"*
-Hal K. Rothman, **Blazing Heritage,** p. 193.

There are many staff specialists in the big parks (i.e.- archeologists, plant and fire ecologists, etc.). At the Grand Canyon (as noted in quote above) the fire ecologist had been disregarded for her research just as Buck had been dismissed for his observations of the "crowning" potential of fire by BJ.

Before the hearing, BJ took Buck aside privately, and warned him to be quiet, not say a word if he ever wanted to work again, anywhere in a park.

(Buck's interjection)- I remember being numb at his words and threat. I couldn't believe this was happening, like in a movie, only real, and it was regarding my future, my passion, what I had worked hard to achieve and where I wanted to go. I just looked at him and thought this was all a bad dream. Then, the Yaz's words echoed in my head at this moment, "hawk totem people, like many who carry strong predator animals, may be shunned by others who sense and fear their inner power. Others will strike first in an attempt to keep the hawk animal at bay."

(Prof continues)- As a seasonal, he had no recourse. BJ, being a permanant, even though incompetent, had the upper hand. Buck was stunned, silent, and contemplating his future, since he had finally found a home and a career. We all were silent at the so called, "hearing." A transcript was read monotonously and obviously edited of the actions transpiring on Lancelot. Many (radio) transmissions were deleted, favoring a more decisive and active BJ. Man, it was a stunner, some real bullshit and a major corruption of ineptitude hidden. Even the person brought in to oversee the "hearing" had no knowledge of fire and was just a figure head filling in. You'd think that the superintendent or an assistant, someone above and in power would've been there. Feeling hopeless, Buck and I looked at each other acknowledging we were powerless and sighed in agreement, "Oh Well!"

"If you don't say everything, then you won't learn from what really happened."
-John Maclean, <u>Fire on the Mountain,</u> p.182.

Len (Wad) was the only one to speak up. He asked some poignant questions, all of which were overlooked and never answered. For this he has always earned my respect and that of every Longshot whoever scratched away at a fire line.

"Credibilty problems are exacerbated through manipulation of the" (National Park) *"service's own ad hoc workgroups, investigative teams...made up of selected colleagues...The manner in which these teams... are assembled generally assures a desired finding or outcome or at least obfuscation of facts that might damage the reputation of the agency."*
-Paul D. Berkowitz (<u>The Case of the Indian Trader</u>, p. 69)

Some good came out of the Lancelot turmoil. Deano became part of the South Rim crew, while a steady hand of a ranger up from Big Bend, Albert, was now the assistant F.M.O. Two very good people, knowledgeable, competent, and trustworthy (assigned to add input to some of the controversial decisions being made by BJ).

We decided as a crew, in order to make it through the rest of the season as best we could (without Lisa, and with Ken being detained more and more to the South Rim for business) to opt out of Billie Joe's antics. In itself, even that decision was a moot point. How do you ever avoid a mad man control freak that monitors your every move?

After the hearing, Buck and the Fox headed down to Phoenix for a Winwood show with some peaches from Georgia they had plucked in the Bright Angel bar the night before. Me, well, Janice had gone off to school while I was heli-slackin' in Nevada and Idaho. However, I did have a four legged gal waiting for me to go campin' with. The thought of waking up to her, running circles of joy seeing me, was keeping me going. Those few dog days left of August were my sanctuary.

"I love my country, but I fear my government."
-unknown

Superintendent Pecker Tracks looked down at his tan loafers, then across the great plains of his desk, and in his most political voice retorted, "It appears that our water figures were incorrect on the environmental impact statement and that there will be no new motel project."
"What!" Brigham Stern blurted.
"In fact, Senator MacSlain called and suggested that all or part of that nine million dollars needs to go into upgrading existing structures and especially your own employee's housing." (Known as the ghetto ironically to us North Rimmers).

Meanwhile, head interpreter chief, Jack McGregor, was smiling somewhat whimsically. He'd just gotten off the phone with one of his Denver Sierra Club buddies. They were going to be filing some legal paperwork that would put a stop to the development on the North Rim due to the water figures he had procured for them. Walking out he was interrupted by a loud pinyon jay looking down demanding tribute.

"Resist much. Obey Little." -Walt Whitman

(Buck) Elephant trap

Due to moisture patterns converging we would typically get a monsoon season of daily afternoon thunderstorms. Monsoon seasons varied, but typically brought an abundance of lightning activity, which had us "chasing smoke" reports. Sometimes substantiated, other times it was just mountain mist hanging in the trees. In any case, we were in charge of checking these reports out.

One such occurance had our initial attack wildland engine crew out, with Tex driving (again) while Jim rode shotgun. The call came in via radio to me, "Send in the McCullough." Now the McCullough chainsaw in our cache was for one thing only. As the Wad had instructed us, these ancient heavy relics were what the old Longshots used. Now, they were only to be used for a serious fuck up, like a fire truck being swallowed in the elephant trap down in the meadow. An innocuous beautiful valley of wildflowers and trees with a sandy, dirt road down the middle. Being in a basin, it was naturally a collecting pool of water when the rains came. In fact, one area of the road became historically known as, "the elephant trap" due to its' ability to swallow up an elephant (and thus a wildland fire truck/engine) during monsoon season rains.

The Fox and I responded in Engine 3 with the McCullough. What a sight!

From up on the hillside looking down at the swallowed engine, with only the front cab showing, was Tex and Prof. I could only laugh as they relayed the story of young Tex asking if he should gun through the trough of water ahead.

Canyon figured he needed more experience driving and manuevering on park roads. Tex, remembering that the park service was all about preserve and protect, don't leave a footprint, take only pictures, and minimal impact was a bit hesitant with his driving. Trying to be minimalist, Tex (really living up to his billing as Bucky, being the youngest) went through the bog, so as not to disturb the wildflowers and vegetation growing beside the road. And then he went under, literally, swallowed up by the massive water trap.

Turkeys chattered, a Kaibab squirrel squawked, while a red tail soared overhead, and butterflies skittered about as we all tried coming up with the least invasive way to extricate the buried fire engine. First, we had to dump out the water that was in the holding tank, all 350 gallons. That meant holding breath, going under muddy water, and opening the hatch. Bucky volunteered as he was the driver, and a very good man. Next, we had to hook up the winch from engine 3 to the immersed one, and so I ran a block and tackle technique with tree protector and cables. The other job was to saw off some tree limbs for leverage and grip. Fox and Prof took turns running the McCullough and selecting thick trees from out of sight of the road (so as not to impair future generations of any visible tree scars).

By this time we were off the clock, but far from having the vehicle emerge. Like the creature from the black lagoon, Engine 2 soon came out drenched in mud and scrapping much of the ground in the ensuing winching operation. Firing her up, she ran, but we all rushed back to rehab the torn up ground. Working well into the eve, we finally parted farewell, journeyed back to the developed area, washed the trucks, showered and took Bucky up on his offer of rounds for us all at the saloon. As the locals inquired of our latest fire conquest, or daring escapade, we all four just looked at each other with a rather nonchalant attitude, and calmly replied, just another day out searching for smokes (with shit-eating grins).

(Buck) Looking together in the same direction

Finally deciding she was ready to tie the knot after several years of courting, Laurel and Gussie announced their plans to wed there on the North Rim. Long anticipated by the rest of us, we were all waiting for Laurel's announcement. Turning away many suitors and broken hearts, she had her man, her dream of a Ranger's Ranger in Gussie. He had served well in his capacity in past parks and was now in charge of the North Rim. People liked him and his style. He was friendly, upwardly mobile, and most importantly, really took a fancy to Laurel. The twinkle in his eyes when they were together was obvious. Just as in love was Laurel, the way she spoke so highly of him, revered him, and shared her happiness when she was with him was evident.

A stage was set up by the volleyball courts outside Gussie's cabin and the administration building. The Peach Pitters were the chosen band to perform for the reception and folks from all over arrived for the big event. Patrick Ways, a former North Rim ranger and now U.S. Marshall down California way was one of the first to arrive. Tall, lean, and with a loud, smirky laugh, his presence was immediately felt as his jovial mood preceded his appearance. Passing the bottle early in the day, he found several to imbibe with his favorite poison, Jack Black, as the priming began. The Wad with his now new steady Jinny arrived, smiling from brim to brim. Ken and his lovely wife Linda were there for the celebration as well. The evening before, they hosted a reunion of sorts at their cabin. Past rangers, firefighters, and park staff showing up for the wedding of the summer gathered for tunes, drinks, eats, stories, and happenin's at their place the night before the big event. Soon enough, an old tradition was re-initiated. With the Wad in the lead, Ken next, followed by an old fire dog, John-boy, I followed suit with the rest of the Longshots in tow as we lined out the front door, arms on the waist of the perrson in front, kicking up feet side to side swaying while singing together, *"hi-ho, hi-ho, it's off to work we go, hi-ho, hi-ho..."* only to circle around the cabin entering the back door with an article of clothing removed. And on it went like this, until we were naked and had folks astonished, laughing their drunk assess off. Other antics followed, like Ken's classic "samarai" cutting of watermelons with his best voice imitation of Belushi doing the "Samarai Taylor." Then it was requested that I perform my infamous handstand pushups while eating a large Milk Bone dog biscuit, much to the dismay of poor ol' Whit (Ken and Linda's pooch). It was great having such a wonderful celebration and we were all thankful for Ken and Linda hosting as they were so busy these days with their park careers and preparing their future for more permanant positions and a family. We missed those fine folks many a time down in the saloon, but understood their reasoning...

"One of the best things about marriage is that it gets young people to bed at a decent hour."
-M.M. Musselman

The big day arrived sunny and bright, but as it progressed, as is so common this time of year, clouds came billowing in that afternoon. The show must go on. And on it did, in fine fashion, many beautiful people from all parks and all places converged to share in the uniting of the love so exhibited by these wonderful folks. Even with downpours from the heavens above, we all gathered in typical park fashion, and came up with solutions to keep the celebrants dry. Tarps attached to the stage kept us huddled and dancing close to each other, temporarily anyway. As the winds gusted, lifting and dumping the water accumulated on bodies underneath, we took turns emptying the tarps at certain intervals to continue the partying outside. Certain speeches and toasts were made, honoring the couple to celebrity fashion, but one I won't forget is Laurel's father. He got up onstage and shared his heartfelt love for his daughter and her new home. How she had taken his advice and followed her heart, seeking her quest and life in the admonishment of Horace Greeley, famous newspaperman,

"Go West, young man, and grow up with the country."

Knowing Laurel and for that matter, all park service gals at that time, they knew that any time, "man" was noted, they took it upon themselves to correct it to the times and their nature, to acknowledge woman as well. And we're all glad she did. She added an innocence, wonderment, and excitement of life in the outdoors at her job as a naturalist.

Festivities continued into the night. Gussie in his mischievous smile and gleaming eyes asked me to do the infamous, "bacon toast." Hard to refuse the big man with such a little boy look of anticipation, I scrambled onstage, fumbling, slurred speech and all, to pull it off. It was hilarious to see so many grown people flopping on the wet ground below, acting and making noises like bacon frying. A sight to behold; weird if you had just arrived and ventured onto this.

"We're all a little weird. And life is a little weird. And when we find someone whose weirdness is compatible with ours, we join up with them and fall into mutually satisfying weirdness-and call it love-true love."
-Robert Fulghum (True Love)

(Prof) Dog Days

The Iter became my new days off partner, and we started to explore the national forest part of the Kaibab Plateau (due to no leash laws). Of course that was in between cerveza's with Buck and the rest of the crew at the saloon. Off season plans were also starting to formulate in everyone's mind. Lisa was now in the spinal center at the University of Washington's hospital in Seattle on the way to a new life in a wheelchair. Pat had pulled some strings and was going up there to trail crew it in Olympic National Park and be near his love for support.

However, there still were fires to be had! Slim (Tim) and myself did the initial attack on four pinyon-juniper fires in a South Rim monsoon lightning frenzy on one afternoon. Those were not only the days when fires were fires and not incidents, they were also the days when their naming was at the discretion of the smoke bum who arrived at the scene first. Hence on that day, the Lost, the Canyon, Moose, and Hummer fires were entered into the record books. The Moose and Hummer were dedicated in my mind to the weekend I took Janice down the old B.A. trail for some illegal camping. So named for the memory of a lawdog gal pulling out a reefer and seducing me in a purely Egyptian manner there amongst the reeds and the creek. So, the dog days and the fires continued on…the Lucky fire, the Fizzle, the Overnighter, and on and on.

One of my fave Buck memories occurred on the Fly fire. Somehow or another, I got to fly solo and for some reason, Buck flew out a bit later. We had taken to wearing feathers in our ball caps during the daily routines around the station. This prompted a "No feathers" memo from the official powers that be (read as BJ). Anyhow, here comes park helicopter 210, flying in with Buck. As Buck gets out of the ship, both sides of his hardhat loomed with big old wild turkey feathers. Together with his dark flight goggles, Buck resembled a big fly, antennae's and all, complete with a huge shit eating grin. Pilot Curly Red was in stitches as he bid adieu and 210 lifted off. I was fetal with laughter on the Ponderosa needles, while Buck, the human fly, was leaning over me just grinning and grinning. The fire was a piece of cake that we had lined and put out within the hour. The windy evening with a prediction for red flag warnings predicated our quick actions despite Billie Joe's protestations. Justification was our following protocol as a red flag warning indicates critical fire weather was expected, so we did what we had to, we milked that puppy 'till morning with some exploratory recon hiking while enjoying some government fire cuisine ala beanie-n'-weanies.

On another front, it was at this time that Buck had fallen prey to the "Swiss Miss" who had popped up at one of our skidrow production dinners. The young enchantress showed up clad only in a towel, fresh from the shower room. Buck wasn't the only tree to fall that night. But he was the only one left as the others decomposed into dust. They had a week to enjoy the forested splendor together. After that party, the Iter and I took off on one of our favorite runs off road, up to Cottonwood Canyon (Utah). In the evening, the ruts were dark and hard to see coming in only to find us waking by a graveyard that I mistook for a corral (in the night). Escalante for breakfast at the Birkenstock Café, onto the Aquaries Plateau, Hell's Backbone, Death Hollow, the Box and other slick rock streamside places of wonder. And so summer passed her torch onto fall and those cool mornings and sunsets of September with my gal.

(Prof/Buck) Oh blah dee, oh blah da, life goes on

"Without music, life would be a mistake."
-Nietzsche

Word of our jam sessions/pot luck dinners at skid row palace began to escalate. We now had several guitars, a keyboardist (from the TW crew) myself blowing harp, and Buck on bongos and various weird assortments of percussion-like instruments. It was entertainment for all as we celebrated into the night (at least until 11 P.M. which was park quiet hour). Folks arrived bearing foods and fav drinks with regards to the designated themes (i.e.- Mexican, Greek, Italian, etc.). The Snake, our neighbor, was a great organizer and delegator, while his roomie, Robbins, was an amazing foodie, intellect and planner. Great flavors, amazing aromas, potent drinks, fabulous music and bizarre dancing, all packed into a tiny place amongst the aspens made for some memorable times.

One such theme was our Greek night. Stuffed grape leaves, souvlaki, baklava, grapes, olives, wines, and ouzo. Buck thought up the idea that we should all be in toga to truly honor the ancient culture. And thus we did. Carrying it a bit further, Buck had tricked Spider woman, now with TW management, into having a live band play at the saloon. Only, he didn't let her know that it was us. Our band of jammin' gypsies arrived early after the feast, thoroughly stuffed, warmed up and bearing togas (naked underneath). Spider woman argued against us being the band, and left to bring upper management in to kick us out. While she was gone, we boogied right into, *"SuzieQ"* and like a rehearsed event, a gorgeous tourist sitting near the band, jumps up and gushes that's her name! This gets a whole crowd up dancing. Nervous looks upon the management's faces disappeared as the tourists kept on buying six packs of Corona's and stacking them gratis for our entertainment. They were happy that money was being spent. A huge success indeed. A fun time by all in attendance. We inherited some groupies that night. Buck was last seen with a Swedish meatball, blonde, blue-eyed and killer accent. Yaa!

(Buck)-Our usual form of entertainment was visiting (people to socialize and places for hiking) or listening and playing music and finally by reading (swapping paperbacks). As a sense of community, when one of us would head down to either Flag (180 miles) or Page or Kanab, we would place a cooler, cash, and our list for groceries with the outgoing party. The Dove and Prof were the music afficieniados. Whenever they returned from civilization, they usually had some new tunes for their cassette player, and turned us on to the groove. Kathan had set up a successful cooperative where fresh veggies and now some fruit was available. The morels (mushrooms) that grew wild next to the Ponderosa's were quickly harvested for butter sauted dishes. In our close knit family we shared what we had and that was often in the form of potlucks. Socializing, we discussed different stories people were reading. Any discarded newspaper (usually USA Today) however old was still news to us. Some of the novels circulating that summer were: various Hillerman mysteries, <u>Lonesome Dove</u>, <u>Milagro Beanfield War</u>, and <u>Clan of the Cave Bear</u> series. Re-reading Abbey was always a ritual, especially the classic, <u>Monkey Wrench Gang</u>.

(Prof)- As days grew shorter, the Iter and I got back to the palace at sunset. The note on my bed this one particular eve said, "Powell tomorrow, monitoring. Saloon tonight, Corona's." So, filling the dog's bowl with Gravytrain, I jumped back into Bertha, and headed down to the saloon. It was a slow Sunday. A couple of tour-ons, a few wranglers, and Buck along with Kathan and Margerite hanging out.

"So, where have you been stranger?" Margerite asked as Buck handed me a cold one. "Out with the Iter in slick rock land." noncommittally.

"Well, you could stop by some evening and have dinner on my tab." she smiled.
"Now you tell me!" as I laughed and felt funny inside thinking that seasonal life is hard on one's love life. I was in my last months of the seasonal mental state. Thoughts of where to go next for employment, the goodbyes, and postponing them in one's mind all added up to be different for each individual.

Margerite was headed to the Everglades, where a lot of canyon TW folk go come winter, the big tourist season there. Even some smoke bums venture out there for the saw grass control burns. Personally, I try not to go east of the Mississippi.

I took a sip of my Corona and looked at Margerite. Her raven tresses and smoldering blue eyes were always a joy to get lost in. "Uh-oh, not that sense again. In love again, are we professor?" as my thoughts swirled.
"I'd like it if you would stay tonight at my place with me," feeling my desire starting to burn with her request.
"Okay," I smiled, to which she gave me a kiss.

Buck and Kathan turned around.
"Powell for four days." voiced the Buck.
"So Dave can come back home from there. I start teaching in a week." Kathan informed me, and asked, "How's Iter?"
"Wonderful, we had a good lost weekend in Utah." I answered.
"Where?" Buck wondered.
"Secret." while taking a pull of my Corona and Margerite's fingers tantalized my ear. Buck finished his beer, Kathan got off her stool.
"We're off." Buck announced, while Kathan gave me a hug.
"Night." she said.
"Morning." Buck barked.
"Later." I laughed with five fingers driving me crazy. I gave Margerite a long kiss or should I say, we both indulged with passionate intensity.
Lips departed, I quipped, "Devil."
"Angel." I saw a light in her eyes and knew she was right.
"Angel." finishing my Corona and we walked back to skid row, hand in hand under the bright moon.

Part Five-
The Homestretch

(Prof) Fall

"The best and most beautiful things in this world cannot be seen or even touched. They must be felt with the heart."
-Helen Keller

The typical fall usually arrives at the North Rim somewhere in September. The first indication is that thermals, as in the underwear kind, are needed to offset the morning chill. Away from the rim's edge, the inner gorge's warming influence is lessened. Shorter daylight signifies aspen, in the first grips of frost, to start their colorful sojourn from green to golden hues. Cool breezes accompany clear skies. For the most part the tourist flow slows, while a lull in the fire season begins, which makes this a really fine time to enjoy the canyon.

September arrived with another lightning bust on Powell Plateau. The fire was initial attacked by the team of Deano and Tex, who by themselves contained it with a single scratch line. That action kept the fire out of the Muav Saddle and Teddy Roosevelt's hunting cabin. To add reinforcements, the Wad and I joined them for a night before they departed. It was an evening that smoke and fire were talked about, dreamed about, lived and breathed about. Thirty-five seasons of fire amongst us. Many stories were shared of times like this.

I can't remember all the specific tales told that night. What I do remember is my walk alone to visit with the flames while the stars burned overhead. With my headlamp and Pulaski, I took off following the line along the the fires edge from the helispot and our camp. I'd spent quite a few nights on the line and on fires in general, but Powell was always my favorite experience. These flames could dance and that they did, casting a spell on the pines, while thrusting their high pulsating flickers and... damn, words are hard to find to completely describe this phenomena unless you've experienced it. Suppose you were dancing to your favorite song with the person of your dreams, and you were their dream person as well. Nothing could feel more right, more beautiful, more joined, than that bond. Likewise, the bond born between lightning and pine, of sun and earth, is one of nature. Such was the spectacle I witnessed. Upon my return to the others, I tried to explain my feelings. The Wad and Deano could only laugh.
"What was burning out there anyway?" the Wad smiled, knowing my sacramental inclinations.

"Hey now." I laughed.

"That's why we're here anyway." Deano somberly went on, "That magic of nature."

"Amen!" echoed Tex.

"Cheers!" I hollered, raising my tin cup of hobo, or should I say, smoke bum coffee. We all took a sip and the stories were passed until one by one we crawled off into our bags.

Morning came and wafting my nose was the smell of bacon frying, followed by potatoes cooking in bacon grease, with onions, and upon inspection, lots of peppers: red, green, and yellow. Cooking everything until well blackened, eggs were scrambled in followed by bread chunks tossed into the whole shebang and voila, a hearty breakfast, washed down with hot, gritty, smoke hobo coffee. Morning also brought 210 with Dana, taking Deano and Tex to a smolder report and telling us that the Wad would be office bound tomorrow and replaced with a forest service legend, the "Mad Cat Killer" of Williams. More commonly known as Bill Campbell, the story begins that he was infuriated by the number of cats that were killing birds in his yard. To remedy the situation he took quick and decisive action. Bill rid the whole east side of town of over forty felines. It would have been more had it not been for a Hazel Wardlow notifying the papers, so the story goes. I would be getting a chance to meet the infamous guy soon.

(Prof) A tale of two plateaus

It would be our last fire together. Not knowing that at the time, it was with a bit of melancholy loading up Len (Wad) and his gear into 210 to fly back to the South Rim.

"Have fun Boomer." he smiled to me while strapping into the harness up front with Dana.

""Always!" I answered, moving off at a forty-five degree angle to the front of the ship in that helitack crouch. 210 lifted into the blue and Dana's voice crackled on my handset, "Dispatch, 210 enroute from Powell Fire to South Rim with one."

"210, dispatch copies, 0734 hours."

I pulled my radio off my hip and on crew net, added, "Happy Trails!"

"Click, click." my radio answered back.

Turning around to help Bill with the gear he'd unloaded, I introduced myself, "Professor Canyon."

"Bill Campbell, good to meet ya."

"Likewise."

"How's the fire going?"

"Slow and steady." I replied, thinking he doesn't look like a homicidal cat killer, rather more like a grade school teacher (clean, kind, pleasant). Hmmmm! As I unloaded the gear in addition to the case of meals-ready-to-eject (MRE's) another case had been stashed away underneath. This one was twenty-four canned beers. Quickly doing the math of four campfire beers a piece for a three night stay and things were brewing up. "Then they better get us the hell out of here." Bill joked with a now cat killer look in his gleaming eyes as I handed him the case.

Like a raven, I replied, "Aww, Awwwww!" (but thinking how would he react if I mewed like a cat, "Meowww!).

We settled into a fire monitor's routine of hourly weather collecting and fire behavior observations such as: flame lengths, the amount of duff consumed, rate of spread, etc. Those days on Powell were like paid vacation to this smoke bum.

Day three awoke me with the radio cackling, "North Rim heliport, we have a smoke report." in a new honey-laden voice.

"North Rim." answered Buck.

"Prepare to copy legal." the honey beckoned.

"10-4"

After giving township, she continued with, "range eight east, southwest quarter, section six."

"North Rim copies, I'll give you a landline from the pit." informed Buck in his best radio voice.

"Fire dispatch copies."

Sure enough Bill and I could see a small faint tendril of wispy white smoke from Walhalla plateau according to the legal we plotted on our map.

"Looks like they can drive to it." stated Bill, scanning the map.

"Gravy." I dolled back.

I should say a bit about Walhalla, which could be considered Powell Plateau's east side twin. However, there is a lone stretch of asphalt on the plateau headed out to Cape Royal, a scenic viewpoint. It's also a beautiful drive. Walhalla is home to impressive Ponderosa glades, though a bit younger than Powell's giants. Stephen Pyne chronicles the saga of some prescribed burns there in his book, "Fire on the Rim, that created quite a few fire sculptures. In fact while Stephen was working on his book and spending a couple weeks with the crew, he and I got sent out to Walhalla, where we played a bit with fire, cutting out mini burn plots. It was a day that I'll always treasure. The memory that stays with me of Pyne was an indefinable childlike essence. Maybe that was his love of fire, his passion so amply stated in Fire on the Rim.

On our final day of monitoring, as we looked on and our fire continued its' mellow dance, dispatch informed us, "a backcountry unit will be driving out to Swamp Point to meet you at 1700," and it wasn't in a honey's voice. So Bill and I packed up our necessities and proceeded to hike across Muav Saddle to the waiting government vehicle. No one was home at the skidrow palace, other than Iter, who was as happy to see me as I was her, performing that holy ritual that dog lovers play: food and a walk. Getting back to the palace, I noticed there was still time for a cerveza at the saloon. Maybe I'd run into Margerite, and we'd have the palace to ourselves later while everybody was out at the fire on Walhalla.

<u>**(Prof) Into the arms**</u>

Leaving Iter and feeling a bit guilty, I told her to "stay," which she always did while I left. Off to the saloon I ventured, parking at the far end of the lot to steal a toke with that high full moon. Basking in the glow, I enjoyed the trail view along the rim as the moon shadows cast on the world below. *I'm being followed by a moonshadow, moon shadow-moon shadow,"* humming in my head the old Cat Stevens song. Now I had to check out the veranda scene of the canyon glow before heading into the saloon.

Approaching the watering hole, the juke box was going full tilt, sounding like there was quite a party on. As I neared, Jerry Jeff was singing, *"...kicking hippies asses and raising hell…"*

Opening the doors, my mind went, "What the ..!"
"Professor!" shouted Buck, standing on a barstool clad in dirty Nomex, suspenders dangling. And there were the rest of the Longshots, along with Deano, Albert, the Wad, Slim, all my smoke bum friends. A big, glorious smile burst upon my bearded face. A pause in the juke box and Buck began...
"You know what I like in the morning when I wake up?" shouted from his barstool perch to the crowd.
"What?" responded the chorus shouting back, knowing all too well the routine.
"English muffins, nice ...and ....hot…mmmm, (he was milking it, play acting with sexual innuendo to this whole routine).
"Ohhh yeah" shouted the masses.
"Butter ooooozing down the cracks... and crevices..., nice... and slow...., mmmm…" emphasizing with pauses as Buck knew where these minds in the gutter were going.
"Yes, and yeah!" hollered the brave respondants.
"and some jam, yeah…" intoned Buck.
"What else?" as we played along.
"Some crisp... hash…browns… and…" further quipped Buck from on high.
"A blowjob!" someone hollered.
"No, although…hmmm, nice... later, but now I want my breakfast and some eggs. And... what else with those eggs? What else is missing?" implored Buck.
"BACON!" as we all shouted in unison and flopped down on the floor, where we all proceeded to flip, gyrate, sizzle, and curl (imitating bacon frying in a pan); otherwise acting ridiculous.

The tourists looked on bemused, as we rose to our feet. Cheap entertainment for the night.

"How about an ice cold Corona with a cool slice of lime?" came a sultry voice I'd been hoping to meet. Turning to face Margerite, I got a quick kiss before I could grab the Corona in her hand.

"I love the smell of smoke on you." she said while I leaned closer and plucked the Corona from her fingers.

Taking a swig, I replied, "That's why I go to them," in my best Bogie accent.

"Well, I've got to get the rest of these drinks to the dining room." as she got real close for an intimate kiss but then grabbed the tray from the bar with a, "See you later."

"You bet." I vowed and off into the arms of my smoke bum friends I went.

As I reached them, the Wad nodded, "Hey Boomer." offering up his bottleneck.

I raised up mine in a clink and wondered aloud, "Who's at the fire?"

"A couple of forest service engines." answered Wad.

"And you'll be there at 0500." added Deano.

"I just got off one." I protested in vain feeling the heat from a quick kiss.

(Buck)-Not a great way to wake up

"Fools act on imagination without knowledge, pedants act on knowledge without imagination."
-Alfred North Whitehead

One particularly humorous story comes to mind with Jim and I on our off days in the fall. Backpacking down into the canyon on an old packer trail from decades ago, a remote back country place with a waterfall and trout in the stream was our destination. Upon our successful arrival, we set camp, caught some trout for dinner cooked over a small fire, and settled down to our sleeping bags in the dry, southwestern, cool evening breeze. As the stars shined overhead, our campfire diminished below us by the stream. Comfy, cozy, curled up in my bag, I munched a granola bar for a snack while reading a book Jim loaned me, "Cudjo" by Stephen King. It was about this monstrous type of killer dog-beast. Anyway, I had fallen asleep, with crumbs on my beard, when I felt something wet, cold, licking my face. Awakening, I saw two, huge eyeballs only inches from me. We were in classic mountain lion country, and so I gave out a huge yell, while at the same time, jumping up in the air, and flailing myself wildly. These yells, whoops, hollers, and upon my galloping crazy movements had the effect of getting Jim not only up, but skedaddled up the boulders to higher ground. I ran after him, for fear of my life where I was camped out. We both ran, climbed, and rushed about forty yards before we stopped, looked back and quietly, secretly, ventured back. Stealthily, we returned, inspecting our site, specifically mine. Above my sleeping bag in a small pinyon pine tree was a creature I had never seen before. Larger than a house cat, with a long raccoon tail, cat face and ears, it had two huge eyes.

It was called a ring-tailed cat, a common creature in canyon country. It must have been cleaning my face of the crumbs that littered my beard from the granola bar I munched on earlier. Reading that horror book also factored in to my subconscious as all I could think of was being attacked by a killer animal. Then there was the memory of the mountain lion crossing in front of our engine on a smoke filled fire road just the week before. The lessons I learned were several: not to eat while in bed, especially camped outdoors and especially with wildlife like lions and bears around. Oh my! Another was I should choose what I wish to read in certain situations. But most importantly, not to panic in situations even when I think the worst. Oh how the prof laughed at that one for a long time.

(Prof) What a great way to wake up, Awww!

Like the flaming golden-orange aspens for one last climax, September's end brought us together to complete our mission, full cycle. Among the closing out projects awaiting us was hazard tree removal from the developed area to keep cabins and people from suffering the calamity of nature and gravity. Then, there was always the bucking and splitting of trees for fire wood. The wood would be stacked for the winter caretakers, like Rolo at the wastewater plant, who had stayed at least a half dozen winters. Some of the wood went to the historic entrance cabin for incoming winter skiers. We also had to order equipment and supplies for the next fire season, no matter how dreadful the thought of working for Billy Joe appeared.

Notified by the naturalist division that our monthly amphitheater presentation for the campers complete with slides, fashion show, and Ken's flamethrower demonstration (appropriately titled: *"Pyro-romanticism"*) was now over. Aww-well. There was still the year end inventory to be taken and the pickling of the cache. Slowly, we were down to a skeleton crew in both the park and T.W. concession employees.

Just as I was walking into the fire pit to ask Buck if we should hit the roads one last time before pickling the saws, the phone rang. Buck picked it up, "Fire pit, Buck here."
Pause, "Yeah, yeah," pause, "yeah," pause, "tomorrow, okay." Buck placed the phone rather firmly back in place with a, "Hmm." escaping his black bearded lips.
"That good." I commented upon my entrance.
Buck turned to face me, "Billie Joe wants us on the South Rim tomorrow afternoon for a farewell chat before we're laid off on Sunday."
"Yeah!" was all I could muster forgetting why I came in.
"Let's grab the saws and hit the roads." commanded a now grinning Blackbeard. This old red beard grinned right on back.

I woke up the next morning with Margerite and Iter curled up on both sides of me, outside underneath an aspen grove in a fern laden ground covering. We'd taken our bedding out underneath the stars after a somewhat private dinner of chili and cornbread with Buck and Molly in yee olde skidrow palace. Dove was gone, back in school at Flagstaff, a destination that I was thinking of. Nice mountain town, college scene for youthful vibrancy, great location for quick escapes, good music, and best of all, many good folks that I already know wintering there.

"Awwwk!" shrieked a raven, stirring me from myself and dreamland. I stroked the Iter with my free hand, feeling her stretch while giving Margerite's tresses a brush of a kiss as they lay by my lips and thought, "What a great way to wake up!"

Sitting up and getting dressed, I heard Buck in the palace calling out to me, "Coffee's on!"

(Prof) The Last of the Fun Bunch

"Everybody who read the Jungle Book
Knows that Riki Tiki Tavi's a mongoose who kills snakes
When I was a young man I was led to believe
There were organizations to kill my snakes for me
i.e., the church, i.e., the government, i.e., the school
But when I got a little older I learned how to kill them myself

I said, 'I need to get Riki Tiki, mongoose is gone'
Riki Tiki Tavi, mongoose is gone
Won't be coming around for to kill your snakes, no more my love
Riki Tiki Tavi, mongoose is gone

People walking around, they don't know what they're doing
They been lost so long, they don't know what they're looking for
Well, I know what I'm looking for but I just can't find it
I guess I gotta look inside of myself some more"
-Donovan

We decided to take a government van to the South Rim. Ken, Buck, Tex, the Fox, Tack and myself were piled in. Buck was driving and I was riding shotgun. I'd been somewhat silent which he noticed, saying as we pulled into Cameron for Navajo taco's, "What's on your mind, old man?"
Just stewing with, "Billie Joe might not like to know." I curtly answered. Buck was silent as we got out of the van, until he shared the song echoing in his head,

"...There's a calm before the storm,

I know, it's been coming for some time..."

(by John Fogerty, *"Have you ever seen the rain?"*).

Ever since we'd gotten in that van to go see Billie Joe, a pressure had been mounting in me. My good friend, Slim (Tim) was an uneasy soul to get along with, and perhaps, because of this Billie Joe had ranted with him on numerous occasions what he thought of the Longshots. I'd kept most of what Slim passed along to myself. So much had happened and was already out in the open why make matters worse? But one thing that Billie Joe had said about me kept coming back repeatedly in my conscience. Perhaps there was some truth to it. Hmm! I was mulling it over.

"Be who you are and say what you feel because those who mind don't matter and those who matter don't mind."
-Dr. Seuss

When the van deposited us, the Longshots took up residence at the fire barracks. Disillusionment had spread like a wildfire. The boiling point had been reached. Curly Red, Deano, Slim and the Wad were all there with a bottle of whiskey to help loosen up the demons in the commons room. The bottle was passed around and around…

I was 'feeling my oats' by the time B.J. showed up with light pleasantries exchanged. Not wasting time, I got right down to it, trying to keep my emotions in check, asking Billie Joe, "So, what did you think of this fire season?"
Billie Joe cocked his head in a questioning manner, similar to a dog, not to insult a mutt's intelligence mind you, just to use an analogy.

B.J. proceeded to ramble, "Oh, busiest fire season in park history, busier than…" and on and on for a few minutes droning while his blood red eyes were darting around nervously.

As soon as he dwindled out of words, I continued my line of attack, "So, did you learn anything?"

His eyes danced around for someone else to respond, yet no one did, so he finally answered, "Yeah, I learned a lot. Busiest season in park history, did I mention that?" and he popped open a can of Bud.

Someone handed me the bottle of Kesslers, I took a chug, passing it on to Buck, who was grinning. I turned back to Billie Joe and asked, "Did you learn anything from us?"

B.J. took another gulp of his beer, looked down and away, mumbling, "Well, perhaps…" and then while taking another swig, Buck chuckled, and B.J. just looked at me.

"So I heard you say that if I just kept my mouth shut, I might learn something!" I emotionally let loose.

"You can't talk to me like that!"
"The hell I can't!" I plausibly answered as Billie Joe turned and ran from the room.

"You chicken-shit!" the Fox yelled out as Deano went in pursuit of B.J.

"I just wanted him to own up." I said to no one in particular as the bourbon made the rounds again. Deano came back minutes later and told us B.J. would meet with us individually the next morning. He never did.

"Dear Mr. Fantasy, play us a tune

Something to make us all happy

Do anything, take us out of this gloom

Sing a song, play guitar, make it snappy."
-Steve Winwood with Traffic (Dear Mr. Fantasy)

We all went to the Wad's and partied there before heading out to the pub, the Bright Angel, and El Tovar. While we were over there someone took a Polaroid of the Longshots: Buck, Tex, Tack, the Fox, Curley Red, the Wad, Ken and myself with whiskey bottle in hand. The last of a dying breed.

"If you don't stand for something, you will fall for anything."
-author unknown

The next day, Sunday, saw us at the El Tovar for a crew breakfast of prime rib hash followed by a quiet ride back to the North Rim for the final pickling of the cache. When it got near to 1800 and time to sign out for the season, Buck took our crew picture down, writing on it, "the last of the fun bunch," before hanging it back. The hall of flames wall in our fire pit was a historical depiction of crews from seasons past. A dedication, a legacy, and a tribute to all Longshots dating back to Pyne's reign.

Grabbing his radio (at Ken's urging) Buck somberly began, "Dispatch, North Rim Longshots."
"Dispatch, go ahead." as a honey-laden voice seductively drawled.
"Dispatch, the Longshots are out of service for the season."
"Dispatch copies, 1800."
Radio clicks went on repeatedly for minutes over the air in response. Tears were streaming down from his face.

There was no looking back. Not knowing this at the time, it was the last transmission ever from the Longshots.

Only forward now to the survivor's party that night. And then the road.

<u>**(Prof) To the Longshots**</u>

"Dance

As though no one is watching you,

Love

As though you have never been hurt before,

Sing

As though no one can hear you,

Live

As though heaven is on earth"
-Souza

Survivors! From the opening on the North Rim when the road is first accessible through the snow plows, to the leaves falling dusted by a winters blanket, we were the survivors. Our reward now was the sun room, down at the Grand Lodge, overlooking the incredible spectacle of a canyon. Our own private dance floor for us to boogie.

Mister Dukes, the blues king from Flag, was the band this time around. I threw my harps in my daypack as Buck and I loaded one cooler full into the back of his pickup. Bending down, I tied my favorite red silk bandana around Iter's neck. She looked proud and happy to be going to a party.
"Can you handle this blaze?" offered Molly passing me a burning spliff.
"Si, senorita!" passing her a cold Corona, while Buck looked on waiting for his cerveza.
"You're driving." I joked, reaching down and handing him a cold one.
Molly and Margerite squeezed between us and off we went with the Iter on our laps.
"Aww Awwk!" laughed a raven, evermore!

Tommy Dukes was hot and the dancing was as always, great! Tex met Kat, who had come up from Ganado, bringing mom and a friend, Uncle Lester with them. Uncle Lester, along with the Grateful Dead were to figure prominently in my life from the end of those eighties and on into the nineties. Kat's mom enjoyed the antics of Buck in his holey, ragged Levi's with red long johns peering from the rips. She also had her fun level cranked a notch as Buck escorted her atop a table to dance a few tunes. Meanwhile, Jake had been famously performing his hands dance. The guy could dance to tunes while balancing on two arms, moving his hands along the floor. The Dove was there with his favorite recipe, a tall blonde. A rag was cut by everyone, from the Ancient Mariner of the trail crew to Dimwit of the law dogs. After sittin' in with Mr. Dukes for some breakneck blues, Margerite pulled me outside for some veranda passion.

I remember my whispering words, while entwined, "I wish I could make you some kind of promise."

"I never asked for any." Margerite gently replied, planting a slow, wet, passionate kiss on my lips. Looking me in the eyes with a goddess smile and wisely speaking, "Let's see where next summer brings us."

"I couldn't say it any better." my response with a hug attached, followed by a kiss, while the twin doors of the veranda burst open.

Out came Buck, Molly, the Fox, Tex, Ken, the Wad, Jenni, Curly Red, and others.

"Thought you both might need something cold." offered Buck, handing Margerite and myself a couple of Corona's. With that done, Buck proclaimed, "To the Longshots!" and we all raised our glasses and bottles in salute.

"To the North Rim!" I added loudly as the tears in my eyes flowed.

"Yeah boy-howdy!" Molly and Margerite drawled.

We all drank up and danced 'till we couldn't dance no more!

"...Can a youth, a man, do more wisely than to go where his life is to be found?..."

-Thoreau

Epilogue

(Buck) And so we ramble

Like the seasons changing, so go lives with the opening and closing of the North Rim. Collectively, due to the new fire mismanaging officer and his ineptness, dishonesty, and lack of leadership, we the Longhots of North Rim fame and honor retired the logo (designed by Gussie and Wad) and the name (with Wad's permission). There would be future North Rim fire crews but never would it be the elite and fabled Longshots, left only for the history books. We could not carry any further the Longshot tradition (steeped in professionalism) hanging under a new command with the antics of an idiot for a leader. His name and reputation was a joke everywhere; he was an incompetent. He was allowed to stay on and manage due to his stature as a permanent employee where firings were rare to non-existent, the nature of the game.

However the tale continued with the friendship of Professor Canyon and Buck. Both very different individuals, they remained united by a brethren of experiences shared together. Young at heart, yet broken in spirit after the tragedies and heartache from the previous fire season, but like the phoenix arising, they would too. Like that spark smoldering in duff, the fire brand re-ignited in the the magic and aura of the North Rim of the Grand Canyon once again. Exploding with passion in the adventure of life many of the same characters returned, if only to relate the next chapters of their journey onward. Reunited, it was with gusto and vigor, and the now, for we don't look back, ever! And...
"Never say never."
-The Wad (r.i.p.)

(Buck's) Foray

"Strange days have found us
Strange days have tracked us down
They're going to destroy
Our casual joys

We shall go on playing
Or find a new town"
-The Doors

The Longshot fire season and career done, I took off, European bound with a German gal. She had long dark hair, big brown eyes, athletic legs, and yes, a yearning for adventure. The fact that she loved the outdoors was just what the professor ordered. Europe was fun. Traveling on trains by night and exploring during the days. Hiking the alps, touring villages, and enjoying the locals while living the Bohemian lifestyle was a splendid respite from the previous crazy fire season.

Refreshed and renewed from Europe, it was time to be thinking of another spring and making some money to live. Calls came in, like Alaska BLM, for a strike team leader. I was to fly in a fixed wing craft and determine from the air whether to let fires below burn or get personnel on them. Since I had never set foot in Alaska, I hesitated with the thought that one could have so much authority from the lower 48. Remembering my manzanita blow up in California chapparel, I figured I would get time to learn the local fuels. Upon further contemplation and thoughts of BJ from Grand Canyon days and his mismanagement from relying upon the air and computers, my decision was clear to turn down this offer. I couldn't and wouldn't ruin the lives of people for the sake of ego satisfaction. Even though the title and pay was an advancement, there was that Longshot pride of quality and honest work emitting inner peace. When the Hotshots contacted me I thought that would be a good fit. Needing my head cleared out from the previous season, the hotshot experience was fantastic for some big fires and grueling work.

"To our families and friends, we're crazy. Why do we want to be away from home so much, work such long hours, risk our lives, and sleep on the ground 100 nights a year? Simply, it's the most fulfilling thing any of us have ever done...We don't just call ourselves hotshots, we are hotshots in everything that we do."
-Michael Kodas in <u>Megafire,</u> pg. 256 (quoting Granite Mountain Hotshot leader, Eric Marsh).

I think that quote speaks for all of us that have been there. There were over a hundred shot crews throughout the nation, almost all out west. Many that I had worked alongside with or had been on strike teams with in the past were outstanding and exemplary in every manner. I didn't get to pick where and for whom I would work. My file was in a general bank of potential employees. Background checks, a phone call interview and I was headed on my way to an exciting summer. It was a good season (for us as firefighters) and that meant that we made lots of "oats," or overtime. It was bad if you were going places that burned. Case in point, Tex and Kat got hitched earlier in the spring and were honeymooning it by trekking and camping out west. When they arrived to Yosemite, it was closed due to the firestorm sweeping the park (incidentally, I was on those fires at the time). It was quite an adventure filled season with ground pounding experiences throughout the nation. By the end of our run, my hips were deteriorating with bone on bone grinding, alleviated by eating ibuprofen like candy. The positives were plenty and that was my focus.

After that season, chief Gussie called me again to head up the new resource crew back on the North Rim for the following year. It was to be another magical mystery tour. But first there was another off season...

<u>**(Buck) End of the line**</u>

By this time, my hip bone was popping out of socket daily, dislocating, and causing excruciating pain. The long brown hair steady gal that had befriended me over the years and had been wanting to get serious was supposedly waiting down south in Cal. Finally thinking about settling down with one girl turned into an awakening experience. However my timing was off, as she moved on with another by my arrival.
Next stop, Flagstaff, to find old friends, cure the heartache, and alleviate the pain.

<u>**(Buck) Flagstaff**</u>

"Wilderness raft guides of the '70's and '80's were often...lovers of freedom with a healthy distrust of rules...somehow hiding out from the increasingly urban, fast-paced latter 20th century. Many felt they should have been born into a time with more elbow room, a time in which a man could build a good life from raw materials and honest sweat, call it his own, and fine print be damned."
-Jo Deurbrouck (from <u>Anything worth doing...)</u>

Bumping into Professor Canyon at the Orpheum, a reunion fest was in order. In a few days a private party was heading down the Grand Canyon for three weeks of wet and wild Colorado River fun. It was the Prof, Tex and myself along with some TW Phantom folk, a Kaibab forester, and some Canadian river runners needing to fill three, 16 foot boats with a crew for their winter permit. Similar in mind, we were up for being a working crew. Rowing the boats and learning the oars, reading the river, and working together as a unit was an exhilarating experience. An epic adventure. A rush at times, captivating always, it opened a whole new world for me (as I gravitated towards this new thrill seeking adventure). This winter trip would allow us to experience the entire canyon for three weeks to ourselves. Self-sufficent, rugged determinism, survival instinct, and cooperation, made our awe inspiring event a success.

Each morning in the cold, shaded canyon, we would slowly don our wetsuits that had collected frost overnight. Usually camped at rapids, we would shove off early and get splashed with the 45 degree water upon our faces getting a nasil douce treatment. A slap in the face greeting that screamed out, "How the fuck are you today, my friend?" Baptized into the allure and aura of this magnificent historical canyon carved by this powerful river before us with such reverence was providential. We endured capsizing, broken oars, sleeting winds, and other hardships.

At Upset Rapid we flipped and I got wrapped underneath the boat in the ropes. It was a close call. I struggled to untangle myself while underwater, fast paced, barely able to hold my breath any further. Suddenly, like a big hand pushing me from below, I emerged out momentarily next to the upturned boat as it eddied out but I continued being swept several miles downstream from everyone. Tripping along the bank trying to reach my party, wet, cold, shivering, in a hypothermic state, I remember how hard the simple task of walking became. They managed to get me some woolies, hot chocolate, and dry before getting my ass back out there (in the eddy) again to help with righting the boat and making frame adjustments from the flip.

On these trips we'd pack everything out that we brought in, so that meant we really had to have our shit together. Literally. It was a revolving duty that we took turns with each evening, setting up the "unit" and then breaking it down each morning. I won't bother you with the shitty details. Boiling and disinfecting water for cooking, cleaning, and drinking were other nightly shared rituals. Yet, through all this, we found ourselves working together cooperatively, contributing during meals and learning about each other. With no receptions down here (in the wilderness) for any distractions, dark came quickly and morning was first light in the sky above. We'd found our strengths among ourselves for different tasks and proceeded as a unit, very similar to the cohesiveness that was formed during our season on the rim above. Other mishaps occured: breaking an oar in the rapids at Crystal, another one at Upset, losing one at Lava, and our bag of clothes and tent soaked due to a poor job sealing it before another flip. Our conditions weren't always ideal; wind driven sleet in our faces as we pushed on the oars for a 20 mile day to camp was grueling. But we were rewarded: layover days to explore hidden side canyons, Anasazi ruins, sandy beaches to ourselves, and Rainbow trout to catch. More so, our souls could rest in the solitude that such a cathedral as the Grand Canyon provides; truly a religious experience. We prayed for our lives at several rapids but most notably at Lava, trying a left run, but not making it entirely, and going more center, and thus getting swallowed up, our entire 16 foot boat, dropping down and out of sight into the hole. Only to be catapulted out. Water, air, looking skyward, liquid speed, it was an "E" ticket. What a ride. We were all stoked. Our fearless leader, Cap Roy, lost one of his oars resulting in a 360 through the rapids for their ride. After all our runs through Lava, we made early camp ten miles further down at Whitmore. Celebration. Jubilation. Inebriation. Champagne, wine, beer, goon juice. Cheers to life! It was a fitting stop for the Prof and myself (Tex could only join us for half the trip, hiking out at Phantom). A time for reflections from our seasons past, lessons learned, friendships solidified, and futures discussed.

A few months later, many of the North Rim faithful reunited for a week long cross country ski trek. Winter snows typically piling over six feet blanketed and closed the North Kaibab road from the Jacob Lake outpost in the forest, sixty miles away from the North Rim. The only access at this time was: skiing, hiking across from the South Rim, or (to the skeleton crew left behind to maintain winter operations in the cabins) a helicopter, if conditions were favorable. We decided to trek in this winter wonderland of snow covered pines, skeleton aspens, and high country meadows dressed in white. No other sounds except the swish of our ski's below us. Peaceful, tranquil, and exhilarating, the twenty plus mile first ski day was invigorating. Sharing the trail blazing, food distribution, and camp set up, we found ourselves easily entertained with each other's company in the evenings. Stories were told, Laurel and the Dove leading mostly there, legends revealed, as Jake and Robbins shared, and entertainment in the wilderness was easy to come by. Our senses were awakened by our intimacy with nature. An owl hooting from a nearby tree, while the moon's glow cast light upon snow crystals glistening in the surrounding landscape. Everyone kept close to the ancestral campfire for warmth. Wood crackling in the burn as flames danced, mesmerizing us into a quiet reflective mood. First night's camp was a variation of some making snow caves, while most of us pitched a large four season tent under the boughs of a large Ponderosa and huddled in for a crowded night of snores, farts, and coughs.

Our second day began overcast and freezing, but the great gliding action atop the crusted snow packed meadows would allow us a thirty mile trek. Beginning to spread out, we went into our meditative trances ("the zone") that so often happens when in the natural world. Taking in the majesty amongst the towering giants surrounding us, a surreal world of silence, only interrupted briefly by our breaths of laboring movement. The Dove had invited a ranger friend along from Rainier on this outing, and his other career was as an opera singer in Seattle. Wow, it was a treat to listen to his rich, tenor voice reverberating across the open expanses as we skied on invigorated by the experience.

Second night and we made it to the vacated entrance cabin at the North Rim. All of us packed in like sardines, sleeping bags this way and that, curled around the wood burning stove. Cozy, warm, and sheltered nicely, Laurel had sprung on us a treat that she had been saving for such a special occasion, a dessert that she made, grasshopper pie. Her instructions to us were straightforward and simple: sit and gather around the pie, spoon in extended hand, and at her command, dig in and eat away. It didn't last long; by my second scooping, nothing but morsels existed, but man, what a treat and burst of sugar high that was. Simple pleasures.

Our third day greeted us with a surprise visit by Rolo and Tom, one of the winter maintenence crew in two snowmobiles with sleds for storage. These were normally used in case of a dire need to exit the rim (for food, supplies, emergency, etc.) if conditions made a helicopter visit hazardous. A welcomed break as we unloaded our 40 pound packs on the sled, and just focused upon our technique. Another dozen miles, with particular attention to "heartbreak hill," a real cardio blast of energy, before we ascended upon the housing units. Winterized, fully supplied, and wood fire blazing, we entered the comfy housing of Rolo and his honey, to share some floor space for a night, a meal, songs, drink, and friendship. Just like summers, the Dove strummed acoustically various tunes as we sipped libations and huddled around the warming fire. All was good, and there was a peaceful, easy feeling.

On our fourth day (according to original plans we'd still be skiing in, but due to favorable conditions and no white outs) we explored our summer haven now draped deep in her winter hibernation. Seeing the few hardy souls was welcoming. It was a crew of six, with Dim still heading the law up there, while mostly others maintained structures and made repairs. For our final night we all gathered in the now vacant lodge, extra expansive with the furnishings all piled in a corner and covered, exposing the handsome wooden floors. Lounging around with popcorn, sleeping bags, and a television/vcr to view, "The Shining"; an appropriate flick for the skeleton crew left behind in isolation for the winter. Many jokes were made that night and well wishes cast out to the remaining colleagues, but morning came early as we were on our downward plunge into the chasm of the Grand. Upon descent, the snows quickly disappeared to the rock layers that revealed geologic time. Shedding winter clothes to shorts, ski's strapped to our packs, our fourteen plus mile hike down to Phantom awaited us. From our previous river trip we had made some friends working down at the bottom of this big ditch. Putting us up for the night, sharing more stories, a great spaghetti fest complimented with French bread, salad, and boxed vino, we enjoyed a common bond with these fellow wanderers. For our upward trek the next day we headed out in darkness upon the trail for the seven mile and several thousand feet climb to the South Rim world. A foot of snow greeted us at the top. Temperatures dictated winter clothing again. For a final farewell, we all headed to the Maswick for some dancing as a band was playing. Jake, in true fashion, was on a handstand dancing amongst us, too tired he claimed to take any more punishment on his aching feet. It was a good trip, a good time, with good people.

Upon our return to civilization, we took in the Flagstaff scene. I returned to school to pursue another degree. The Dove was there likewise. Tex and Kat were in the neighboring town. Canyon was incommunicado to scout new lands to explore, play music, and work odd jobs. Jake the Snake became one of my new roomies in a house we rented with some others. And then there was this river goddess. A Canyon guide, and damn good one. She was living downstairs from our place up above. Isn't life Grand?

"When is a man educated?
When he can look out upon the universe, now lucid and lovely, now dark and terrible,
with a sense of his own littleness in the great scheme of things, and yet have faith and
courage. When he knows how to make friends and keep them, and above all, when he
can keep friends with himself.

When he can be happy alone and high minded amid the drudgeries of life. When he can
look into a wayside puddle and see something besides mud, and into the face of the most
forlorn mortal and see something divine.

When he knows how to live, how to love, how to hope, how to pray--is glad to live…and
has in his heart a bit of song."
-Joesph Fort Newton

(Buck/Prof) Meanderings

"Whatever does not destroy me makes me stronger."
-Frederich Nietzsche

(Buck)- Tex, Prof and myself returned to the rim over the next two seasons, none of us
in fire. I took the temporary position of resource protection leader with Tex as my
assistant. We were thrilled to be working under Gussie, and we had an assortment of
interesting projects. Hazard tree reductions in the developed area, restoring eroded trails
and constructing wooden railings to restrict vehicles off fragile vegetation.

A couple of incidents were noteworthy. The new fire crew hired under BJ's supervision
had totally dismantled the fire cache. In disarray, it was a confusion of parts, tools,
equipment scattered and strewn about. I was forlorn, as former cache and saw manager
in Longshot days, I organized and cross-referenced everything by common name and
part number, neatly labeled and accessible. No more, it was now a mess.

One morning while walking to the office for reports, I heard the dispatch cackle about a
North Rim emergency reported, a fire up on Walhalla Plateau. Tourists driving down the
road saw flames from the shoulder. Noticing the engines sitting out, unattended, fire
cache closed, and no one around, I asked Tex to track down anyone on the fire crew. No
luck, so we fired up the ol' engine, and took off down the road letting dispatch know that
the two active (still red-carded) resource personnel were responding to the fire in the
critical area.

Upon arrival, a small plane had crashed into the 80 feet tall Ponderosa's. Apparently
flying at night, the pilot plus one passenger, had cleared the rim at over 8,000 feet, but
had failed to account for the tall trees. Partly lying in the trees, other parts scattered
about the forest floor were the remains of plane and persons burned beyond recognition.

Flames engulfed over an acre and were rapidly spreading. Quickly, Tex and I pulled hose and put down a wet line to keep the flames from spreading further. At that instance, BJ's voice boomed over the radio to me to get the f*#k out of there. Further informing me that I was no longer on the fire crew and that I was not to ever respond without his prior approval. I reiterated that I had cleared with dispatch, tried locating fire crew to no avail, and was responding as an intracrew assist and active fire boss. BJ further demanded us to remove ourselves from the incident, and hike back (the eight miles) to the developed area, leaving the engine there as well as the fire. We continued to extinguish the flames with tourists pulled over on the road observing. Radio transmission instructed the patrol rangers to come out and tape the scene for an investigation as there was no medical emergency response required. The two of us hitched a ride back with some tourists, never seeing anyone from the fire crew respond as we departed.

Another sad incident was in the fire pit (office). The wall of flame (pictorial history) was removed and discarded, never to be found again. Years of pics from great crews and historical documentation, gone. Inquiries led to no answers. No one knew what happened. We could only guess.

Tex and I focused upon our resource jobs, some patrols as well as search and rescue responses (or so we thought). The powers to be had other plans. All fire was now out of our realms and the Longshots were retired. BJ approval for fires was a pre-requisite, and that meant kissing ass and BOHICA (bend over here it comes again)!

BOLO (be on the lookout). A young TW employee gal had gone missing and the call came out with a description and last whereabouts. After work while jogging trails, I came upon her, weak, and dehydrated. Giving her my water, and checking some vitals, all was stable. We walked slowly out together, talking to calm her shattered and scared ego. Upon arrival to my truck, I notified dispatch via radio of the situation and that the missing hiker was found. Then the call came back; I was to vacate the girl immediately, leave her at the trailhead until other rangers arrived. The reason given later was that I had not been checked out by the South Rim EMS director (whereby the previous seasons I was always utilized). This was getting confusing.

As resource leader, I instructed several underneath me. When a newbie arrived, a gal, one with no experience, and one that I trained that year, I was as always, only all too glad to assist. However, by the end of the season she was hired with permanant status to my still seasonal position. It was time to seek new employment. I was informed that my work ethic, experience, and attitude were all outstanding, it was just that I wasn't filling any quota's for the feds. It was time to move on. No hard feelings, but a sense of betrayal, as I was always under the impression, that the "best person for the job" would be the one hired and not to fill a "quota system" as the reason for employ.

Slowly, transformations began with new personnel throughout. The guard was changing. The animosity for taking a stand and supporting a "no-development" cause was appearing throughout the park towards its followers. Reigning from above, shit flowed downhill.

"Because the NPS system of recruitment, retention, and rewards is focused on the top layers of the organization, the integrity of virtually any program area, from administration to budget, from maintenance to fire management and suppression, resource management, and environmental stewardship itself, can be compromised by a single, powerful manager. This is particularly so in the case of a high-profile project..."
-Paul D. Berkowitz (The Case of the Indian Trader,p.72)

The North Rim held off development for a number of years, but eventually all good things come to pass.

"Man always kills the thing he loves, and so we the pioneers have killed our wilderness."
-Aldo Leopold (Sand County Almanac)

Chief Ranger Gussie moved on to higher ranks and then retired, only to pass away too early before enjoying the fruits of his dedicated, long, laborious service to the national parks. His beautiful and faithful wife Laurel following alongside him working the parks as he climbed to success. He was a good guy, always employing the best, and allowing those employed a free hand in dealing with situations, never micro-managing.

Rolo, left the North Rim for other parks.

Jake, left the Park Service, becoming a teacher.

Robbins, left the Park Service as well, becoming a noted author, editor, and contributor to many publications, books, and manuals on the Southwest natural areas.

Dove left the Park Service becoming a nutritionist.

(Prof) continues-

Slim (Tim) hanging out in the fire dorms, met a Belgian woman working at the Youth Hostel, just a few steps down through a grove of junipers. Settling in San Francisco, they both got married and became accountants, had a daughter and fostered another. Slim never worked another fire season.

Tack went on to fame as a backcountry ranger, transferring agencies to BLM, where she carved out a long, successful career.

Pat and Lisa got married, settled in a park in the southwest, raised two wonderful daughters. Lisa, confined to a wheelchair, worked in the natural history division while Pat continued on very successfully serving various roles in maintenance, rescue, and EMS. We still run into each other now and then when I'm wandering about down there.

Tex and Kathan got married and raised two wonderful kids, settling in the southwest. He works outdoors with rivers and streams, while she runs a school. They keep in touch with Buck over on the other side of the Rockies.

Curly Red, left the park as helicopter pilot a few years later. He flew testing runs for a company up in Colorado. Hooked up with Buck a few times. Settled down in Idaho, lived in a cabin in the woods as a photographer for awhile. Only to tire of that and return to the air again, his passion. He flies fire, rescue, and relief missions throughout the nation. When not flying, he can be found on snow covered slopes chasing that adrenaline rush through extreme skiing.

The Fox, as far as I know, never got married, nor settled down, nor raised two wonderful kids. According to Buck he left for Hawaii for the winter, came back visiting only to leave again for islands in the tropics. A postcard Buck received stated, "Still hanging in there, hope you are too. I will get in touch with you soon. Stay loose, and remember, rock n' roll never dies." Followed a few weeks later by another card, " Well Buck, what can I say? The wahines were waiting, and it was feeding time for the Dragon. I am a little awed by the selections on the menu, but like I always say, try a little of this, a little of that, you know, one at a time. Hang loose, bro! Aloha, the Fox." Told Buck that he never would return to fire after the fiasco with B.J. He had enough. Never to be heard from again.

Ken, the last of the Longshot leaders, followed the park scene, growing in stature with assignments. With his beautiful wife Linda, they had two wonderful boys and he rose to fame as an excellent fire management officer at other parks until his early death.

The Wad, well he and Jinny settled down and raised two fantastic boys. Buck and I flew in Curly Red's private fixed wing four seater to their Yosemite wedding. It was a big affair in the meadows of the Redwoods and granite peaks, cascading waters, and historic structures. He became a guru of fire, respected, admired, well liked and sound until his untimely passing at a much too early age.

B.J. continued working a few more years at the canyon and then fell out of touch. Scuttlebutt went around that he was promoted a grade level to take the fire role in far north Alaska. Unofficially designated, "gates of hell" due to its remoteness as no roads reach the area, no trails traverse it and no campsites exist. The winter experiences extreme cold, howling winds, and months of darkness. In the summer, clouds of biting bugs and life-sucking swamplands compete with the man-eating animals. In the boreal forest and tundra subject to wildfires, most vegetation responds quickly in the permafrost table of this wild arctic ecosystem. Fire is allowed and encouraged there. Because of the vast and remote location very few fire suppression efforts occur. Seems that justice would have prevailed in no man's land until a search found one Billie Joe Sagebrush in the records. Not quite sure if this was him.

With a reputation as his, it wouldn't behoove anyone if he had changed his name. Who knows, maybe it was the lack of anyone to boss or lord over. Maybe it was the long, isolated stretches of loneliness and time by himself that he discovered the truth. Apparently this listed BJ found his calling as a right wing, televangical preacher in the Southeast. Hmmm, I wonder...

Myself, well, Iter and I ended up in Flagstaff that winter after some rambling in Northern and Southern California. I moved on (still temporary) with the government in prescribed fire management under Deano in Lassen Volcanoes National Park. It was there that I fulfilled a dream and closed out the fire part of my seasonal life in a lookout tower. Incredible! For a couple of years I worked at the Vermillion Cliffs Bar and Grill on the Arizona strip. Like Abbey, I would "Hail a few Mary's," when the urge required. Never settling, marrying or raising two wonderful kids, I took my parents' advice, sticking with dogs as my companions in the real world of canyons, pines, rivers and streams. Couldn't stay away long, so I continue to work and write from the few remaining fire towers during my summers.

Buck, well, he survived a summer of hotshot fascism (as he noted before) became a teacher, married I don't know how many times, has raised one fantastic son that I know of, and has a beautiful daughter somewhere out there (from a Mormon mom). He enjoyed a brief rep as a Wildman of Colorado. YBH! We stayed in touch over the years harassing each other in teasing manner which is our dance. Once, I shared with him that on my travels passing through Nevada, I visited a brothel to have sex. Buck immediately hammered me with questions. Astonished, he stated he never had nor would he ever pay to get laid. I had to remind him that with his divorces, he had paid a lot more to get screwed. Rebuttal quickly brought the desired result, quiet. As always.

Yet, it wasn't until the twentieth anniversary of that final Longshot summer that we got together again in House Rock Valley. I was working at Vermillion Cliffs Bar and Grill again. Buck, having been through the ortho knife way too many times, just survived the removal of a brain tumor and needed to re-build his memory cells. So up to the North Rim we went to sign in at the Tipover Springs tank, now a rusty old relic, very much like us. It was a great visit and while there Buck took my manuscript with him.

"To me, the fireground is a sacred locale, a place of power that is rich not only in tradition, history, and ecological imperatives, but also in sources of emotion and meditations that I can only describe in terms of reverence and awe."
-Peter Leschak in <u>Ghosts of the Fireground.</u>

While he was there, a storm blew in on the North Rim. It was early June and drought conditions were present. The result was some lightning strikes that hit pay dirt and the U.S. Forest Circus decided to let it play out and burn.

As we cruised around, I pointed out how young and thin the national forest was in contrast with the old growth we'd seen in the park. Why would anyone let a lightning strike burn in drought conditions? The seasonal dryness was so bad that year that Jacob Lake, at 8,000 feet, in early January had no snow. When the forest circus fire information gal came down to tell us in the community of the "let burn" decision, I gave her my background in fire and voiced my concern, seeing no need for it in the clear and young pine stands.
"We have three hundred trained professionals." the gal retorted.
"You can have 3,000. However, when that fire decides to crown, 3,000,000 wouldn't be able to stop it, only mother nature can." yours truly, burger burner stated.

Buck departed and the fire continued to spread. I continued to voice my concerns. For a week the fire stayed on the ground. However after a wind shift the fire decided to stop messing around. You could see the glow of orange in the night sky from our bar and grill, 30 miles away, while ashes rained down on us. The park was evacuated!

The North Rim was first evacuated back in the year 2000, during the Outlet prescribed burn, when condtions changed due to high winds, and the fire was reclassified as a suppression response. (Noted in Hal K. Rothman's book, <u>Blazing Heritage,</u> p. 195).

Some things in bureaucracies just keep repeating. Is history ever referred to?
After a rain deluge a damper was put on and the road was re-opened. I took a drive. For over eight miles along the highway, all those young pines were now sticks. Charred remnants as far as the eye could see in every direction. It cost at least eleven million dollars in suppression costs. What I found strange was that some of the fire folks I talked to didn't think it was a bad call. Ecologically, I felt it was a bad call. Mother Nature always has the last laugh.

(Buck)- I would agree that fire is a much needed natural occurance that has been suppressed for almost a century creating choked, unhealthy forests. Whether by mechanical means, presribed burns, or allowing some lightning caused fires to assist in maintaining a more natural ecosystem, normally I would support the decision to let fires burn, however, never in a drought condition. Dangerous and stupid!
"...fire cannot easily be made to conform to bureaucratic measurements. It is always a risk, always a danger, whether it burns or it is suppressed. All the planning in the world cannot obviate a disastrous change in weather or geographic conditions."
-Hal K. Rothman, <u>Blazing Heritage,</u> p.202

"Officials often promote strategies to manage wildfire based on economic or political considerations rather than science. The 'fire-industrial complex' that developed to combat the blazes is today worth billions of dollars and is often driven more by business interests than ecological or safety considerations."
-Michael Kodas in <u>Megafire,</u> (p.14).

(Prof)-Why did I do it?

"Many men go fishing all of their lives without knowing that it is not fish they are after."
-Thoreau

I'd been around ten fire seasons of smoke and flame, driving engines, flying choppers, making supervisory decisions affecting life and limb. Eight dollars an hour (in the early '80's) with no benefits. Why did I come back? Maybe the call of the wild, the flames, the smoke bum friends, camaraderie, five months off, but perhaps the real reason is the woods, canyons, and unexpected joys of life away from suburbia. To me, it's not about the money. I don't live to work, I work to live. The added benefit of employment in America's grade "A" real estate, a national park was a bonus. Most people work all year round just to take a two week vacation to a place that I called home for almost a decade. *"How we spend our days is, of course, how we spend our lives."*
-Annie Dillard

(Buck) Simply stated

"...simplicity is a good counselor and isolation not a bad educator…"
-Joseph Conrad
Living life simply and simply living. Enjoying a warm cup of coffee on a cold morning while getting the engines ready for road clearing was a satisfying moment. Hiking in wilderness areas that probably have never seen modern man before was awe inspiring. Witnessing the almighty wild fire infernos, some that make my ass cheeks pucker just thinking about them was breathtaking. Rolling along four wheel drive roads with wildlife, trees, and no one else for miles was blissful peace. Looking back, I am glad for the simpler times. We had occasion to converse and find mutual acquaintances for off days' jaunts. Many instances this mystical place led to romance, however fleeting, however shallow for some of us, others found their partners for life (as noted). It is a magical place. It was a simpler time. You could drive for hours down two lane highways and not encounter another person. When you got tired, or tipsy, you pulled over, crawled in the back of your pick up or maybe just to the ground, sleeping on the side of the road in a forest. Lacking many of the time saving conveniences found outside of our hamlet in the woods (like microwaves and dishwashers) we still found time to interact with each other. Distractions like television and radio station chatter were not available in our remote location. Even with the big lug of a computer we had, it was strictly utilized for Affirms (fire weather and reports). Modern technology like the internet and cell phones weren't around, yet we communicated more directly in person, face to face.
"...part of Buddhist practice is learning to perceive the ways we are all connected to one another, just as each moment is tethered to the past and the future. Like a stand of aspens, all phenomena emerge aboveground from the same root."
-Colleen Morten Busch (<u>Fire Monks, p. 83</u>)

(Buck) And a spirit of adventure
Jon Krakauer's book, <u>Into the Wild,</u> about a young man's search, while bold, was
reckless to the point of death. Nevertheless, the young man captures the essence of the
adventurous spirit, *"So many people live within unhappy circumstances and yet will not
take the initiative to change their situation because they are conditioned to a life of
security, conformity, and conservatism, all of which may appear to give one peace of
mind, but in reality nothing is more damaging to the adventurous spirit within a man
than a secure future. The very basic core of a man's living spirit is his passion for
adventure. The joy of life comes from our encounters with new experiences, and hence
there is no greater joy than to have an endlessly changing horizon, for each day to have
a new and different sun."*

Yes, a way of life for youth and not for everyone. Longshots? We did it for the draw of
fire and the magic of the canyon, along with the adventure, excitement, camaraderie, and
romance of the old west. Thoreau's Walden is still popular today as he critically views
the lives of people, *"making a living"* rather than in *"living."*
"We should come home from adventures every day."
-Thoreau

Outside influences surrounding me was a pressure felt of rushing through life to become
someone successful. To experience life is to know it and who you are in it (the Lost
Generation found). I know of several that were waiting for their "golden years," or when
they were financially set, to experience adventures and life. With their nose to the
grindstone working within months of retiring, they passed on, with bucket lists of wishes
sitting idle and undone. How sad!
"We don't stop playing because we are old; we grow old because we stop playing."
-George Bernard Shaw

The youth, I believe, is a time for experiencing a variety of life, so that as we age we can
continue to carry the joie de vivre, and have no regrets.
During the Yukon Gold Rush of the 1890's, less than *"one-half of 1 percent of all
stampeders realized their dreams of finding vast quanitites of gold. Yet, for many...an
interesting thing happened. Once...home...they realized that the journey had been
valuable in other ways...they had pushed themselves to do things they never would have
thought possible. As they grew older, many...looked back with nostalgia...and considered
it the most exciting time of their lives."*
-David Meissner and Kim Richardson <u>(Call of the Klondike,</u> p. 146).

It's never too late. The journey is ongoing.
"A journey of a thousand miles begins with a single step."

-Lao-tze

Interestingly enough, not one of us on the Longshots or associated like-minded companions have ever experienced a need for a mid-life crisis. We lived in our youth, and continue to do so in our lives.

(Buck) Was it worth it?
" 'to thine own self be true"
-Shakespeare (Hamlet)

To answer that, I beckon you to visit the North Rim sometime. Camp out at Point Imperial and wake up to a rising sun as it appears illuminating Mount Haydn on the east rim. Bike a dirt road past the Basin, taking in the aspen and ponderosa lined meadow with wildflowers in bloom, turkeys, deer, and red tail hawk overhead. Head out to Powell Plateau for a sunset, and capture the multitude of colors (indescribable) as the bathtub ring of rock layers are bathed in days last light. Hike down into it. Experience the waterfalls, the cool shade of a cottonwood tree in the heat of the day. Get on a boat and tackle the river as Major John Wesley Powell did. Go back in time again and check out the Anasazi ruins at Nankoweap. Fish it for some huge trout and try the professor's recipe, trout ala Mexicana. Get some air, fly it, experience the vastness of this area. In the evening, make time for the shooting stars and to meet new and different people from all over the world, first from the veranda, then a real old fashion saloon.

I would do it all over in a minute. Numerous occasions I tried leaving, to get a "real job" according to my family, only to come back, countless times for the magic, the aura, the mystique, the romance, the tranquility, and peace of the natural world. A magical, mystical tour. I've been happy in the flash of time granted me in this endeavor. No amount of money could ever be offered to buy me a different life. My memories and moments, friendships, and experiences were all worth it. Cest la vie!
"Don't cry because it's over. Smile because it happened."
-Dr. Seuss

(Buck)-My observation and some thoughts

"I'd love to change the world
But I don't know what to do
So I'll leave it up to you"
-Ten Years After (*"I'd love to change the world"*)

Away from the politics and people business of running parks, the Grand Canyon is fine. As humans start messing with a good thing, shit happens!

Fire has changed too. More challenges with fire today due to the wildland urban interface (areas in wilds where people, in trying to escape the busyness of life, build houses, cabins, retreats). A nice concept, but it's not always stewardship. More so it's becoming ownership and elitism at the cost of human lives.

While working with fire authorities in Northern Colorado during the last decade, we encountered many new developments in the forested mountainous regions. Beautiful, expensive homes with little regards to the hazards of wildfire. Mitigation efforts were available and free from the state and federal agencies. Most folks wrongly thought that meant clear cutting around their private places. Our concerns were for human lives first, property second. Not if but when that lightning came and caused fire in the area, our responders (in engines) would be able to pull up to the residence, pull hose and easily turn around for their escape route. Most of the places had narrow drives, tight corners, and no easy exit. During fires, when the sun is choked out and daylight turns to night, smoke fills the air and visibility becomes poor. Add that to an emergency response and having to escape a fire inferno, and many of these sites were red lined on our maps for, "let burn." Meaning, if the homeowner didn't take the precautions to mitigate, we weren't going to risk human lives in a losing battle to save a structure. It was hard getting folks to understand that being in such wilderness settings had inherent risks.
"I turn around and look at who I have with me. I know what their capabilities are, their strenghts and weaknesses. I think, do I want to do this? Generally, I've got young people in their 20's with me ... Do I want to explain to their spouses and families why they're in the burn center, or they're dead? And for what? For trying to save a frickin' house that can be rebuilt."
-Steve Carlson commenting in C.B. Busch's book, <u>Fire Monks,</u> p.117.

"If more of the tab for wildfire protection was paid by the people who live in flammable landscapes, they would be less likely to build in the path of wildfires."
-Michael Kodas in <u>Megafire,</u> p. 312 (quoting Ray Rasker of Headwaters Economics, a think tank that studies the cost of the nation's wildfires.

If you go to the forest, you are going to encounter bears, mountain lions, wildfire and changing weather patterns. Shit happens! Nature follows its natural laws. When we go outdoors to experience nature, inherent dangers exist out in the wild. Be prepared for it. The national parks are not a Disneyland experience.

Even though this story is somewhat about fire management back in its infancy, that was then. I don't yearn for those days. I'm glad I experienced it. They were life altering, adventurous, and wonderful, however my life has continued to evolve as well. My greatest two loves-fire and the North Rim are still there. Fire has changed although I still appreciate and reminisce when I see it. The North Rim I still visit, but it too has changed. The new community of people are making their own stories, fashioning friendships and forming lives as it should be. The canyon will always be there, long after I'm gone, just as fire will always shape the landscape and the two will always capture the souls of other wayfaring strangers. No regrets.

"There are only two assets we have, love and time. Lives are measured by how we spend our time and how we spend our love..."
-John Maclean, <u>Fire on the Mountain,</u> p.257, quoting Barbara Roberts, Oregon's governor at the public eulogy for Prineville Hot Shots.

<u>(Prof) Signing out-</u>

To this day the North Rim calls me and rarely a circle around the sun goes by while I'm still around that I don't heed the call and end up there. All I've tried to do here is tell a tale of a life determined by the seasons, a story of a time gone when smoke bums like myself were fortunate to live in such a place as the Skidrow Palace. Happy trails and remember, destroy all memory and leave no footprints. HA!…pass me that…would you? Thanks for reading our story.
Prof (Jim Boomer) Canyon
"the aim of life is to live, and to live means to be aware joyously, drunkenly, serenely, divinely, aware."
-Henry Miller

(Buck)- Professor Canyon wrote much of this many years ago. I edited, took liberty with his original words/story, and added my insight, reflections, and memories resulting in this combined retelling. While trying to search the North Rim and NPS files for our '80's fire logs, an interesting dilemma occured. No records were found. Luckily, Tex had copied our fire reports while he was briefly stationed there for an assignment back in the days. It seems that records are readily available from before and even after BJ's stint, but not during. Coincidence?

<u>(Buck's)Afterword</u>

"Feel kindly toward everyone, but be a close friend only with good people."
-Confucius

Reflectively, our fun bunch was a meeting of the time, place, ideas and people; a harmonic convergence that impacted us the rest of our lives. The fun bunch continues, only not associated with a crew identity, and not tied to a partying life that the mention of the phrase conjures up. I believe it is within the beholder, anyone, to find that positive, fun-loving nature. Some people are just plain fun to be with, they laugh heartily, don't obsess what others think about them, and are comfortable with who they are, friendly, gregarious, positive and humble. Free to be who they are. Forever young!

<u>**(Buck) In solitude (Retrospective)**</u>

"And in the end, it's not the years in your life that count. It's the life in your years."
-Abraham Lincoln
I've experienced fire. Huge conflagrations of forest burning up, smoke pluming to form clouds and daylight blocked with darkness, flames, heat, and confusion surrounding me. Muscles aching, lungs gasping for air, sweat pouring down my already soaked clothes, body craving water, headache flaring from carbon monoxide released by incomplete combustion of woody fuels, all part of it. The trains rolling overhead, the sound of a crowning fire, as it sweeps rapidly and fiercely destroying what took years to form. There's no amount of forces available to put a major wildfire out. We draw our line in the dirt, only to have it burned over. We bomb it from the sky, and it buys us temporary time to try to make headway and take a stand. We ferry in more troops in the battle to contain this wild natural thing we call fire. Resources roll out in the form of engines with water and foam to cool off hotspots, or to coat human structures that have a fighting chance to withstand the inferno and embers that travel at insurmountable speeds. Gale force winds add another temporary element of nature to our already complex natural cycle. Many times we humans just get in the way of the natural cycle of things.

Try to control a wild-fire. Interesting, the word, "wild," add that to fire, and it should tell you that you can't always control what is wild. Like trying to control what is natural. Hurricanes and tornadoes also happen naturally in our country. How effective are we (at controlling) when we are experiencing these storms of nature? Yet we don't seem to heed these cycles and just seem to say, "screw it, I'll build where I want to." I think this is a natural human tendency, to play god, to think we can control everything about our lives and the world around us. Humans could but usually don't follow their own code of honor and must resort to obeying rules imposed by others while nature just follows its natural laws.

I know that sometimes I have tried to control things beyond my capability only to have them backfire on me. In my life I have made many adjustments to the fires burning within. In comparison, when natural fires have burned, scorched the land, smoldering subsided, winds abated, with time, comes healing. New growth slowly takes hold, wildflowers spring up amidst blackened stumps, skies clear, sun shines, and the cycle is repeated. On wildfires, if we are clever now with our past, we know that preventing natural occurrences from happening damages the balance in an ecosystem. Thus forests become clogged, overcrowded, unhealthy, and sick. I too become sick if my thoughts become clogged with worry or I obsess over situations that are out of my control. What can I control? I have come to learn that is only me. I can control me. No one else. Nothing else. I must let the natural occurrences of life happen. Sometimes, I must face the fires in my life, and some I will effectively battle and put out, others, will be conflagrations of overwhelming intensity that I have to wait out and let it happen, riding out the natural cycle. In the great Yellowstone fires of 1988, all types of resources were utilized for months to battle the blazes only to have the winter snows fall to finally extinguish the flames for good. Nature doing its thing. Not always liked by us, not always approved, but required, for cleansing.

I've been cleansed too many times for my comfort. But with age sometimes comes wisdom, and I feel now at my final quarter of life I am beginning to understand cycles of my nature more fully. I am a person that resonates with nature. It has been in my blood since I was a youngster. Live and learn! Living life to me is just being in the here (wherever you are) and the now (not yesterday nor tomorrow). Like nature though, I've cycled through the fierce and calm of my life. With time, I've found the flow of my soul and what resonates with me personally is the outdoors. The outdoors were always my place of refuge.

"Wherever a man may happen to turn, whatever a man may undertake, he will always end up by returning to the path which nature has marked out for him."
-Goethe

I liked the camaraderie of the outdoor folks I worked with, at least the ones in the field, who were like minded. To be true to thine own self I had to get out of my ego and controlling anxiety, allowing myself to go with the flow rather than fight the currents of my life. Lost relationships, but what the heck, it was about taking care of myself first before I could serve others (just like they teach you on the airplanes with the oxygen masks). I am at peace with myself now and am learning to take in life with ease and grace. Thinking way back to that time with the red tail hawk and the Yaz giving me his insight, I remember some words that held no meaning then, "Ancients recognized this bird of prey as a messenger. Just as the hawk circles overhead, searching, you too are to look at your life from a higher perspective, an overall view." By writing this and looking back, I think that I have finally found meaning for me. We all walk our own path...

I initially wrote this for myself to be read in my golden years (if so happens) hoping to re-tuck a bit of that magic era in my memory banks for my rocking chair days (when there is only the past left). Long ago a flick came out, titled, *Little Big Man*, with Dustin Hoffman as an old Indian survivor (of Little Big Horn). He recalls his past and learned experiences. I fathomed that portrayal (of an old fart) for this re-telling. As a monumental impact, that past life (fastly fading) positvely influenced my evolution today. This is one story, there's many out there, this just happens to be Prof's with my interjections.

Thanks Stephen, Len, and Ken, for instilling the Longshot life and all that it stood for. Thanks Gussie, for trusting us under your management.

It all helped shape the person I became. I was proud to be a part of the longstanding tradition that was once formed on that magical side of the canyon.

Thanks Tex, and fellow North Rimmers, for the friendship and memories.

And to Cap'n John, thanks for being the inspiration that started it all.

Canyon, you are the spark for all of this, your wisdom, training, wit, and talent as well as humor, sarcasm, and insight are the reason for such a reflection. More so, the trails we treaded, the camps we set, the fires we fought, and the experiences we shared were truly monumental and grand!

I love you all dearly. Peace and may you all have sun shining on you, trails to hike, and wild places to explore.

"You cannot travel on the path before you have become the path itself.
-Buddha

Appendix

Ramblin', rolling stone, gypsy-nomad

-(Prof) Jim Canyon

Grabbed that pack
not looking back
out the door
under blue sky
left my family
left my friends
don't ask
just listen to the breeze, maybe you'll see
only the birds
keep their balance
keep their grace
in flight, in songs.

grabbed my pack
lost the game
other people play
that I love
ah, love.
Left my lover
left my friends
for those one night stands
of no one, only the moon
I can't expect you to understand
the touch of your hand
takes a drink of water
giving sight, sweet light

Grabbed my pack
into the cool winter morning
into the cool crisp frost
every breath a cloud of prayers to the great spirit of
rain falling in the desert
the smell of life
breathe the miracle, taste of mortality
consumes me and my feet may carry me
Its' love keeps me walking

grabbed my pack
not looking back
is that you calling

grabbed my pack
is that you

grabbed my pack
I'm waiting,

I'm waiting

grab your pack
let's take that journey… It's truly a miracle.

<u>Professor's trout ala Mexicana recipe</u>

1. Catch fresh trout,
2. Slicing belly open, scoop out entrails (doesn't get any fresher than that folks)
3. Season with salt, pepper,
4. Still in skin, wrap in foil or lacking foil, just put over coals (slightly above). In the wilderness he uses rocks to prop the fish over the coals below.
5. Cook until done, varies by weight/size, but done fish are flaky and white opaque.
6. Holding fish by the head, pull up on snout/head and keep pulling until dorsal spine is out. This action will pull most if not all the bones out.
7. Now, you can eat it out of the skin.
8. For final touch, and reason this is ala Mexicana is the salsa added to the fish. Use fingers if in wilderness, or if you are fortunate to have fork/spork use this utensil to eat this delectable wild fish, freshly caught.
    Shhhhhh! It's a secret where to catch these, ask the prof if he'll share...